INVISIBLE GIANTS

INVISIBLE GIANTS

FIFTY AMERICANS
WHO SHAPED THE NATION
BUT MISSED THE HISTORY BOOKS

EDITED BY MARK CARNES

OXFORD
UNIVERSITY PRESS

2002

OXFORD

UNIVERSITY PRESS

Oxford   New York
Auckland   Bangkok   Buenos Aires   Cape Town   Chennai
Dar es Salaam   Delhi   Hong Kong   Istanbul   Karachi   Kolkata
Kuala Lumpur   Madrid   Melbourne   Mexico City   Mumbai   Nairobi
São Paulo   Shanghai   Singapore   Taipei   Tokyo   Toronto
and an associated company in
Berlin

Library of Congress Cataloging-in-Publication Data available upon request
ISBN 0-19-515417-7

Book design: A Setback Design

1 3 5 7 9 8 6 4 2

Printed in the United States of America
on acid-free paper

CONTENTS

CONTENTS

INTRODUCTION

This book consists of biographical essays on fifty "invisible giants" of the American past, each selected by a prominent person in contemporary America. The "invisible giants" were chosen from among the 18,000 historical figures contained in the *American National Biography* (ANB). Those who selected a subject explained their reasons in a brief introduction; in return, they received the satisfaction of rendering their "invisible giant" less so in consequence of being included in this book. We chose selectors whose interests were wide-ranging. Because their judgments were to be expressed in writing, we particularly sought accomplished writers. Although we made no systematic attempt to define "invisible giant," we explained that we were looking for the type of figure who, though often overlooked in history books, warranted special consideration.

The *American National Biography*, published by the American Council of Learned Societies and Oxford University Press, consists of twenty-five million words and twenty-five volumes, including a recent supplement. It begins, alphabetically, with an essay on Alexander Aarons, producer of *Lady, Be Good!*, and ends with one on Vladimir Zworykin, inventor of the picture tube and, in the minds of many, the "father of television." (Zworykin, no fan of his invention, contended that his greatest contribution to television was the "off" switch.) In between are people, all dead, who have shaped the nation in countless ways. The ANB includes every prominent American most people can think of and many thousands most have never heard of. (A parlor game: find an American who died sometime ago, has some claim to national significance in any field of endeavor, and is not in the ANB. If you "win" [few do], please send me a short note or e-mail, and we shall consider including your person in the on-line version of the ANB in the next published supplement.)

Major figures in the ANB receive extended essays, many written by the finest historians in the nation—and beyond. But the unique value of the ANB lies in its wealth of information and contemporary perspective on historical figures about whom most scholars may know little. A random sorting of any fifty ANB subjects would provide plenty of food for thought— and a chance to sample the fascinating diversity that has made this nation. Another way of browsing the ANB is to use its index of "occupations" and "realms of renown." The list begins, alphabetically, with "abolitionists," "abortionists," "accordionists," and "accountants" and closes with "yachtsmen," "zionists," "zoo curators," and "zoologists." In between are "bobsledders," "comb players," "insect pathologists," "outlaws," "weavers," and hundreds of other fields.

This book presents an alternative culling of these less famous subjects, one that illuminates the connections between past and present. All works of history do this, if only because good historians search for contemporary relevance amidst the rubble of the historical record. But this book further underscores the dialogue between past and present by relying on contemporary figures to select its contents. Those making the nominations are themselves important in American life; many will likely be included as subjects in the *American National Biography* in what we hope to be the distant future. Their pleas for remembering an "invisible" person constitute an implicit indictment of our having forgotten him or her. Moreover, the selectors may be sending signals to future historians about themselves. If so, some of their messages are surprising.

Harold Bloom, for example, one of the nation's foremost literary critics, might have chosen his "invisible giant" from among the eight hundred novelists whose biographies appear in the ANB, including many worthies tottering on the edge of oblivion. He chose instead Joseph Smith, founder of the Mormon Church. "No other religious imagination of the nineteenth century was as comprehensive and daring as Smith's," he wrote. Historian Edmund S. Morgan, though known chiefly as a scholar of the Puritan world, also chose a nineteenth-century religious visionary (and a contemporary of Joseph Smith): Charles Grandison Finney, the preacher who inaugurated the Second Great Awakening and sparked, as Morgan observed, "the movement that led to the abolition of slavery." Andy Rooney, commentator for 60 *Minutes*, chose Walter Lippmann, a journalist and literary stylist whose *A Preface to Morals* (1929), Rooney wrote, is "better than the Bible and easier to understand." That Rooney, a humorist, should celebrate the unflaggingly earnest Lippmann reveals something new about both. Camille Paglia, who has attained prominence through her iconoclastic feminism, might have chosen someone with equally flamboyant intellectual credentials; instead she selected Gisela Richter, a sober and unassuming scholar of Greek sculpture: "If academe is ever to revive," wrote Paglia, "we need to recover Richter's noble ideal of profound erudition."

Other choices suggest a more comfortable fit—as if past and present are engaged in a companionable chat. Novelist A. M. Homes's work is characterized by a keen sensitivity to the resonance of contemporary icons; she chose Frank Winfield Woolworth, founder of the five-and-ten-cent empire, for his indirect influence upon her imagination. His stores were "a phantasmagoria, an education, a treasure chest of temptation, a wide expanse with counters that went on forever, wooden floors, oiled to keep dirt from sticking, the whole store filled with the scent of fresh popped popcorn, of roasting peanuts, the sweet tweak of dark chocolates." Wilma Mankiller, a Cherokee Indian who grew up amongst a people who were losing their culture, has sought to reanimate their way of life as a visionary and political leader. She drew inspiration from

Handsome Lake, who, appalled by the cultural collapse of the Iroquois as a result of the incursion of British settlers in the late eighteenth century, revitalized Iroquois beliefs and practices. Sherwin B. Nuland, author of *How We Die: Reflections on Life's Final Chapter* and other books on surgery, praises William Halsted, a pivotal figure in the profession early in the twentieth century. "It is because of his teachings," Nuland wrote, "that I chose [surgery] as my life's work." Nuland's appreciation of his subject further prompted him to ponder Halsted's mixed reputation—his addiction to cocaine and morphine, and the development of the radical mastectomy for treatment of breast cancer, a procedure that later generated controversy.

Biography endures because people seek historical figures as role models. Many selectors chose "invisible giants" who shaped their own growth, providing guidance, inspiration, or intellectual patronage. William F. Buckley, Jr., championed Alfred Jay Nock, an essayist and cultural theorist who believed that the preservation of civilization depended on a virtuous elite. Helen Gurley Brown, who spearheaded the growth of *Cosmopolitan*, nominated DeWitt Wallace, who pioneered *Reader's Digest*.

Sometimes the need for biographical forebears is so great that we search for them unconsciously. Thus Simon Winchester's insistent impulse to be on the move, reflected in his peripatetic writings *Fracture Zone: A Return to the Balkans*; *Korea: A Walk through the Land of Miracles*; and *The Map That Changed the World*, surfaced even on vacation in North Conway, New Hampshire, where he discovered the letters and manuscripts of General Adolphus W. Greely, Arctic explorer. Despite the fact that Greely's most famous voyage ended in disaster and scandal, Greely became Winchester's "personal hero." Historian David M. Kennedy similarly happened upon dusty boxes and cartons that proved to be "the answer to a researcher's prayer": the papers of Robert Latou Dickinson, "a fascinating human being, a pioneer in the scientific study of sexual practice, a proponent of often daring reforms respecting women's attire, diet, exercise, and erotic fulfillment." These materials were incorporated in Kennedy's pioneering dissertation on birth control in America in the early twentieth century, published as *Birth Control in America*.

But if the historical subjects in this book were so important, why are so many of their names unfamiliar? An "invisible giant" is, after all, an oxymoron. Some of the selectors addressed this point directly. A few bemoaned the cultural forgetfulness of these United States of Amnesia, in the words of expatriate Gore Vidal. Others suggested that their figures were out of step with their times. Jacques Barzun combined both explanations to account for the invisibility of John Jay Chapman, a "literary genius whom America has yet to value—and enjoy, for he is immensely enjoyable." Chapman wrote cultural criticism, however, when the nation's self-criticism was mostly political and social. Chapman "came at the wrong time, and those whom contemporaries fail to honor (or attack) slip altogether from the communal memory," Barzun opined. Andrew Greeley, a steadfast advocate of reform of the Catholic Church, selected John England, the first Catholic bishop of Charleston. England embraced Enlightenment thinking, separation of church and state, ecumenicalism, and a less centralized church structure. His views, which did not prevail in his own time, constituted "a prophecy of what would come—a prophecy, one might add, whose fulfillment remains central to Greeley's life.

Harold Evans honored Oliver Evans, an inventor who in the late eighteenth century conceived of motorized vehicles, devised high-pressure steam engines, and outlined the mechanics of air-conditioning. Unfortunately, Evans's concepts anticipated the requisite machine tooling and technical

knowledge. "It is extraordinary that he is such a neglected figure," Harold Evans explained." Of course, like so many innovators, he attracted the scorn of the traditionalists and the envy
of inferiors, all the more reason why our generation owes him
his due."

On the other hand, some historical figures have become
invisible only with the passing of time. Gary Giddins observed
that writer James Gibbons Huneker "dominated American
arts criticism between 1890 and 1920 to a degree unmatched
before or since." He became "the forgotten man of American
letters" only when his lush style was superseded by the spare,
sober prose of a new generation of writers such as H. L.
Mencken and Edmund Wilson. Similarly, Henry Louis Gates,
Jr., noted that poet Paul Laurence Dunbar was once "the most
famous black writer in the world." His reputation declined
when the "poetics of respectability" derided the use of
African-American dialect, a genre that had been corrupted by
its racist appropriation in vaudeville and minstrelsy. Now,
Gates contended, Americans can appreciate Dunbar's "resplendent vernacular voice."

Stature is in the eyes of the beholder. So, too, is visibility.
When Ed Koch selected Malcolm X as an "invisible giant," we
demurred. Malcolm X did not strike us as invisible. Who could
forget the sardonic smile that lurked below those earnest
black-framed eyeglasses? And if our recollection of the man
has morphed with that of Denzel Washington's portrayal of
him in Spike Lee's movie, did that not constitute further proof
of Malcolm's visibility? But Koch, of course, prevailed. We
remember the early, racist Malcolm X but have lost sight of the
man who, late in his short life, learned to embrace all races.

Most of the figures in this book, and in the ANB, have made
positive contributions to American life. But the past teaches
painful lessons as well as inspiring ones. Sometimes its giants
are fearsome. Sometimes we choose not to look at the past

because we do not like what we may see. Several years from now, once we have acquired sufficient perspective on the events of September 11, 2001, Mohamed Atta, ringleader of the terrorists who flew jetliners into the World Trade Center, will likely be added to the ANB. He courted posthumous attention, and it will doubtless pain the editor to gratify Atta's wish. But the ANB is a historical tool, not a "who's who" of the great and good. It includes corrupt politicians, gangsters, and murderers. To illustrate this point, I selected as my "invisible giant" the anarchist Leon Czolgosz, who for one brief moment emerged from shadowy oblivion to shoot President McKinley. Shortly afterwards, Czolgosz was executed; within a few years he had been nearly forgotten. His story appears in the ANB because it had become part of the nation's history. Of what particular use it may be to contemporary readers, or those who happen upon it in the future, one cannot say. Our dialogue with the past is open-ended.

The ANB is a vast repository of information and historical judgments. General readers and scholars alike will seek and find in it an infinite range of meanings and purposes. This book provides one set of meanings, derived from a tiny sample of the whole. Many of the giants of the past are at least partly self-made; we can't help but see them because they loomed so large during their lives. But every generation finds its own heroes and villains—indeed, its own meanings. We constantly reinterpret our history, and thus discover historical figures who speak to our own times with uncanny clarity. As stated in its motto, the *American National Biography* seeks to tell "the history of the nation through the lives of its people." We must listen to their stories to better understand our own.

The ANB was the work of over 7,000 authors, several hundred scholars who served as associate editors, and a veritable army of fact-checkers and copyeditors. This book, too, was a collective endeavor. At Oxford University Press, Casper Grathwohl,

Senior Editor in charge of Trade Reference, conceived of this project and executed many of the details. Benjamin Keene, Associate Editor, corralled the wayward selectors and organized the editing. Paul Betz edited and prepared the manuscript, and Joellyn Ausanka faithfully shepherded it through production.

MARK C. CARNES

INVISIBLE GIANTS

Johnny Ace

[9 JUNE 1929–25 DECEMBER 1954]

I *can remember the first time I heard Johnny Ace's dulcet tones pouring from my stereo in the early eighties. My mother had been a huge fan of the fallen singer before he was struck dead by a bullet from his own gun in a game, she told me, of "Russian roulette." I was intrigued by his fame, by his short life, and by the story of how he died so needlessly, so tragically, by his own hand. I promised my mother that if I ever came across his album — this was long before compact discs were the widespread and popular items they now are — I would make the purchase and send her a tape of the recording.*

It is easy to imagine my surprise and delight when I spotted a record collection of Ace's few hits spun out during his brief career. The album's cover art featured the crooner's smoothly dark face, cropped by a red-and-white ace of diamonds card. I fetched the few dollars the album cost from my pocket and headed home to hear the voice my mother so movingly remembered as inspirational and exciting. The outstanding song, the one for which Ace is known, is the one I listened to repeatedly: "Pledging My Love." It is a love song to be sure, but one that is nonetheless marked by a mournful yearning at the heart of Ace's piercing tenor. I was struck by his youthful passion and his earnest delivery, and as I sat in my living room, alone, listening to Ace's wonderful art, I felt connected to my mother in a new way. It was fascinating to me that a long-dead icon who enjoyed a painfully brief career full of promise before succumbing to his own risky behavior would unite us.

It would take me another twenty years before I understood fully what Ace meant to my mother and many in her generation. I learned this by writing a book on another figure, Tupac Shakur, whose life and art bore striking similarities to Ace's own. Both had huge gifts; both left too soon by engaging in self-destructive acts;

3

and both were crowned "the black James Dean." Shakur is now globally recognized, while Ace is a comparatively obscure figure whose legacy lives on only in the memory of those whom he moved. Besides my mother, that number now includes me. One can hope that very soon another generation will appreciate his unique sound and significance.

MICHAEL ERIC DYSON

Johnny Ace, musician, songwriter, and rhythm and blues star, was born John Marshall Alexander, Jr., in Memphis, Tennessee, the son of John Marshall Alexander and Leslie Newsome. His father earned his living in Memphis as a packer, but his lifework was as a commuting minister to two rural Baptist churches in East Arkansas. At LaRose Grammar School in south Memphis, John, Jr., as his family called him, displayed both musical and artistic talent. He mastered the piano at home but was allowed to play only religious music there. Along with his mother and siblings, he sang in the choir at Bethel African Methodist Episcopal Church. Becoming restless at Booker T. Washington High School, he dropped out in the eleventh grade to join the navy and see the world. His sisters recall military police coming to the house in search of their brother and remember his brief period of enlistment in terms of weeks, ending in an "Undesirable Discharge" in 1947. His mother was furious. "I can't keep up with you," she scolded, "and *they* can't keep up with you."

It is possible that Alexander never had a job in the conventional sense, and he did not seek employment after his failed navy attempt. He did, however, find kindred spirits on Beale Street. Joe Hill Louis, "the Be-Bop Boy," may have started him out as a professional musician, or the credit may belong to Dwight "Gatemouth" Moore, but by 1949 he was the piano player with the Beale Street Blues Boys (later the Beale Streeters), a band that backed B. B. King when he performed live. In 1950 Alexander wooed and married Lois Jean Palmer, a ninth grader at Booker T. Washington High School, and moved her into his parents' home. A son was born to the couple that year and a daughter in 1952. Alexander's mother, who disapproved of his lifestyle and his occupation as a blues musician, embraced his wife and children but refused to let him sleep at the family home.

In 1952 David James Mattis, the program director at the Memphis all-black radio station WDIA (the "Mother Station of the Negroes"), founded Duke Records and changed Alexander's name to Johnny Ace. When Bobby "Blue" Bland could not sing a song scheduled for recording at the WDIA studio (it was subsequently revealed that Bland could not read), Mattis wrote new lyrics to an existing rhythm and blues hit, and Ace "faked out" a new melody. The result was "My Song" (Duke 102), a "blues ballad" (*Billboard* called it a "heart ballad"), which Ace sang in a vulnerable and innocent soft crooning style. Though the recording lacked professionalism in sound quality, the charm of Ace's voice made it an immediate hit with the limited audience that had access to it. "My Song" attracted the attention of Houston entrepreneur Don D. Robey, a black man who owned Peacock Records and controlled a booking agency specializing in "chitlin circuit" venues. Robey became a partner and quickly the sole owner of Duke Records, moving the entire operation to Houston. He aggressively promoted Ace's "My Song" to the top of the rhythm and blues charts and groomed him as a national headlining rhythm and blues act, carefully cultivating the kind of polished, first-class, uptown image that Berry Gordy would later emulate at Motown.

Ace's career, which lasted less than two and a half years, produced eight rhythm and blues top ten records, including three number-one hits: "My Song" (1952), "The Clock" (1953), and "Pledging My Love" (1955). Primarily he lived the nomadic life of a road musician, with no permanent home or routine beyond a string of temporary hotel stops, traveling coast to coast with a backup band and an opening act, blues singer

Willie Mae "Big Mama" Thornton. In 1954 he may have performed as many as 350 one-nighters, sometimes driving as far
as 800 miles between shows. According to Evelyn Johnson, the
head of Buffalo Booking Agency and the closest thing to a personal manager that Ace had, the singer was shy, childlike, and
unassuming. "Sweetest thing since sugar," she recalled, "but he
didn't care about nuttin', honey." At a pawnshop in Florida he
purchased a .22 caliber pistol to amuse himself and alleviate
the boredom of the road. On Christmas night 1954, while back-
stage during intermission at a "Negro Christmas Dance" at
Houston's City Auditorium, Ace began "snapping" his pistol at
the heads of people in his dressing room. According to Thornton, he put the pistol to his own head and uttered his last
words: "I'll show you that it won't shoot." Authorities ruled the
cause of death to be "playing russian roulette—self inflicted."

Ace's last record, "Pledging My Love" (Duke 136), first advertised in *Billboard* on the day of his death, represented neither
rhythm nor blues, but the slow ballad became a rhythm and
blues triple crown hit (number one in retail sales, radio airplay,
and jukebox action), the most played rhythm and blues record
of 1955, and generated more than half a dozen tribute records
to the romantic legend of Johnny Ace. In addition, the record
crossed over to the pop charts to become a pop hit as well. For
the first time in the postwar era, white record buyers (primarily teens) chose this ballad by a solo black male singer signed to
an independent rhythm and blues label as the unique and
definitive performance of a *popular* song against which all subsequent performances were ruthlessly judged. Arguably,
"Pledging My Love" represents the transitional record
between rhythm and blues and rock and roll.

Johnny Ace died a rhythm and blues star and was resurrected
as a rock and roll legend. He has been called rock's first "casualty," "the first fallen angel," and "the colored James Dean." For
disc jockeys he remains "the Late Great Johnny Ace."

J.M.S.

James Agee

[27 NOVEMBER 1909–16 MAY 1955]

I selected James Agee less for his literary contribution, which was distinctive and important, than for what he stands for. On the vast spectrum of the American sensibility, that conjectural abstraction that shows us who we, collectively, are, and which ranges from John Wayne and General Patton on one end to Emily Dickinson on the other, James Agee represents, in his writing and his person, our conflicted and susceptible romantic nature. In considering this writer, we contemplate a tender, empathetic soul—sometimes violent in its stresses and longings—which expressed itself either in pure distilled lyricism, in the Pulitzer Prize–winning A Death in the Family, *or in a far more complex way in the epoch-making documentary he made with photographer Walker Evans. Reading* And Let Us Now Praise Famous Men, *we feel an engaged, powerfully emotional man trying to rein in his affective nature in the interest of a more objective presentation. His bid finally fails—James Agee cannot stop being James Agee—but the result is all the more moving. We confront the precision, the sharp registrations of his descriptions and his portraits of tenant farmers and their families, but at the same time we detect the self-restraining impulses of a suffering witness just behind. Agee's early death—he was in his mid-forties—robbed us of an authentic American dreamer.*

SVEN BIRKERTS

James Rufus Agee, writer, was born in Knoxville, Tennessee, the son of Hugh James Agee, a construction company employee, and Laura Whitman Tyler. The father's family were poorly educated mountain farmers, while the mother's were solidly middle class. Agee was profoundly affected by his father's death in a car accident in 1916. He idealized his absent father and struggled against his mother and

7

Portrait of James Agee by Walker Evans, 1937. *(Library of Congress)*

her genteel and (he felt) cold values. "Agee's mother wanted him to be clean, chaste, and sober," the photographer Walker Evans, a close friend, observed. "So of course he was none of these things." The father's death inspired the adult Agee to spend nearly two decades, on and off, recreating in words "my childhood and my father as they were, as well and as exactly as I can remember and represent them." The resulting manuscript, which Agee could never bring himself to finish, was published posthumously as *A Death in the Family* (1957) and won the Pulitzer Prize and his greatest fame.

Laura Agee responded to her husband's death by intensifying her religious commitment. In the summer of 1918 she moved her little family (Agee had a younger sister) to St. Andrews (near Sewanee), Tennessee, to live among members of the Episcopalian monastic order of the Holy Cross. The following year she enrolled Agee in St. Andrew's School, which was run by the order. At the school Agee met Father James Harold Flye, who became his spiritual adviser and lifelong correspondent. *Letters of James Agee to Father Flye* (1962) is the best introduction to Agee the man and one of the great letter collections in American literature.

St. Andrew's was a school for farm boys from Appalachia, few of whom went on to college. More was expected from Agee, and in 1925 he entered Phillips Exeter Academy as a sophomore. He graduated three years later and enrolled in Harvard College. At these schools he wrote most of his poetry (collected in *Permit Me Voyage* in 1934) and short stories. In his senior year at Harvard he wrote a parody of *Time* magazine that appeared in the *Harvard Advocate*, of which he was president. On the strength of the parody, he was offered a job as a reporter at Time Inc.'s *Fortune* magazine.

Agee stayed with *Fortune* from 1932 until 1937, writing articles on topics as varied as steel rails, orchids, Saratoga Springs, and the Tennessee Valley Authority. Like many intellectuals during the depression, he was politically leftist in his sympathies (he wrote that he "felt allegiance or part-allegiance to catholicism and to the communist party"), although he was never doctrinaire or politically active. His radicalism was of the spirit: he longed to feel and communicate the pain of those on society's bottom rung.

He got his chance in the summer of 1936 when *Fortune* assigned him and Walker Evans to do an article with text and pictures on southern sharecropping. He and Evans gathered material in Alabama over two months. When they returned to New York City, Agee prepared an article that, he told Father Flye, "will be impossible in any form and length *Fortune* can use."

Rather than a typical, and typically condescending, exposé of the sharecroppers' plight, Agee wrote a piece that was a mixture of lyricism, painstaking description, scathingly personal confession, and moral outrage. *Fortune's* editors tried reworking the article, held it for a year, then turned it down. Agee, on a small advance from Harper & Brothers, left the magazine and expanded the article into his masterpiece, *Let Us Now Praise Famous Men*, which was rejected by Harper & Brothers and was not published until 1941 by Houghton Mifflin. The book received mostly favorable reviews but sold only 600 copies. Agee never again tried to write anything so innovative.

In 1939 he joined *Time* as book reviewer, and two years later he moved to movie reviewing. His fame as a film critic rests, however, on the longer reviews he did for the *Nation* from

December 1942 until July 1948. In these columns he mastered a new approach to commenting on movies — chatty, knowledgeable, opinionated, good-humored. "Of the movies I have seen lately the one I like best was *To Have and Have Not*," he wrote. "It has so little to do with Ernest Hemingway's novel that I see no point in discussing its 'faithfulness'; it is, rather, a sort of call-house version of *Going My Way*." His reviews were collected in *Agee on Film* (1958), one of the first books to present a movie reviewer's work as of permanent literary value.

By the mid-1940s Agee had been married three times (to Olivia Saunders, 1933–1938; Alma Mailman, 1938–1941; and Mia Fritsch 1943–), fathered two children (two more would follow), and become a legend in New York magazine circles. A night person and an insatiable talker, he was undisciplined about everything except the writing that he had to do on deadline. He was addicted to alcohol, cigarettes, and benzedrine (his wife Mia once said his motto was "a little bit too much is just enough for me"), and he took no care of his health (movie director John Huston said Agee went to the dentist only to get teeth removed).

In the late 1940s he began to write movie scripts (and, later, ones for television). Of the scripts produced, his greatest successes were *The Quiet One* (1949), a documentary about a troubled black boy in New York City; *The African Queen* (1951), on which he collaborated with director Huston; a five-part TV series about Abraham Lincoln's early years for the prestigious "Omnibus" program (1952–1953); and *The Night of the Hunter* (1955), the only movie Charles Laughton directed. By the early fifties, though, Agee's excesses had ruined his health. He suffered a series of heart attacks and recurrent angina, which kept him from writing the end of *The African Queen* or joining its filming on location, and which so weakened his work on *The Night of the Hunter* that Laughton had to rewrite the script.

In his last months Agee went back to writing about himself. He had published a short novel about his adolescent religiosity, *The Morning Watch* (1951), which provoked little interest, and he probably expected no better of his writing about his childhood and his father's death. In 1955 he died of a heart attack in a New York taxicab, with no will, no insurance, and only $450 in the bank. He considered his life a failure and a waste of talent, but the posthumous publication of *A Death in the Family*, his film criticism, a second edition of *Let Us Now Praise Famous Men* (1960), and his letters to Father Flye earned him a reputation, which seems certain to endure, as an important and original writer.

W.S.

Jessie Daniel Ames

[2 NOVEMBER 1883–21 FEBRUARY 1972]

Historians are generally drawn to people whose impact on history is clear and unequivocal, and there is much justification for that preference. But history is also the product of struggles by courageous individuals who stand against the temper of their time and bear witness to injustice. During the long, dark period of racial segregation and oppression from the end of Reconstruction to the beginning of the modern civil rights movement, there were relatively few white Americans who were willing to work openly and actively on behalf of racial justice. Jessie Daniel Ames, a white southern woman, emerged from an unlikely background to become — at great personal risk — a powerful, committed, and effective leader in mobilizing opposition to lynching in the South.

ALAN BRINKLEY

Jessie Daniel Ames, antiracism reformer and suffragist, was born Jessie Harriet Daniel in Palestine, Texas, the daughter of James Malcolm Daniel, a train dispatcher and telegraph operator, and Laura Maria Leonard, a teacher. James and Laura Daniel were pious parents who stressed the importance of education but showed little affection for their children. They openly preferred their younger daughter, Lulu, and Jessie suffered deeply from a lack of self-confidence. When Jessie was four, the family moved to Georgetown, Texas, an impoverished and often violent community. There Jessie attended local schools and, later, Southwestern University.

Fearful of spinsterhood, Jessie married Roger Post Ames in 1905. Roger Ames, a friend of Jessie's father, was a U.S. Public Health Service physician. The marriage was not a happy one; the couple were sexually incompatible, and the Ames family felt Roger had married "beneath" him. Rather than face pressure from his family, Roger pursued medical research in South America, deserting his wife for most of their marriage. With the exception of several trips to South America, Jessie lived with her wealthy married sister in Tennessee. In 1914 Roger Ames died of blackwater fever, leaving Jessie with the care of their two children and with a third on the way.

At age thirty-one Jessie Daniel Ames began her public career to support herself and her children. She and her mother ran a local telephone company. As Ames grew more confident, she developed an interest in social justice issues and began to work for woman suffrage. She was elected treasurer of the Texas Equal Suffrage Association in 1918 and worked to secure suffrage for women in primary elections. In an effort to organize woman voters, Ames became founding president of the Texas League of Women Voters and served as a delegate to the national Democratic Party conventions from 1920 to 1928. By working in organizations such as the Federation of Women's Clubs and the American Association of University Women, Ames sought to further women's participation in the reform movement.

Through her participation in woman suffrage, Ames discovered the limitations of the reform movement. She grew increasingly sensitive to the contradictions of a movement that served a predominately white constituency in a South domi-

Jessie Daniel Ames in Austin, Texas, May 24, 1965. "The daughters of the South are not content with hurling denunciations," wrote one newspaper of Ames's Association of Southern Women for the Prevention of Lynching, "they are militantly marching out to make war upon the barbarism that has flourished in their name." (Ames Papers, Southern Historical Collection, Library, University of North Carolina, Chapel Hill)

nated by the Ku Klux Klan. To educate herself about racial issues, Ames enrolled in courses at the University of Chicago and began to address racial concerns. Her work against racial injustice began in 1922, when she became the director of women's work for the Commission on Interracial Cooperation (CIC) in Atlanta, where she held various positions until the 1940s.

By 1930 Ames was alienated from suffragist colleagues and began to concentrate on antiracism work. In that same year she founded the Association of Southern Women for the Prevention of Lynching (ASWPL) as a volunteer organization within the CIC, although the ASWPL eventually outgrew its parent organization. The ASWPL grew out of Ames's belief that lynching was the most visible symbol of black oppression within southern society. With the aim of exerting social control over blacks, whites used the threat of lynching as a form of coercion for enforcing labor contracts. Ames believed that the fear of violence against white women by black men was used to justify lynching as a means of protecting white women. The goal of the ASWPL was the eradication of mob violence by whites against blacks within southern society, through educational efforts that attacked the justification for lynching and through encouraging women to refute the stereotype of themselves as vulnerable creatures in need of protection. The cornerstone of Ames's educational campaign was the compilation of statistics from her own research into 204 lynchings over an eight-year period: only 29 percent of the victims were accused of crimes against white women.

Ames traveled extensively throughout the South as the chief organizer for the ASWPL and formed local chapters by working mainly through Protestant women's missionary societies. She also formed alliances with Jewish women's groups, the Young Women's Christian Association, and organizations such as the Parent-Teacher Association. The ASWPL gained support from both the white and the African-American press.

"The daughters of the South are not content with hurling denunciations," wrote one newspaper, "they are militantly marching out to make war upon the barbarism that has flourished in their name" (Hall [1979], p. 164).

To her contemporaries Ames appeared "animated, positive, and full of determination" (Hall [1979], p. 262). Her chief contributions were her dedication as a single-minded reformer and her genius as an organizational founder. Ultimately Ames's desire to preserve her autonomy within the ASWPL prevented the organization from working more effectively with other organizations on related causes. Though outraged by racially motivated violence, Ames failed to collaborate with black reformers or to significantly include blacks within the ASWPL. Though quick to respond to persons less fortunate than herself, Ames was unresponsive to the issues raised by blacks themselves. Ames became increasingly alienated from the emergent liberalism of the late 1930s and early 1940s, and as the number of lynchings decreased the ASWPL itself dissolved in 1942. Ames's attempts to reinvigorate the organization failed, and she was forced to retire from the reform movement.

In retirement, Ames moved to Tryon, North Carolina, and from 1944 to 1968 devoted her energies to local Democratic politics. Having always been busy, she found that the loss of her life's work took its toll, and her old feelings of insecurity returned. In addition to the rigors of her public career, Ames faced personal trials most of her life. Her youngest daughter contracted polio in 1920. Money was always a problem, and the situation worsened when her mother's resources were wiped out in the Great Depression. Influenced by her own experience, Ames ensured that all her children were educated and were financially independent. Severe arthritis eventually forced her to return to Texas to be near her daughter. Jessie Daniel Ames died in Austin, Texas.

S.A.K.

Roger Nash Baldwin

[21 JANUARY 1884–26 AUGUST 1981]

R oger Nash Baldwin's pioneering struggle for civil justice offers us a valuable lesson: one person's action can help change the world. So many basic American liberties we take for granted can be traced back to Baldwin's uncompromising recognition of humanity in practice. A life to be celebrated.

RICHARD AVEDON

R oger Nash Baldwin, civil libertarian and social activist, was born in Wellesley, Massachusetts, the son of Frank Fenno Baldwin, a leather manufacturer who owned several companies, and Lucy Cushing Nash. The lines on both sides of the family went back to the Pilgrims. Baldwin attended Wellesley public schools. As a boy he lacked prowess in sports and developed interests in music, art, and nature. He was regarded as "different," which made him seek, early in life, "unconventional, nonconformist avenues of expression" consistent with the intellectual heritage of Ralph Waldo Emerson, Henry David Thoreau, and other New England icons. His family were free-thinking Unitarians.

Baldwin earned bachelor's and master's degrees from Harvard University. He became a sociology instructor at Washington University in St. Louis in 1906 and worked in a neighborhood settlement house there. He soon became chief probation officer of the local juvenile court, where he achieved a national reputation in part through his book, written with Bernard Flexner, *Juvenile Courts and Probation* (1914).

In 1909 Baldwin attended a lecture by Emma Goldman, the anarchist, who later became an important figure in his life. Goldman opened up a new literature to Baldwin and introduced him to new sorts of people, who included not only anarchists but also, as he said, "some libertarians, some freedom lovers and some who had no label—like me." These people were bound together by "one principle— freedom from coercion," and many of them were commit- ted to nonviolence.

In 1910 Baldwin became secretary of the Civic League of St. Louis, a reform group that addressed issues of municipal government. Bald- win said later that he got his "first impulse to civil liber- ties" during this period when

Roger Nash Baldwin (left) with Leonard Bernstein and Felicia Bernstein, celebrating Baldwin's eightieth birthday. *(Library of Congress)*

the police denied Margaret Sanger, the birth-control advocate, the right to hold a meeting in a public hall. In St. Louis Bald- win also had his first exposure to issues of racial prejudice. After failing to obtain approval of a special course for blacks at Washington University and after white voters approved a seg- regationist housing ordinance, he concluded, "In cases where minority rights are concerned, you can't trust the majority."

In April 1917 Baldwin joined the American Union against Militarism (AUAM), a New York organization of prominent reformers, writers, editors, church people, and lawyers who opposed World War I. The next month he organized the Bureau for Conscientious Objectors within AUAM to advise conscientious objectors and to help them receive favorable treatment under the new Selective Service Act. The bureau took a more aggressive stance than some AUAM directors could accept, and—after changing its name to the Civil Liber- ties Bureau—it became an independent organization. Its work broadened to include freedom of speech, press, and conscience and the defense of citizens who were prosecuted under the 1917 Espionage Act, including members of the Industrial Workers of the World (IWW), who were accused of calling strikes to obstruct the war effort.

In September 1918 Baldwin was called to register for the draft. After he "respectfully declined to appear" for a physical examination, saying that he was opposed "to any service whatever designed to help the war," he was arrested. At a hearing he made a long and eloquent statement in which he said: "I regard the principle of conscription of life as a flat contradiction of all our cherished ideals of individual freedom, democratic liberty and Christian teaching. . . . I cannot consistently, with self-respect, do other than I have, namely, to deliberately violate an act which seems to me to be a denial of everything which ideally and in practice I hold sacred." After complimenting Baldwin for stating his position honestly, the judge sentenced him to a year in the penitentiary. Baldwin's stance earned praise from many liberal organizations, and Emma Goldman said he "has proved himself the most consistent of us all." The socialist leader Norman Thomas said that the hearing "was one of the rare experiences of a lifetime." Baldwin's time in jail was relatively pleasant, and he turned it to his advantage. He carried on an extensive correspondence, wrote poetry, and, as a trusty, worked in the prison's kitchen and garden. He also found time to start a Prisoners' Welfare League and to befriend inmates, some of whom became lifelong friends.

After his release in July 1919 Baldwin married Madeleine Doty, a writer and lawyer who was a pacifist and feminist. Less than two months later, with his wife's encouragement, Baldwin left for the West with only a few dollars to see how he would fare as an unskilled laborer. He passed several months this way, joined both the IWW and the Cooks and Waiters Union, took part in a steel strike as a union spy, and felt the satisfaction of experiencing firsthand what he had previously known only theoretically.

In January 1920, after his return to New York, he and his allies transformed the Civil Liberties Bureau into the American Civil Liberties Union (ACLU). The union's statement of purpose included reference to freedoms endangered by government repression, especially against labor—free speech, a free press, the right to strike, criminal justice, immigration equity, and racial equality. As executive director, Baldwin put together a diverse board of prominent liberal activists, including Jane Addams, Helen Keller, Scott Nearing, Norman Thomas, Helen Phelps Stokes, A. J. Muste, John Haynes Holmes, Felix Frankfurter, Oswald Garrison Villard, and his closest associates, Albert DeSilver (who acted as associate director) and Walter Nelles (who acted as counsel).

Under Baldwin's direction and with the aid of volunteer lawyers, the ACLU participated in a variety of controversial cases. These included challenges to the roundup and deportation of radical aliens; the defense of John T. Scopes in the famous Tennessee "Monkey Trial" in 1925, when the case was lost but the cause won; the Nicola Sacco–Bartolomeo Vanzetti murder case; a successful challenge to the banning of James Joyce's *Ulysses*; and the protection of the First Amendment rights of communists and socialists, union members and Henry Ford, the Ku Klux Klan and Jehovah's Witnesses. The common element, Baldwin said, was that the Constitution protected people you "feared as well as those you admired."

In the late 1920s and early 1930s Baldwin made two trips to the Soviet Union and wrote extravagant praise of that country, which he later came to regret. Although he joined no party, he worked closely with communist and other left organizations during the Popular Front period of the mid-1930s. A few years later, after a change in mind, he acted decisively to remove communists and their supporters from the board of directors of the ACLU. In the most notorious case, Elizabeth Gurley Flynn, a communist leader who had been a board member from the founding of the ACLU, was removed after a celebrated "trial" at the Harvard Club of New York City. In 1940 Baldwin drafted, and the board of directors passed, a resolution that required ACLU officials to aver that they were not adherents of communism or fascism and that they supported the civil liberties of all peoples, including those outside the United States. This resolution became, ironically, a model for government loyalty oaths that the ACLU challenged during the McCarthy period. (In the 1970s the ACLU repealed the 1940 resolution and voted to restore Elizabeth Flynn to its board of directors posthumously.)

World War II did not provoke the same pacifist protests or government repression as World War I had. During the war, Baldwin was largely occupied with the legal challenge to the Roosevelt administration's decision in 1942 to round up Japanese Americans on the West Coast, many of them citizens, and send them to camps in the interior. The effort to declare these actions unconstitutional failed in the Supreme Court, although years later evidence appeared that the government concealed information that the program was not essential to national security.

In 1947 Baldwin went to Japan at the invitation of General Douglas MacArthur to help instill in the Japanese an understanding of democracy and civil liberties. The previous year Baldwin was a founder of the International League for the Rights of Man (later the International League for Human Rights). After he retired, Baldwin was the ACLU's coordinator of international work, serving as a liaison to the United Nations and participating in discussions concerning U.S. possessions and territories. For many years he taught a civil liberties course at the University of Puerto Rico.

To appreciate Baldwin's contribution, one must recall the state of civil liberties in 1920, when the ACLU was founded. Post–World War I euphoria was yielding to "normalcy" and nativism, culminating in a resurgence of the Ku Klux Klan and the Palmer Raids, mass round-ups of aliens suspected of radi-

calism, which often ended in trials and deportation. The
Supreme Court had yet to uphold a single claim of free
speech; state criminal trials were virtually beyond constitutional protection; racial minorities, women, and other disad-
vantaged groups found almost no judicial support; workers
were unable to organize legally; and sexual privacy was forty-
five years from constitutional recognition.

In 1950, when Baldwin retired as ACLU executive director,
the modern foundations of the Bill of Rights were in place.
Under his supervision, volunteer lawyers such as Clarence
Darrow and Arthur Garfield Hays had, among other things,
helped abolish the worst of company police forces, achieved
initial victories for free expression and religious liberty, and
assisted in laying the groundwork to end segregation in
schools and other parts of American life.

Throughout his life Baldwin was an active outdoorsman. He
spent weekends in a rustic house in New Jersey, where he
watched birds, canoed, hiked, and observed nature. He was
active in the Audubon Society as well as in the National Urban
League and the National Conference of Social Welfare. Baldwin divorced his first wife in 1935 and in 1936 married Evelyn
Preston, also a reformer. They had one child, and he adopted
her two sons. He died in New Jersey.

That Baldwin was able to organize, lead, and put to work—
for a pittance or merely a pat on the back—so many talented
people speaks not only to the principles they shared but to his
special character. He was cantankerous and obstinate. He was
also vigorous, puckish, courtly, joyous, vain, determined, loyal,
and tough. His qualities gave the civil liberties movement, in
the words of one writer, "a special blend of passion and ration-
ality, of biting dissent and tolerance for the beliefs and causes
of others."

Baldwin did not consider himself an intellectual but rather
a manager, a practical man, and above all an inspirer of others.
But if he was not an intellectual, he certainly was a philoso-

pher. He knew life and he knew people. He urged everyone to live as if each individual could make a difference in a complex, stubborn, and often cruel world. He believed that each person might save the world a little, and—perhaps more important— would be saved by the effort to do so.

Baldwin was not a religious man. Nevertheless, he viewed the Sermon on the Mount as an extraordinary declaration of humanity. He patterned his pacifism after Gandhi's, and, like Gandhi, he went to jail in witness to his beliefs. His life exemplified the high purposes of religion: to transmit a sense of generational continuity, of caring, and of love. He concerned himself with people not only in the mass but one by one. He genuinely cared about other people and, always with a sense of humor, gave them confidence in what they were.

N.D.

George Bancroft

[3 OCTOBER 1800–17 JANUARY 1891]

Vaguely remembered today as the first consequential American historian—remembered but not read—George Bancroft was also in his own time a political boss, a cabinet officer, a diplomat, a presidential ghostwriter, a parlor radical, and a bon vivant. His grand achievement was his ten-volume History of the United States—*an epic of democracy that vitally shaped America's conception of itself. Based on diligent archival research, it was written, alas, in a rhetorical style that fatigues modern eyes and ears.*

An admirer of Andrew Jackson, Bancroft dispensed federal patronage in Massachusetts in the 1830s. As secretary of the navy in the 1840s, he founded the Naval Academy at Annapolis and issued the orders in the Mexican War that led to the annexation of California. After Lincoln's assassination, he was chosen to give the official eulogy before Congress. He was minister to Germany during the Franco-Prussian War in 1870, and his pro-Prussian sympathies provoked Victor Hugo to write a scathing poem denouncing him.

Besides working away at his history for half a century, he rode horseback in the afternoon and gave lively dinners in the evening. Henry Adams, a young friend (and a brilliant historian who today is not only remembered but read), said of him, "Old George Bancroft was never more than forty." He died in 1891 at the age of ninety. John Adams was president when he was born, and Theodore Roosevelt attended his memorial service. He should not be forgotten.

ARTHUR SCHLESINGER, JR.

George Bancroft, scholar and diplomat, was born in Worcester, Massachusetts, the son of Aaron Bancroft, the founder of Worcester's Second Congregational Society and later president of the American Unitarian Association, and Lucretia Chandler. The eighth of thirteen children,

George passed his childhood in a frugal rural household dominated by paternal activism. In 1811 he entered the Phillips Exeter Academy in New Hampshire, run by Benjamin Abbot, a family friend. Attending with a scholarship, Bancroft received a solid grounding in classics, which prepared him for Harvard, where he enrolled at the age of thirteen.

Under the presidency of John T. Kirkland, another family friend, Harvard was struggling to develop from a glorified boarding school into an institution of higher learning. Bancroft thrived in its structured environment, immersed in a curriculum fostering self-control, reasonable faith, and virtuous citizenship. Financial aid allowed him to concentrate on his studies. The seriousness of his few friends, who were among the younger faculty, rubbed off on Bancroft, and he became something of a prig. Under the tutelage of Levi Hedge and others, he acquired proper tastes in literature, a smattering of science, and a good knowledge of Greek and Latin. Moral philosophy, the underpinning of the curriculum, a mixture of Lockean rationalism and Scottish Common Sense philosophy, shaped his mental outlook. The English oration he delivered at his 1817 commencement on the dignity and philosophy of the human mind indicated his high class standing and proper outlook.

A ministerial career seemed appropriate given Bancroft's interests and education. He began the requisite M.A. studies and sought respite from theology in the novels of Sir Walter Scott and Maria Edgeworth. On Edward Everett's recommendation, Kirkland offered Bancroft the opportunity to study at the Georgia Augusta university in Göttingen, and Bancroft sailed for Europe in June 1818. The course of his education over four years was somewhat unfocused, but philology, biblical criticism, German and French literature, ancient and oriental languages, and modern history vastly broadened his intellectual horizons. Awarded a doctorate by the Georgia Augusta in 1820 but unwilling to face an uncertain future in Cambridge, Bancroft next embarked on a grand European tour, including an extended stay at Berlin to hear Hegel and Schleiermacher lecture. He visited Paris, traveled through Italy, and met distant relations in London. Immense curiosity about America as well as letters of introduction allowed Bancroft to meet Goethe and Alexander von Humboldt, Washington Irving, and Lafayette. In June 1822 the educational pilgrimage ended, and Bancroft sailed for the United States ready to begin life in earnest.

At first Bancroft embarked on a desultory ministerial career, aware it would lead nowhere. He also antagonized several former benefactors who disagreed with his belief that a European doctorate deserved special consideration. His Georgia Augusta education was deemed fit at most for a Greek instructorship at Harvard, a one-year appointment which Bancroft was forced to accept. In an experience as unhappy as his foray into the pulpit, he joined several younger faculty members who sought to reform Harvard after European models. Their plans produced no immediate results, and in the winter of 1822, together with Joseph Cogswell, Bancroft set out to establish an intermediate educational institution patterned after the German Gymnasiums he had visited, incorporating innovative educational methods to stimulate young minds. Round Hill in Northampton was a pathbreaking experiment that appealed to parents progressive enough to entrust their boys, at sizable expense, to two young schoolmasters. In 1824 Round Hill enrolled 25 boys, and in 1827 the number had grown to 135. But the chores, administrative details, and financial worries soon forced Bancroft once again to look elsewhere for a profession. Meanwhile, the publication in 1823 of a volume of his poems had revealed budding literary ambitions.

In 1827, after an elaborate courtship, Bancroft married Sarah Dwight, the daughter of a prominent merchant-banker. Her family's social standing and political connections fueled Bancroft's ambition and increased his resources, prompting him to sever his ties with Round Hill. He wrote extensively for the *North American Review* and other magazines and translated Arnold Hermann Ludwig Heeren's *Reflections on the Politics of Ancient Greece* from German, becoming one of the main transmitters of European literature to the United States. Bancroft also began to dabble in local politics. The clergyman-schoolmaster was on his way to becoming a man of action and a scholar.

Bancroft's fluid political views attracted attention from both National Republicans and Democrats, but he wanted to publish at least the first installment of his *History of the United States* before making a serious political commitment. He began assembling materials in 1832, chiefly to explain the United States to its citizens, harnessing the past to elucidate the present. In 1834 the first volume appeared and was a great literary and scholarly achievement. Democratic in tone, it carried a reassuring message to readers worried about the future. Current upheavals, Bancroft showed, had antecedents. The United States had surmounted earlier trials, and it would again. National Republicans and Democrats united in praise of the book, and the volume sold well.

Bancroft implied in the *History* that the voice of the people was the voice of God. This and several pro-Democratic pronouncements elicited overtures from local workingmen's associations as well as from the Democratic organization. After weighing options for several months, Bancroft chose to align himself with the Democratic Party, whose ideology was more compatible with his views, its structure more flexible in accommodating demands, and its ranks less crowded with ambitious youngsters ready to lead. Bancroft developed an extensive friendship network with local workingmen, labor, and anti-Masonic leaders. He ran for the Massachusetts General Court as an independent, but the scurrilous opposition from the National Republicans, who tagged him a turncoat radical, contributed to his defeat and strengthened his credentials as a Democrat.

His effort to unseat Springfield's congressional representative also ended in defeat, but the irrepressible Democrat persisted in forecasting a rosy future for the state and the nation. In 1837 a financial panic exposed the shallowness of his predictions, but the death of his first wife, who never recovered from the birth of their third child, overshadowed the political aftershocks. Overcome by grief, Bancroft escaped to Montreal for a few weeks, then returned to immerse himself in party activism. Bancroft was appointed collector of the port of Boston, a post he turned into a power base, remodeling party machinery and improving its electoral chances. He also was able to use patronage to further the careers of Nathaniel Hawthorne and Orestes A. Brownson.

Bancroft moved to Boston, where in 1838 he married the widow Elizabeth Bliss, with whom he would have one child. A gracious lifestyle included extensive scholarly activities to prepare the next installments of the *History*, hosting foreign dignitaries, and managing Democratic Party activities. In 1839 the Democrats won the governorship, thanks to Bancroft's adroit exploitation of the liquor law controversy, and the second volume of the *History*, in which Bancroft developed the Democratic message embedded in his first volume, was published the following year.

In 1840 William H. Harrison's election as president created unprecedented though temporary Democratic unity. Bancroft shrugged off troublesome questions about the nation's political system. Could *vox populi* be construed as *vox dei* when the people opted for "Tippecanoe and Tyler too"? Timorous Democrats like Brownson developed doubts, but Bancroft, embroiled at this inopportune moment in an acrimonious legal suit with the Dwights over his first wife's inheritance, thought the answer an unqualified yes. Meanwhile, the Liberty Party was draining Democratic strength by exploiting slavery's political impact, which Bancroft preferred to ignore. The more his friends edged toward abolitionism, the more Bancroft dis-

tanced himself, disliking rabble-rousers, mistrustful of visionary reforms, and opposed to radical solutions. Bancroft abandoned local for national politics. In 1844 he was a leading figure at the Baltimore Democratic National Convention, which
nominated James K. Polk for the presidency. The annexation
of Texas, Manifest Destiny, and the future of Oregon seemed
the slogans of the hour, and Bancroft, running that year for the
Massachusetts governorship, altered his political pronouncements accordingly. He campaigned for Polk in New York, tried
to reconcile embittered Van Burenites, and still found time for
his *History*. He lost the gubernatorial race, but Polk's victory
brought Bancroft to Washington, D.C., where he joined the
cabinet as secretary of the navy.

As secretary Bancroft acquired first-hand experience at
conducting foreign policy in a democratic society. He also
helped found the U.S. Naval Academy at Annapolis and tried
to streamline the Navy Department. Bancroft was instrumental
in the acquisition of California, ordering the Pacific Naval
Squadron in June 1845 to occupy San Francisco and other
ports in case of war, and he defended President Polk against
the charge that the president was party to a nefarious southern
plot to extend slavery. Bancroft believed that the Mexican War,
of which he was an enthusiastic supporter, was a god-sent
opportunity to enlarge the national domain for liberty. The
vociferous antiwar sentiment, the shifting political alliances
the war created, and the strange bedfellows it produced
astounded Bancroft. After eighteen months in office he had
had enough of Washington; and when Polk offered him the
ambassadorship to Great Britain, Bancroft jumped at the
opportunity.

Bancroft spent three years in London, where he proved
himself a reliable diplomat, closely following instructions
from Secretary of State James Buchanan. Bancroft ably
defended U.S. policy against English criticism while moving
with ease within polite society. He also followed the 1848 revo-

lutions on the Continent and the Chartist demonstrations in London, certain that they were the death knell of the Old Regime. Meanwhile, a tribe of secretaries and friends supplied materials for the future volumes of the *History*.

News from the United States about political realignments, the rise of the Free-Soil Party, and Democratic splinterings in Massachusetts augured an uncertain political future. When Whig Zachary Taylor's 1848 presidential victory ended Bancroft's service in London, Bancroft moved to New York, where, as a gentleman of means, he wrote the next four volumes of his *History*. He and his family divided their time between a gracious residence in the city and a house in Newport, Rhode Island, where Bancroft indulged his passion for roses and horseback riding. In New York he was host to prominent visitors, supported charitable associations, and observed politics from a distance. He helped shape plans for Central Park, defended animal rights, and closely followed the ups and downs of his investments.

After 1854 Bancroft resumed his public role, horrified to discover that what he had always believed an impossibility—the demise of the United States—seemed about to materialize. The *History* volumes published during this decade articulated a message to all extremists about the impossibility of deviating from the nation's providentially assigned course. They also reminded readers that progressive schemes aimed at overturning ancient abuses needed time to mature. Those who hoped to accelerate the normal pace of historical development would be disappointed. Bancroft's faith in providential guidance as well as his continued travels in the United States further reassured him that the Union ultimately could not fall apart.

When events threatened to prove otherwise, however, Bancroft fastened on the Democratic Party as the last unifying, nationwide political institution. His hopes were placed successively in President James Buchanan, the Supreme Court (until the Dred Scott decision), and Stephen A. Douglas, for whom he wrote speeches during Douglas's 1860 presidential bid. Once the South seceded, Bancroft became a convert to vigorous prosecution of the war, a position he sustained throughout the conflict, amidst shifting prospects and failures that Bancroft attributed to President Abraham Lincoln's incompetence, to Republican stupidity, and to Copperhead treachery. He joined Republicans and Democrats in founding the Union League and blamed the war on a southern conspiracy. When the war's magnitude became evident, Bancroft resorted to the doctrine of affliction to justify the pain, divinely inflicted suffering being, he thought, a prelude to national regeneration. As the conflict expanded, he bemoaned northern defeatism and southern "fanaticism." By the summer of 1862 he opted for emancipation. The draft riots in New York in the summer of 1863 astounded him, and, though still a Democrat, he voted for Lincoln the following year. In his eulogy on Lincoln before the House of Representatives in February 1866, Bancroft implied that the president had wished to punish slavery while sparing the slaveholder. Bancroft aided President Andrew Johnson in drafting his first annual message, and he supported Johnson's reconstruction policy.

The publication of the ninth volume of the *History* in 1866 embroiled Bancroft in a nasty war of words with irate grandsons of revolutionary figures who detested his current politics and his treatment of their ancestors. Johnson's offer of the post of U.S. minister to Prussia in 1867 enabled Bancroft to return to Germany, where he felt at home. While there he cultivated the acquaintance of musicians, artists, and scholars. President Ulysses Grant kept Bancroft in Berlin, where the historian witnessed first-hand Bismarck's adroit handling of opponents at home and abroad. Bancroft considered Bismarck to be Germany's George Washington and was an enthusiastic supporter of Prussia in its war with France and a vociferous defender of the newly united Germany. He remained in Berlin for seven years.

Upon his return to the United States in 1874, Bancroft settled in Washington, D.C., determined to complete his historical projects. In the remaining years of his life, he played the part of local celebrity who knew everyone worth knowing, and he was frequently called upon by prominent tourists. The tenth volume of the *History* appeared in 1874 to the customary approval, although by then younger scholars were challenging several Bancroftian interpretations of the nation's past. Undismayed, Bancroft embarked on other tasks in addition to working on the constant revisions of his *History*. The Centenary Edition appeared in 1876, in six volumes, followed in 1882 by a two-volume edition of documents relating to constitutional ratification. The last version, appearing between 1882 and 1884 and subtitled *Author's Last Revision*, incorporated the previously published volumes into a final whole. He also authored articles and notes as well as a biography of Martin Van Buren (1889). In 1885 the two-year-old American Historical Association elected Bancroft its president. By 1889 Bancroft's health had worsened, and he died two years later in Washington.

Bancroft's *History of the United States*, a multivolume sermon, assumed the certainty of providential guidance, the transitory significance of the individual, popular conservatism, and the durability of the nation's political institutions. It documented how divinely ordained natural laws sustained growth, and it articulated a national consciousness, providing historical substantiation for an optimistic faith. A self-sustained process of orderly reform, inherent in national evolution, spared the country after 1776 the need for further revolutions. Bancroft's influence in his lifetime reflected the popularity of this message.

L.H.

Béla Bartók

The Hungarian-born Béla Bartók is, by any reckoning, one of the most original, profound, and influential composers of the twentieth century. He was one of the first modern composers to real-ize the importance of collecting folk music, which, often with his col-league Zoltán Kodály, he gathered throughout Eastern and Central Europe and as far away as North Africa. These folk melodies became the basis of much of his music, transmuted with the utmost sophistication, but never academically overcerebral. A man of the highest integrity, Bartók, though Aryan (albeit with a Jewish second wife), would have nothing to do with fascism at home or abroad and refused various prizes.

His last and supreme compositions were created during summers at Saranac Lake or winters in Asheville, North Carolina. In 1944, he published important studies of Serbian and Romanian folk music. The great Third Piano Concerto is deliberately simpler than its predecessors, a legacy for his wife. Still working on his Viola Con-certo, and starting his seventh string quartet, he died in a New York hospital. Interred first in Westchester, his remains were later reburied in Hungary.

JOHN SIMON

Béla Bartók, composer and pianist, was born in Nagyszentmiklós, Hungary (now Sînnicolau Mare, Romania), the son of Béla Bartók, the headmaster of an agricultural school, and Paula Voit, a schoolteacher. Bartók received his first piano lessons at age five from his mother, who, after the death of Bartók's father in 1888, supported the family through a succession of teaching positions. At age nine, Bartók began composing short pieces for piano, and in 1892 he made his first public appearance as a pianist. His family settled in Pozsony (Bratislava) for five years between 1894 and 1899, and Bartók studied harmony and piano there with László Erkel and Anton Hyrtl.

From 1899 to 1903, Bartók attended the Academy of Music in Budapest. He studied piano with István Thomán and composition with Hans Koessler. Although Bartók was attracted early on to the music of Wagner and Liszt, he discovered more direction for his own stylistic development in the works of Richard Strauss. He was also influenced by a growing nationalist movement. Both influences are manifest in compositions from Bartók's student years, for example his symphonic poem *Kossuth* (1903).

While a student, Bartók commenced a successful career as a concert pianist. Following graduation, he studied and gave concerts in Berlin as well as in Vienna. Beginning in 1903 with his Violin Sonata and later with *Kossuth*, Bartók programmed concerts of his own compositions. In 1905 Bartók entered his Piano Quintet (1904), Rhapsody for Piano (1904), and Violin Sonata in the Rubinstein competition in Paris, where he received only a disappointing certificate.

In 1904, while making his first notation of a Hungarian peasant song, Bartók discovered a folk music of which he, and his musical compatriots, had been virtually unaware. He then began the lifelong task of collecting, cataloging, and analyzing folk melodies, in much of which he was joined by Zoltán Kodály. Together they amassed thousands of peasant songs, some of which they published, beginning in 1906 with *Twenty Hungarian Folksongs*. Bartók's collecting extended over many years and into remote villages in his own and neighboring countries. In folk music, Bartók discovered the means to create his own uniquely Hungarian style, one that combined folk elements with the main trends in contemporary music. He was also strongly influenced by the music of Debussy, in which he found traits similar to those he admired in peasant songs, such as modal melodies and exotic harmonies.

In 1907 Bartók was appointed to a piano professorship at the Academy of Music in Budapest. In 1909 he married his sixteen-year-old student Márta Ziegler, with whom he had one child.

Bartók's interest in the folk idiom is evidenced in a large quantity of piano music including *Fourteen Bagatelles* (1908); his first Violin Concerto (1907–1908); *Two Portraits* (1909) and *Two Pictures* (1910), both for orchestra; his String Quartet no. 1 (1908); and several folk song arrangements. After the collapse of the Hungarian Music Society, formed in 1911 by Bartók and Kodály to promote contemporary Hungarian works, and the rejection of his opera *Duke Bluebeard's Castle* (1911) by the national opera competition, Bartók withdrew from public life, and his output decreased. He continued his folk music studies with increased enthusiasm.

During World War I, Bartók, exempt from the military on medical grounds, continued collecting folk music and returned to composing, producing the Piano Suite, op. 14 (1916), the String Quartet no. 2 (1915–1917), two song cycles (1915–1916), a number of pieces based on Romanian song, and his first unqualified public success, the one-act ballet *The Wooden Prince* (1914–1917).

After the war, Bartók found himself out of sympathy with the government. Restrictions on traveling hampered his collecting, and questions about his patriotism arose over his work with minority cultures. His status in Hungary improved, however, as his international reputation grew considerably, owing to the concert tours he made each year to England, Germany, the Netherlands, France, Switzerland, and Italy.

In 1923, after a divorce from his first wife, Bartók married Ditta Pásztory, who became a concert pianist; they had one child. Between December 1927 and February 1928, Bartók made a concert tour of the United States, during which he gave the New York premiere of his Piano Concerto no. 1. That same tour, his *Contrasts* for violin, clarinet, and piano was commissioned by Benny Goodman. He then toured the USSR (Dec. 1928–Jan. 1929). On his fiftieth birthday Bartók received the medal of the Légion d'honneur and the Corvin Medal.

In 1934 Bartók ceased teaching and accepted a research post at the Hungarian Academy of Sciences that enabled him to devote more time to his folk music collection, which included some 13,000 Hungarian melodies. He wrote and lectured on his work and took part in international congresses.

Following *The Miraculous Mandarin* of 1918–1919, Bartók's compositions of the 1920s and 1930s include two violin sonatas (1921, 1922), *Village Scenes* (1926), the first and second piano concertos (1926, 1931), the third through sixth string quartets (1927, 1928, 1934, 1939), *Cantata profana* (1930), *Mikrokosmos* (1926–1939), Music for Strings, Percussion and Celesta (1936), Sonata for Two Pianos and Percussion (1937), the Violin Concerto no. 2 (1938), and Divertimento (1939). Of his work after 1926 Bartók observed in an interview in *étude* (1941) that it became "more contrapuntal and also simpler on the whole. A greater stress of tonality is also characteristic of this time."

Eventually, Bartók's antipathy toward fascism and renewed questions over his political allegiance led to his decision to leave Hungary. He made another concert tour of the United States in April–May 1940 and returned the next October to stay. He was appointed to a research position at Columbia University to work with the Milman Parry collection of Serbo-Croatian folk songs. Columbia also awarded him an honorary doctorate.

Bartók's American years were discouraging; for two years he composed no new music. With his wife he gave a few concerts, the last being the premiere of the Concerto for Two Pianos, Percussion, and Orchestra by the New York Philharmonic (21 Jan. 1943). Funding for his Columbia position was discontinued. During his final years, Bartók was supported through the help of friends and ASCAP (American Society of Composers, Authors, and Publishers). His final compositions include the

Concerto for Orchestra (1943), commissioned by Serge Koussevitzky; Sonata for Solo Violin (1944), commissioned by Yehudi Menuhin; the unfinished Viola Concerto for William Primrose; and the Piano Concerto no. 3 (1945), on which he worked until the moment he was taken to the New York hospital where he died.

Following his death, the Béla Bartók Archive was set up as a permanent department of the Hungarian Academy of Sciences. Along with Kodály, he is credited with the awakening of serious interest in the folk musics of his homeland. He did not establish a school of composition but is regarded as a major individualist and as one of the leading composers of the twentieth century.

E.K.

Sterling A. Brown

[1 MAY 1901–13 JANUARY 1989]

Sterling A. Brown's poems strike me as being among the most alive of American poems. His fury holds steady and sings; his humor cuts true; his music compels, by its formal inevitabilities and its free-wheel improvisations. How many poems in English have the moral force, the balance, the irony, the brilliant metric change of pace of "Old Lem"? And, with all their fierceness — clothed in it, and in their stringent, flexible rhythms and harmonics — his poems embody so much love for courage, and for the sensual, and for human honor.

SHARON OLDS

Sterling Allen Brown, professor of English, poet, and essayist, was born in Washington, D.C., the son of Sterling Nelson Brown, a minister and divinity school professor, and Adelaide Allen. After graduating as valedictorian from Dunbar High School in 1918, Brown matriculated at Williams College, where he studied French and English literature and won the Graves Prize for an essay on Moliere and Shakespeare. He was graduated from Williams in 1922 with Phi Beta Kappa honors and a Clark fellowship for graduate studies in English at Harvard University. Once at Harvard, Brown studied with Bliss Perry and notably with George Lyman Kittredge, the distinguished scholar of Shakespeare and the ballad. Kittredge's example as a scholar of both formal and vernacular forms of literature doubtlessly encouraged Brown to contemplate a similar professorial career, though for Brown the focus would be less on the British Isles than on the United States and on African-American culture in particular. Brown received his M.A. in English from Harvard in 1923 and went south to his first teaching job at Virginia Seminary and College at Lynchburg.

Sterling Brown and his world (1940s): (from left) Jean Himes, Chester Himes, Sterling Brown, Backlin Moore. *(Photographer: Chick Solomon; Schomburg Center for Research in Black Culture)*

Brown's three years at Virginia Seminary represent much more than the beginning of his teaching career, for it was there that he began to immerse himself in the folkways of rural black people, absorbing their stories, music, and idioms. In this regard, Brown is usefully likened to two of his most famous contemporaries, Zora Neale Hurston and Jean Toomer (with whom Brown attended high school). Like Hurston, Brown conducted a kind of iconoclastic ethnographic field-work among southern black people in the 1920s (she in Florida, he in Virginia) and subsequently produced a series of important essays on black folkways. Like Hurston and Toomer, Brown drew on his observations to produce a written vernacular literature that venerated black people of the rural South instead of championing the new order of black life being created in cities in the North. And like Toomer in particular, Brown's wanderings in the South represented not just a quest for literary material, but also an odyssey in search of roots more meaningful than what seemed to be provided by college in the North and black bourgeois culture in Washington. After

Virginia Seminary, Brown taught briefly at Lincoln University in Missouri and Fisk University before beginning his forty-year career at Howard University in 1929.

Brown's first published poems, frequently "portraitures" of Virginia rural black folk such as Sister Lou and Big Boy Davis, appeared in the 1920s in *Opportunity* magazine and in celebrated anthologies including *Countee Cullen's Caroling Dusk* (1927) and James Weldon Johnson's *The Book of American Negro Poetry* (1922; 2d ed., 1931). When Brown's first book of poems, *Southern Road*, was published in 1932, Johnson's introduction praised Brown for having, in effect, discovered how to write a black vernacular poetry that was not fraught with the limitations of the "dialect verse" of the Paul Laurence Dunbar era thirty years earlier. Johnson wrote that Brown "has made more than mere transcriptions of folk poetry, and he has done more than bring to it mere artistry; he has deepened its meanings and multiplied its implications." Johnson also showed his respect for Brown by inviting him to write the *Outline for the Study of the Poetry of American Negroes* (1931), a teacher's guide to accompany Johnson's poetry anthology.

The 1930s were productive and exciting years for Brown. In addition to settling into teaching at Howard and publishing *Southern Road*, he wrote a regular column for *Opportunity* ("The Literary Scene: Chronicle and Comment"), reviewing plays and films as well as novels, biographies, and scholarship by black and white Americans alike. From 1936 to 1939 Brown was the Editor on Negro Affairs for the Federal Writers' Project. In that capacity he oversaw virtually everything written about African Americans and wrote large sections of *The Negro in Virginia* (1940), a work that led to his being named a researcher on the Carnegie-Myrdal Study of the Negro, which generated the data for Gunnar Myrdal's classic study, *An American Dilemma: The Negro Problem and Modern Democracy* (1944). In 1937 Brown was awarded a Guggenheim Fellowship, which afforded him the opportunity to complete *The Negro in Ameri-*

can Fiction and *Negro Poetry and Drama*, both published in 1937. *The Negro Caravan: Writings by American Negroes* (1941), a massive anthology of African-American writing, edited by Brown with Ulysses Lee and Arthur P. Davis, continues to be the model for bringing song, folktale, mother wit, and written literature together in a comprehensive collection.

From the 1940s into the 1960s Brown was no longer an active poet, in part because his second collection, "No Hidin' Place," was rejected by his publisher. Even though many of his poems were published in the *Crisis*, the *New Republic*, and the *Nation*, Brown found little solace and turned instead to teaching and writing essays. In the 1950s Brown published such major essays as "Negro Folk Expression," "The Blues," and "Negro Folk Expression: Spirituals, Seculars, Ballads and Work Songs," all in the Atlanta journal *Phylon*. Also in this period Brown wrote "The New Negro in Literature (1925–1955)" (1955). In this essay he argued that the Harlem Renaissance was in fact a New Negro Renaissance, not a Harlem Renaissance, because few of the significant participants, including himself, lived in Harlem or wrote about it. He concluded that the Harlem Renaissance was the publishing industry's hype, an idea that gained renewed attention when publishers once again hyped the Harlem Renaissance in the 1970s.

The 1970s and 1980s were a period of recognition and per-haps of subtle vindication for Sterling Brown. While enduring what was for him the melancholy of retirement from Howard in 1969, he found himself suddenly in the limelight as a redis-covered poet and as a pioneering teacher and founder of the new field of Afro-American studies. Numerous invitations fol-lowed for poetry readings, lectures, and tributes, and fourteen honorary degrees were bestowed on him. In 1974 *Southern Road* was reissued. In 1975 Brown's ballad poems were collect-ed and published under the title *The Last Ride of Wild Bill and Eleven Narrative Poems*. In 1980 Brown's *Collected Poems*, a vol-ume edited by Michael S. Harper, was published in the National Poetry Series. Brown was named poet laureate of the District of Columbia in 1984.

Brown had married Daisy Turnbull in 1927, possibly in Lynchburg, where they had met. They had one child. Brown was very close to his two sisters, who lived next door in Washington. They cared for him after Daisy's death in 1979 until Brown entered a health center in Takoma Park, Maryland, where he died.

Brown returned to Williams College for the first time in fifty-one years on 22 September 1973 to give an autobiographical address and again in June 1974 to receive an honorary degree. The address, "A Son's Return: 'Oh Didn't He Ramble'" (*Berkshire Review* 10 [Summer 1974]: 9-30; repr. in Harper and Stepto, eds., *Chant of Saints* [1979]), offers much of Brown's philosophy for living a productive American life. At one point he declares, "I am an integrationist . . . because I know what segregation really was. And by integration, I do not mean assimilation. I believe what the word means—an integer is a whole number. I want to be in the best American traditions. I want to be accepted as a whole man. My standards are not white. My standards are not black. My standards are human." Brown largely achieved these goals and standards. His poetry, for example, along with that of Langston Hughes, forever put to rest the question of whether a written art based on black vernacular could be resilient, substantial, and read through the generations. Despite his various careers, Brown saw himself primarily as a teacher, and it was as a professor at Howard that he felt he had made his mark, training hundreds of students, pioneering those changes in the curriculum that would lead to increasing appreciation and scrutiny of vernacular American and African-American art forms. In short, Brown was one of the scholar-teachers whose work before 1950 enabled the creation and development of American studies and African-American studies programs in colleges and universities in the decades to follow.

R. S.

A. P. Carter and Sara Carter

[15 DECEMBER 1891–7 NOVEMBER 1960; 21 JULY 1898–8 JANUARY 1979]

I grew up on the music of the Carter family. Their first-ever recorded versions of our region's old songs forever shaped my sense of narrative and place. Visionary genius A. P. Carter was the first to understand the value and importance of the Appalachian area's traditional music; he put his family in the car and took them to record for Ralph Peer at the historic Bristol Sessions of 1927 in Bristol, Tennessee. Country music as we know it—or as we knew it, to be exact—was born there. Though Sara and A. P. Carter and his sister-in-law Maybelle Carter (who formed the original group) have long since been eclipsed by subsequent stars—including their own family members Johnny Cash and June Carter Cash—we must not forget their importance. They gave voice to an almost invisible people in a poor, isolated part of America, articulating their values, beliefs, and passions; documenting their history and their lives. This music has evolved and changed over the years, yet it continues to sing the working man's—and woman's—song, expressing our frustrations and our dreams. Their legacy of language, story, and song continues to make us mindful of who we are, as it delights and inspires us today.

LEE SMITH

Musicians and songwriters A. P. Carter and Sara Carter were the founding members of the early country music singing group the Carter Family. A. P. Carter was born Alvin Pleasant Delaney Carter near the Appalachian hamlet of Maces Spring, Scott County, Virginia, the son of Robert C. Carter and Mollie Arvelle Bays, both local farmers whose families had been in the region since the late eighteenth century. As a youth, A. P. was exposed to music by both sides of his family. His father had been a well-known local

The Carter family: (from left) Maybelle, A.P., and Sara. *(Country Music Hall of Fame and Museum)*

banjo player who later turned to sacred music; his mother's family included an uncle, Flanders Bays, who taught rural singing schools for area churches; and his mother was a repository of old ballads, both those brought over from Great Britain and newer ones derived from Native American sources. By 1913 A. P. was singing bass in a local church choir and had learned to play both the guitar and fiddle—the latter in a light-bowed, skirling style associated with older Scotch styles. A restless and curious young man, A. P. traveled to Indiana in around 1910–1911, worked on a railroad crew near Richmond, Virginia, for a time, and eventually returned home, suffering from typhoid fever. His schooling consisted of sporadic attendance at local country schools in the Poor Valley. By 1915 he was trying to make a living selling fruit trees to area residents.

Sara Carter was born Sara Daugherty in Flat Woods, near the modern town of Coeburn, in Wise County, Virginia, the daughter of Sevier Dougherty, a sawmill operator, and Elizabeth Kilgore. When her mother died prematurely, young Sara was reared by her aunt and uncle, Milburn and Melinda Nick-les, in the Copper Creek area of nearby Scott County. There she became interested in music and learned to play the auto-harp — a stringed instrument then new to the folk music of the mountains — from her neighbor Eb Easterland. Family history tells that one day, probably in 1914, while Sara was at a rela-tive's house playing her autoharp and singing the train-wreck ballad "Engine 143," A. P. appeared with his fruit trees for sale. The pair hit it off and, after an exchange of letters and visits, were married in 1915 at Milburn and Melinda Nickles's house in Copper Creek.

For the next several years the young husband and wife entertained informally in the area; they would sing many of the old songs and ballads, but, unlike many of the older singers who sang unaccompanied, Sara and A. P. sang in har-mony and backed their singing with guitars or autoharp. Much of this early work was at churches and most of it yielded little money; neither of them yet thought about trying to make a liv-ing from their music. By 1925 they were being joined by a third musician, Sara's first cousin Maybelle Addington. She was a skilled guitar player and singer as well, and after she married A. P.'s brother Ezra, she joined the group and the Carter Fami-ly was born.

By this time phonograph records were making their way into the mountains, and the Carters began to hear recordings of some of the old tunes that they had been singing. The com-mercial record companies, looking for authentic mountain music to put on their new discs, were sending talent scouts into the Appalachians, and in early 1927 A. P. and Sara audi-tioned for the Brunswick company in nearby Norton. The company wanted to develop A. P. as a fiddle player, but he felt his talents were as a singer and song arranger and spurned the offer. A. P. was by now interested in making records, though, and began to correspond with Ralph Peer, the artists and repertory (A&R) man from the Victor Talking Machine Company. When Peer decided to come to nearby Bristol, on the Tennessee-Virginia line, to set up a field studio and record local talent in July 1927, he invited the Carter Family to come in for an audition. This they did, and one of music history's most important events ensued: a session that yielded the first recordings by the Carters as well as by Jimmie Rodgers, the two acts that would in effect define modern country music.

Most of the Carter Family vocal arrangements were built around Sara's lead singing, and it was her voice that impressed Peer. On many of the early recordings, vocal duties were shared by her and A. P.; on later arrangements, Sara and Maybelle carried the burden of the singing, with A. P. occasionally (to use his own words) "bassin' in." Their very first professional recording was an old folk lyric, "Bury Me under the Weeping Willow" (Victor 21074), and it was typical of their repertoire: an old song known in the mountains for years but rearranged by A. P. Within a few years they would record numerous songs for Victor that would become country music, folk, and bluegrass standards: "The Storms Are on the Ocean" (Victor 20937, 1927); "Keep on the Sunny Side," their theme song (Victor 21434, 1928); "Wildwood Flower" (Victor 40000, 1928); "John Hardy Was a Desperate Little Man" (Victor 40190, 1928); "I'm Thinking Tonight of My Blue Eyes" (Victor 40089, 1929); "Wabash Cannonball" (Victor 23731, 1929); and "Worried Man Blues" (Victor 40317, 1930).

From 1927 until 1941 the Carter Family recorded more than 300 songs for RCA Victor (and its Bluebird subsidiary), Decca, and the American Recording Company. Their songs and their sparse but elegant arrangements made them the most famous singing group in country music history. While A. P., and occasionally Sara, would create original songs, most were older tunes that had been arranged or even rewritten by A. P. At one time it was assumed that old folk songs made up most of their repertoire, but recent research has revealed that the Carters often performed popular songs from the late nineteenth century that were published in songbooks or as sheet music. Many of the gospel songs came from the paperback shape-note songbooks published by companies like James D. Vaughan of Tennessee.

During the height of their popularity, the Carters were often separated and beset with personal problems. As early as 1931 Maybelle and her husband were living as far away as Washington, D.C., where her husband's work took him; the group sometimes came together only for recording sessions. Then, in early 1933, Sara and A. P. separated, with Sara returning to Copper Creek and working with A. P. only on professional occasions. They would later divorce, and in 1939 Sara married one of A. P.'s cousins. Both Sara and Maybelle were busy raising their families during this time as well.

The Carter Family career also encompassed radio shows throughout the 1930s, many of them on the various "border radio" stations in Texas, such as XERA in Del Rio. Such stations skirted federal broadcasting regulations by having their transmitters across the Rio Grande in Mexico, allowing them to broadcast at hundreds of thousands of watts. These stations carried the Carter Family music to every hamlet and home in the southern United States. During these years—the late 1930s—the Carters involved their children in the group. Sara's daughter Janette performed, as did Maybelle's children Helen, June, and Anita.

The Carters broke up permanently in 1943. A. P. returned to Maces Spring to open a country store; Sara moved to California with her new husband. Maybelle started her own career featuring herself and her daughters. Though A. P. and Sara were effectively retired from music, they did reunite in 1952 for a series of recordings on the independent Acme label, but these recordings were not commercially successful. Through the offices of Johnny Cash, who had married Maybelle's daughter June, Sara and Maybelle did a reunion album in 1967.

C.K.W.

John Jay Chapman

[2 MARCH 1862-4 NOVEMBER 1933]

*O*ne has only to read the first ten pages of A Glance towards Shakespeare *to know that one is in the presence of a master critic and prose writer. John Jay Chapman is a literary genius whom America has yet to value—and enjoy, for he is immensely enjoyable. His vision is uniquely enlightening and entertaining, and his style simply original. His range, too, is notable. It goes from city politics to poetry and philosophy and from estimates of great American figures to an extraordinary utterance at the scene of a lynching. In 1912 Chapman went to Coatesville, Pennsylvania, at the risk of his life to hold a "prayer meeting" after the cruel death of a young Negro. Chapman was also a pioneer in the civil rights movement through his short biography of William Lloyd Garrison, as fresh today in word and thought as it was ninety years ago.*

I first encountered Chapman when M. A. DeWolfe Howe, who liked to guide my reading in Americana, gave me a copy of his just-published collection of Chapman's letters. It too makes good reading. Then Edmund Wilson published his fine essay in praise of Chapman, after which came two anthologies of his writings. The question why such an unmistakable literary power has been so long overlooked brings the usual answer: he came at the wrong time, and those whom contemporaries fail to honor (or attack) slip altogether from the communal memory. It takes repeated efforts to reinsert the name and the work in the web of history.

By wrong time, I mean that Chapman was a "cultural critic" long before the term was coined. In his day, American self-criticism was overwhelmingly political and social. Few or none understood that preconceptions and attitudes about art, education, history, philosophy, and religion also influence politics and social life and constitute a subject to be widely discussed by capable thinkers. Now every newspaper columnist is a cultural critic. By going to Chap-

man for a lesson or two, they might install him at last in the niche he deserves. This country has not such a surplus of great critics and great letter-writers that it can afford to neglect Chapman.

JACQUES BARZUN

John Jay Chapman, essayist and poet, was born in New York City, the son of Henry Grafton Chapman, a well-to-do stockbroker and later president of the New York Stock Exchange, and Eleanor Jay, the great-granddaughter of John Jay, the first chief justice of the United States. From 1874 to 1877 Chapman studied at St. Paul's School in Concord, New Hampshire, where he suffered a nervous breakdown. After then being tutored privately for college, he entered Harvard in 1880 and profited intellectually by touring Europe as an undergraduate. He received his bachelor's degree in 1885 and studied at Harvard Law School for the next two years. In January 1887 he mistook the harmless attentions of Percival Lowell, the future Orientalist and astronomer, toward Minna Timmins, his own close friend, and he beat Lowell with a heavy cane. Learning of his error in judgment, Chapman punished himself by burning his left hand in a coal fire so severely that it had to be amputated. After vacationing in Europe that summer, he was admitted to the New York bar the following year. He married Timmins in 1889 and lived with her in New York; the couple had three children. He practiced law in New York until 1898 but preferred to read and involve himself in political reform.

Partly because his wife was half Italian, Chapman studied Italian literature and published "The Fourth Canto of the *Inferno*" (*Atlantic Monthly*, Nov. 1890) and "Michael Angelo's Sonnets" (*Bachelor of Arts*, June 1895). In the 1890s he also published *The Two Philosophers* (1892), a comedy based on an incident involving the Harvard faculty, and essays on William Shakespeare (1896), Robert Browning (1896), and Walt Whitman (1897). A major work was his "Emerson Sixty Years After"

(*Atlantic*, Jan.–Feb. 1897). In March 1897 he also began to edit and privately publish a monthly periodical titled the *Political Nursery*, rebuking Tammany Hall chicanery in New York City and promoting suggestions by the local Good Government Club. He was to discontinue the magazine in January 1901. Chapman's wife died in 1897. A year later he married Elizabeth Chanler; the couple had one child.

By the time Chapman published *Emerson and Other Essays* in 1898, Ralph Waldo Emerson had become the single most important influence on his self-reliant moral, social, and intellectual stance. His *Causes and Consequences* (1898) and *Practical Agitation* (1900) reflect his disgust at the unholy alliance of party politics, commercialism, and conservative writers. No longer a Republican but now an independent, he was outraged when he and others persuaded his friend Theodore Roosevelt in 1898 to run for governor of New York as an independent only to see him switch back to the Republican Party. Meanwhile, Chapman was viewing with dismay America's steady drift toward imperialism after the Spanish-American War.

Chapman was stricken in 1901 with a mysterious physical and nervous breakdown, was bedridden for a year, and walked only with crutches for a year after that. He was devastated when his nine-year-old son drowned in Austria while the family was vacationing there in 1903. During this period he received psychological help from his friend William James.

Chapman's work on the stage began in 1907 with seven plays he wrote for children. Mostly comic, romantic, and unoriginal, they feature lost children, witches, hermits, knights, and the like, have passages of blank verse, and praise idealists and reformers. The plays, which were performed by vacationing groups and in schools, were published in 1908 and 1911. Chapman also wrote three adult dramas, one of which, *The Treason and Death of Benedict Arnold: A Play for a Greek Theatre* (1910), retains its value. It depicts a heroic figure gone tragically astray, and its use of varied rhythms, episodes, chorus, and intermezzo provides variety and excitement. Writing plays was undoubtedly of therapeutic value to Chapman.

In 1910 he suddenly felt well again. He published *Learning and Other Essays* that year and took a trip to Italy and North Africa the next. In 1912 he made a penitential pilgrimage, in an effort to cleanse the American soul, to Coatesville, Pennsylvania. He rented a room in a vacant store, advertised a meeting, and on 18 August read a moving address to memorialize the unusually brutal lynching one year earlier of Zacharia (or Ezekiel) Walker, an African American who killed a white man during a robbery. Chapman's speech urged love in response to hate and reverence for human nature and in the process exposed a dark corner of the American soul. He spoke to an audience of two people. Getting a better response was his spirited, well-documented *William Lloyd Garrison* (1913), in praise of unpopular, but occasionally necessary, violent action against evil, in this instance abolitionist Garrison's war against slavery.

In June 1914 Chapman and his wife visited his son Victor, an architecture student in Paris. In July the couple were in Germany. When that country invaded France, the Chapmans returned home via London, but Victor joined the Lafayette Escadrille and was killed in action in June 1916—the first American aviator to die in World War I. Earlier, Chapman had published *Deutschland über Alles; or, Germany Speaks . . .* (Nov. 1914), in which he mostly let Germany condemn itself by quoting bellicose German statesmen, writers, and militarists. He also more sanely, if vainly, asked American leaders—including President Woodrow Wilson in person—to seek, first, disarmament, and then, after America entered the war, unvengeful treatment of Germany, the predestined loser.

After Victor's death, Chapman never regained his previous creative energy. He edited and published Victor's letters from France (1917). He revealed surprising prejudices, wanting names of German students kept off the Harvard War Memorial

(1917), objecting when a Roman Catholic was seated on Harvard's Board of Overseers (1924), and opposing the nomination of Alfred E. Smith as Democratic candidate for president because of his Catholicism (1927). To his credit, however, he published a book on Shakespeare (1922), *Letters and Religion* (1924), a study of Dante (1927), and three books concerned with Greek literature (1928, 1929, 1931). He visited Europe three more times (1919, 1925, 1930). He died in Poughkeepsie, New York.

Chapman was a brilliant, honest man of letters and advocate of reform. His interests were varied, and each of his twenty-five books is distinctive. His main, self-imposed challenge was to understand and reform the American mind. Everything he wrote is graceful, vigorous, and implicitly autobiographical.

R.L.G.

Leon F. Czolgosz

[1873–29 OCTOBER 1901]

*H*e *was restless and rootless. He lacked a steady job and went mostly unnoticed in groups. He used aliases less for conceal-ment than to confer illicit significance upon an unremarkable per-sona. He was uncomfortable with women and did not date. He learned to hate, and was drawn to famous people who articulated grandiose visions of destruction. He craved their approval and sought to win it through a shocking act of violence. On a bright September day in the first year of a new century, he committed mur-der, and in so doing changed the world.*

He was Leon Czolgosz, who assassinated President William B. McKinley on September 6, 1901; McKinley died a week later, precip-itating a crackdown on radical groups in the nation. Czolgosz came to mind while I was reading an account of Mohamed Atta, ring-leader of the terrorist group that flew jetliners into the World Trade Center and the Pentagon, killing more than 3,000, on September 11, 2001.

I understand neither Czolgosz nor Atta. How can one live to kill? How make sense of Czolgosz's muddled utopia, an amalgam of anarchist chaos and socialist planning? How make sense of Atta's ghoulish paradise, inhabited by "black-eyed virgins" who beckon from atop a pile of innocent dead?

The beliefs of these two young men would have been mutually incomprehensible. Yet I suspect that each might have found in the other a kindred soul: socially awkward, impressionable, empty—and terrible.

MARK C. CARNES

Leon Franz Czolgosz, assassin of President William McKinley, was born in Detroit, Michigan, the son of Paul Czolgosz, a menial laborer. His mother's name is unknown. His parents emigrated from southern Poland to the United States just prior to Leon's birth. As a boy Czolgosz shined shoes and sold newspapers. In 1880 the family moved to Rogers City in northern Michigan, but after five months they settled in the Polish community in Posen. Czolgosz intermittently attended public and Catholic parochial schools and developed a lifelong interest in reading, chiefly Polish magazines. In 1885 his mother died in childbirth. That year the family moved to Alpena, near Detroit, and in 1889 to

LESLIE'S WEEKLY
McKINLEY EXTRA

Vol. XCIII—EXTRA NUMBER.   New York, September 9, 1901   PRICE 10 CENTS

The first photograph taken of Leon Czolgosz, the assassin of President William McKinley, in jail, 1901. *(Library of Congress)*

Natrona, a predominantly Polish community near Pittsburgh. There Leon worked in the searing heat of a glass factory, earning seventy-five cents a day. In 1892 the family moved to Cleveland, where he found a job tending machinery at the Newberg Wire Mills. He was a steady and quiet worker who managed to save $400, which he contributed to a family fund to buy a farm. On one occasion the wire spool snapped, slashing and scarring his face.

The depression of 1893 forced many firms to cut wages, including the Newberg Wire Mills, and its workers went on strike. Czolgosz joined them and was fired, but the following year he successfully applied for a job at the plant using the alias Fred C. Nieman. The strike and its aftermath affected him profoundly. Formerly a devout Catholic who read the Bible regularly, Czolgosz abandoned religion and was increasingly

53

drawn to radical groups, first to a Polish socialist club that met in a room above the small saloon his father bought in 1895. Czolgosz joined the organization though seldom took part in its discussions.

In early 1898 Czolgosz experienced some sort of health-related or emotional crisis. He seemed tired and depressed and complained of stomach and lung problems. In August he quit the wire mill and moved to the family farm near Cleveland. Mostly he lounged in his room and read newspapers, especially the anarchist *Free Society*. He was especially fascinated by an account of Gaetano Bresci, an anarchist from Paterson, New Jersey, who in 1900 shot and killed King Humbert I of Italy. Czolgosz kept the article by his bed.

In the spring of 1901 Czolgosz asked his family to return the money he had put up for the farm so that he could seek work in the West. They initially balked but eventually advanced him seventy dollars, which financed his subsequent travels. On 5 May he went to Cleveland and was moved by a speech by the anarchist Emma Goldman. Introducing himself as Fred Nieman, Czolgosz also approached Emil Schilling, treasurer of the Liberty Club, the anarchist group that published *Free Society*. Schilling and other anarchist officials were put off by Czolgosz's ignorance of anarchist doctrine and his incautious queries, such as when he asked whether the group was "plotting something like Bresci." In late July Czolgosz took advantage of low excursion rates to travel to Buffalo, site of the Pan-American Exposition. He took a room in a boardinghouse in West Seneca, outside Buffalo, probably in the hope of finding work. McKinley's decision to visit the exposition was not made public until August.

About this time, too, the officers of the Liberty Club learned that Czolgosz had not given them his real name, and they assumed the worst. The 1 September issue of *Free Society* warned readers that a probable government spy, "well dressed, of medium height, rather narrow shouldered, blond, and about twenty-five years of age," had recently attempted to infiltrate the organization. The article may have driven Czolgosz to take desperate action to prove his loyalty. Early in September he bought a 32-caliber Iver Johnson revolver.

On 5 September Czolgosz attended the exposition. It was "President's Day," and Czolgosz was infuriated: "I thought it wasn't right for any one man to get so much ceremony," he said later. The next day Czolgosz returned to the exposition, concealed his revolver in a handkerchief, and took a place in line at the Temple of Music. When his turn came to shake hands with the president, Czolgosz pushed McKinley's arm away, thrust the revolver forward, and fired two shots through the handkerchief. McKinley stiffened and then slumped into the arms of his aides. Soldiers and Secret Service men knocked Czolgosz down and beat him. "Be easy with him, boys!" McKinley called out. Lengthy surgery proved ineffective; the president died eight days later.

Before the end of the month, Czolgosz was put on trial for murder. When medical experts sought to determine his sanity, he flatly admitted his culpability: "I fully understood what I was doing when I shot the President." He took no part in the trial other than to utter the word "guilty," a plea the judge could not accept. Czolgosz's court-appointed lawyers called no witnesses, and the trial lasted only eight hours. The jury deliberated thirty-four minutes before pronouncing him guilty. He was sentenced to death by electrocution. There was no appeal. On the morning of 29 October, as he was being strapped into the electric chair, Czolgosz's explanation of his actions was terse: "I killed the President because he was the enemy of the good people—the good working people. I am not sorry for my crime." He died in the Auburn penitentiary.

Czolgosz's act provoked a crackdown by federal and state law enforcement agencies on anarchists and socialists; prompted Congress to amend immigration laws to exclude anarchists and other radicals; and forced the Secret Service to

tighten security for the president and other key federal officials. Although most radicals distanced themselves from Czolgosz, Emma Goldman called him an idealist who hoped for a
better world.

In 1902 psychiatrist Walter Channing argued that Czolgosz
had been insane. He cited Czolgosz's shyness, his preference
for solitary pursuits such as reading, and his avoidance of
women. Nineteen years later L. Vernon Briggs expanded on
Channing's analysis and claimed that Czolgosz suffered from
"dementia praecox," or paranoid schizophrenia. But Czolgosz's
act, though unreasonable, was not wholly irrational. McKinley's administration was in fact beholden to powerful business
interests whose excesses came at the expense of poor people
and helped precipitate Progressive reforms. Assassination,
moreover, was consistent with the violent political doctrines of
the Russian anarchist Mikhail Bakunin. Yet it is difficult to dis-
cern a rational purpose in Czolgosz's action if only because his
political beliefs were confused. Though he endorsed violence
and anarchy, his favorite book was a Polish translation of
Edward Bellamy's *Looking Backward* (1888), which evoked a
genteel socialist utopia, and Czolgosz had joined and sympa-
thized with many socialist organizations, whose goals were
antithetical to those of the anarchists.

Neither pathological nor exclusively political, Czolgosz's act
was essentially that of an awkward and dull-witted young man
who rarely attracted much notice, except for one day when,
energized in some complex way by radical rhetoric, he set forth
on a path that fatefully intersected with that of the president.

M.C.C.

Robert Latou Dickinson

[21 FEBRUARY 1861–29 NOVEMBER 1950]

*R*obert Latou Dickinson died in 1950. I first encountered him some sixteen years later, in the course of researching my doctoral dissertation, later published as Birth Control in America: The Career of Margaret Sanger. *Propelled by no more than a hunch and a hope, I made my way one bitterly cold day in 1966 through fresh-fallen snow across Central Park to the New York Academy of Medicine on Fifth Avenue and the office of Dr. Christopher Tietze, once Dickinson's own. To my delight, Tietze pulled from a shelf in his closet several long-neglected cardboard boxes of papers relating to Dickinson's involvement with Margaret Sanger and the birth control movement in the 1920s and 1930s. Those dusty cartons proved the answer to a researcher's prayer. They introduced me to a fascinating human being, a pioneer in the scientific study of sexual practice, a proponent of often daring reforms respecting women's attire, diet, exercise, and erotic fulfillment, and a gifted artist who often illustrated his own medical publications and exhibited his work at the New York World's Fair in 1939–1940. He was also the leading gynecologist of his day.*

His papers proved incomparably rich in educating me about the historical development of the medical profession in the early twentieth century, about the technical history of contraceptive devices, and about the myriad difficulties that beset Margaret Sanger's extraordinary struggle to make contraception an accepted part of clinical practice. In that struggle, Dickinson was often her only ally in a profession that was itself struggling to define responsible therapeutics and to establish its scientific respectability. His integrity, imagination, energy, and courage made him scarcely less crucial than Margaret Sanger herself to the eventual acceptance of artificial contraception in American society.

DAVID M. KENNEDY

Robert Latou Dickinson, gynecologist and sexologist, was born in Jersey City, New Jersey, the son of Horace Dickinson, a hat manufacturer, and Jeannette Latou. During Dickinson's childhood the family business was located in Brooklyn, New York, where the Dickinsons and Latous were civic and cultural leaders. Dickinson enjoyed a privileged childhood in Brooklyn Heights, with summers on an uncle's Connecticut farm. When he was twelve, his father took the family to Europe for four years, during which the children were privately tutored and attended schools in Switzerland and Germany. The Dickinsons returned to the United States in 1876. Robert entered Brooklyn Polytechnic Institute and completed the equivalent of the last years of high school in 1879.

Dickinson considered a career as a commercial artist, but an interest in medicine had been inspired by a childhood boating accident that left an eight-inch scar on his abdomen, and he entered the medical school of Long Island College Hospital in 1879. Although he completed the course work in 1881, his receipt of the M.D., which then served as a license to practice, was delayed a year because candidates were required to be at least twenty-one years old. Dickinson spent his twenty-first year as an assistant to Alexander J. C. Skene, whose *Treatise on the Diseases of Women* (1888) dominated the textbook market in gynecology for a decade and featured 161 illustrations by Dickinson.

Dickinson began building a successful private practice in 1882, but his strong interest in the reform politics of Brooklyn mayor Seth Low drew him into service as a Republican ward captain, ambulance surgeon, examiner for the police and fire departments, and unsuccessful candidate for the office of coroner. In 1886 Long Island College Hospital hired him as a lecturer in obstetrics, and he remained an active teacher there and at other local hospitals until he retired from clinical practice. As Skene's protégé, Dickinson took great pride in developing new techniques for both surgery and teaching, which he described in more than one hundred publications. His writing competed with his busy schedule as a healer but provided an outlet for his talent as an illustrator and his desire to raise the standards of his profession. In 1890 he married Sarah Truslow, a banker's daughter and Packer Institute graduate with whom he shared an Episcopalian commitment to the Social Gospel. They had three children.

Early in his practice Dickinson began to make detailed records of female sexual anatomy and to interview his patients systematically about their sexual experience. Convinced that women were frequently the victims of sexual maladjustments deriving from ignorance or dysfunctional social values, he published a series of articles that described autoeroticism in women, urged his colleagues to counsel patients actively on the need for sexual fulfillment in marriage, advocated dress reform and physical education, and declared his conviction that birth control was essential to strong families. Dickinson became convinced that his ideal of the doctor as marriage counselor was just as important to the future of his specialty as were advances in basic scientific research. Known as a Christian gentleman and orthodox physician, Dickinson commanded a tolerant reception for his unorthodox work, but he chafed constantly over the reticence of his colleagues in matters of sexual reform. He successfully lobbied for election as president of the American Gynecological Society in 1920 in order to secure a platform from which to make his case for sex research and counseling as an essential medical responsibility. The experience represented by his own database of more than 5,000 heavily illustrated patient records convinced him that he should turn from his lucrative ordinary practice to full-time sexology. Following service in World War I in the medical section of the National Council of Defense (1917) and as medical adviser to the Army General Staff (1918–1919), he closed his Brooklyn office-home and moved to Manhattan, where he lived on his investments and devoted all his time to sexual reform.

In 1923 Dickinson founded the Committee on Maternal Health (in 1930 "National" was added to the name) to provide an institutional sponsor for the campaign for medical sex research and marriage counseling. His first agenda item was to conduct a clinical study of contraceptive methods that would disprove irresponsible claims by medical leaders that safe and effective contraceptive practice was not possible. Even Dickinson's group of distinguished physicians could not obtain a license for a birth control clinic in New York State, but through cooperation with Margaret Sanger, the founder of the American Birth Control League (1921) and of the unlicensed Birth Control Clinical Research Bureau (1923), Dickinson played a key role in the publication of the first definitive studies on the effectiveness and safety of contraceptive practice. He waged a long lobbying campaign that led to a 1937 American Medical Association resolution that recognized contraception as a legitimate and essential part of medical practice.

During the 1930s the National Committee on Maternal Health emerged as a clearinghouse for information on human fertility. A series of definitive monographs, such as Dickinson's *Control of Conception* (1931), *A Thousand Marriages* (1931; with Lura Beam), *The Single Woman* (1934; with Beam), and *Atlas of Human Sex Anatomy* (1933), served as handbooks for doctors interested in sexual counseling and as justifications for shifts in medical opinion. Committee publications on the physics and chemistry of contraception helped to define standards for commercial products, while studies on sterility and abortion brought new issues to the table for professional debate. Dickinson was also an active member of the Committee for the Study of Sex Variants, which conducted major studies of lesbianism, described in G. W. Henry's *Sex Variants* (1941). He wrote introductions and provided illustrations for works ranging from sex education pamphlets for adolescents to academic benchmarks such as Clellan Ford and Frank Beach's *Patterns of Sexual Behavior* (1951). As the most influential person in American sexology before Alfred Kinsey, Dickinson received and answered hundreds of letters from colleagues asking his opinion on sexual issues they encountered in their practices. In collaboration with sculptor Abram Belskie, he developed a series of sculptures depicting the cycle of conception, fetal growth, and birth that was viewed by more than two million people at the 1939 World's Fair, in one of the most successful efforts at sex education ever staged.

Dickinson was characterized by directed exuberance in both work and play. His artistic skills and love of nature—he was an avid walker, cyclist, and sailor—were reflected in hundreds of sensitive medical illustrations, as well as in *Palisades Interstate Park* (1921) and the *New York Walk Book* (1923; with Raymond Torrey and Frank Place). Dickinson blended the ethical idealism of his New England ancestors with great social skill in raising funds and mobilizing colleagues in support of his goal, the maintenance of stable families in a changing world. His career as a sexologist was inspired by an essentially religious vision of a richer existence if barriers to erotic fulfillment could be removed. He was a mediator of the transition from the Victorian code of "civilized sexual morality" to the embrace of personal erotic fulfillment characteristic of modern society, yet he maintained a strong, prescriptive commitment to his ideal of heterosexual, monogamous, married parents as the cornerstone of social order. He died in Amherst, Massachusetts.

J.W.R.

Dorothy Draper

[22 NOVEMBER 1889–10 MARCH 1969]

*M*y infatuation with the interior designer Dorothy Draper began with my love of hot dogs. When I was young I would eat one thing and one thing only—hot dogs with mustard. I also had a favorite place to eat my meal and that was Howard Johnson's. The grilled dogs satisfied my stomach. But the colors of the restaurant, a combination of bright orange and turquoise blue, dazzled in my eyes. Dorothy Draper, the restaurant's designer, was brave enough to pair these colors.

I developed my most significant attachment to Dorothy Draper during the long summer days in a small northern Michigan town. These days were often slow, dull, and depressing. But there was always one day I looked forward to: the day my mother, my sisters, and I spent on Mackinaw Island. My sisters loved the horseback riding, the boat rides, and the chocolate fudge. But I had eyes only for Grand Hotel. It is a beautiful white Victorian fortress. The outside took my breath away, but the inside made my heart beat fast. There was no doubt about it—Dorothy had been there. The long halls, the dining rooms, and the shops were all decorated in bright colors, long stripes, and soft florals. Each wall, floor, and furniture covering seemed so whimsical they seemed to possess their own distinctive, enticing scent. We usually settled in some corner where we ordered tea and cakes. I would nestle in comfortably on some big over-stuffed yummy chair covered in the softest, brightest fabric the back of my knees had ever felt. Dorothy Draper was not only a maverick in my profession, she was the magician who entertained and inspired the imagination of a growing girl.

KATIE BROWN

D orothy Draper, interior decorator and columnist, was born in Tuxedo Park, New York, the daughter of Paul Tuckerman and Susan Minturn. She grew up in the environs of New York in an exclusive resort community where her parents were among the founding members in 1886. Educated primarily at home with a governess and tutor, her formal schooling was minimal, including two years at the Brearley School, a private girls' school in New York City. Annual trips to Europe gave her a cosmopolitan

Despite the infamous slur leveled at Dorothy Draper by Frank Lloyd Wright, who referred to her as an "inferior desecrator," her reputation remains unchallenged with respect to the influence of her style on commercial hotel design. 1930s photo. *(Dorothy Draper & Co./Carleton Varney Design Group)*

exposure to the world, and she was presented at Sherry's in 1907. Although she did not have any academic design training, her background and upbringing among the elite families of the Northeast contributed to her subsequent success as a decorator. She had complete confidence in her taste, and her social connections proved to be important in acquiring future clientele.

In 1912 she married George Draper, with whom she had three children before their divorce in 1930. Her interest in interior decorating began when she successfully renovated several houses that she owned in Manhattan and Washington. Eager to apply her energies and natural flair beyond her own domestic environment, she started a small business in 1925 called the Architectural Clearing House in which she coordinated the renovations of friends' houses with the assistance of local architects. In the early 1930s, through Douglas Elliman, a real estate developer, she received the commission to decorate the lobby of the Carlyle Hotel in New York City, the first of many important hotel commissions. The lobby displayed many features that came to represent her trademarks, including large square black and white marble floor tiles, chintz fabric and wallpaper in oversize patterns, and the display of busts and other classical forms as decorative elements.

In 1929, as her business grew with the successful renovation of several apartment house lobbies in the classical–Art Deco idiom, the name of the firm was changed to Dorothy Draper and Company. Draper's natural talent for public relations as well as her reputation in the area of nonresidential design resulted in the 1937 commission for the entire thirty-seven story Hampshire House apartment hotel in Manhattan, the largest commercial decorating contract to be given to a woman at that time. She believed that the entire project should be conceived comprehensively and designed everything from the interior architecture to bellboy liveries and china. Combining furniture styles and design motifs of various historical periods, she tried to make the impersonal public spaces more home-like, creating the atmosphere of a London townhouse instead of the customary hotel look, which was monochromatic and undistinguished. While stark contrasts of black and white, fanciful plasterwork in the neo-baroque style, large expanses of mirror, and innovative uses of materials such as patent-leather and metal gave these spaces theatrical drama, the walls and furniture of bedrooms were decorated with a patterned fabric of huge cabbage roses in brilliant reds and emerald greens. This fabric became a well-known signature of the Dorothy Draper style, produced by the fabric house of F. Schumacher & Co., which sold more than a million yards of this bright-colored chintz throughout the 1930s and 1940s. Wallpaper with wide pink and white stripes, chenille bedspreads, and white organdy curtains completed the Draper scheme and became ubiquitous in tasteful American bedrooms. Another innovation at the Hampshire House was the use of sliding glass doors instead of shower curtains in the bathrooms.

Draper was known for her vivid use of colors. Large, strong, and bold were her catchwords. From the 1930s to the mid-1950s her innovative design statements could be seen in all kinds of environments. In the striking use of scale and light, her style reflected the influence of the surrealist movement. Besides hotel interiors, Draper's work included clubs, restaurants, retail stores, and some private homes. She became a national celebrity largely due to her newspaper columns and publications. From 1939 to 1946 she wrote for *Good Housekeeping* magazine, and later she wrote a syndicated column for Hearst newspapers, "Ask Dorothy Draper." The author of three books—*Decorating Is Fun* (1939), *Entertaining Is Fun* (1941), and *365 Shortcuts to Home Decoration* (1965)—she also had a radio show called "Lines about Living," and she appeared on the covers of *Time* and *Life* magazines.

Some of her best-known commissions include the Gideon Putnam Hotel in Saratoga Springs (1933), Arrowhead Springs resort in California (1939), the Drake Hotel (Camellia House Restaurant) in Chicago (1940), the Mayflower Hotel in Washington, D.C. (1944), the Quitandinha Hotel in Petropolis, Brazil, and the "Dorotheum" restaurant-cafeteria of the Metropolitan Museum of Art in New York City (1954). Most of her work for those buildings has been altered beyond recognition. Her surviving tour de force is the Greenbriar resort in White Sulphur Springs, West Virginia, which was totally redecorated in 1947 with all her trademark motifs. She was also the color coordinator for the 1952 Packard Automobile, parts of the International Hotel at Kennedy Airport (1958), and the interior of the Convair 880 airplane (1960).

One reason given for her particular fondness for large-scale patterns and grandiose architectural detailing was her statuesque height, which was close to six feet. Her commanding presence was frequently crowned by a stylish hat, and her influential design aesthetics earned her the title of the grande dame of American interior decorating. Like most of the first generation of women decorators in America, she lacked the credentials of a professional designer. But because of the enormous impact her firm had on the industry, she was eventually admitted to the American Institute of Decorators (AID) in the early 1950s. Despite the infamous slur leveled at Draper by Frank Lloyd Wright, who referred to her as an "inferior desecrator," her reputation remains unchallenged with respect to the influence of her style on commercial hotel design. In 1960 she sold her company to Leon Hegwood (who has since died) and the designer Carlton Varney; the latter continued to use her name in the design of commercial interiors. Draper died in Cleveland, Ohio, and is buried in Newport, Rhode Island.

P.C.M.

Paul Laurence Dunbar

[27 JUNE 1872–9 FEBRUARY 1906]

I *first heard Paul Laurence Dunbar's poetry as a child. My father, born in 1913 and blessed with a photographic memory, was fond of reciting long passages of poetry, to my brother and me, as we sat around the television in our living room, or at my bedside as I struggled to go to sleep. While my father's repertoire was quite broad— he loved poems such as Kipling's "If," Longfellow's "Psalm of Life," and Whittier's "The Barefoot Boy"—his absolute favorite poem, without a doubt, was Paul Laurence Dunbar's "In the Morning," with Dunbar's "The Party" a close second. In other words, I was raised on Dunbar's lyrics, especially this one:*

> *Lias! Lias! Bless de Lawd!*
> *Don' you know de day's erbroad?*
> *Ef you don' git up, you scamp,*
> *Dey'll be trouble in dis camp.*

Recently, I asked the statesman Vernon Jordan (born in 1935) what his favorite poem was. Without missing a beat, he began to recite "In the Morning," his eyes aglow just as my father's were. And when I had children, born in 1980 and 1982, whenever I had to wake them up for school, I found myself reciting "In the Morning" to them, just as my father had done for me. And I would not be surprised if they find themselves reciting these same lines to their own children someday, just as I did to them.

The tradition of black people memorizing poetry written by black writers is strong, indeed, and merits a study of its own. And of these poets, with the possible exception of Langston Hughes, no one's verse is more frequently quoted out loud than Paul Laurence Dunbar's. "The Party," "When Malindy Sings," "An Ante-Bellum Sermon, "When De Co'n Pone's Hot," "A Negro Love Song," and

"Sympathy" are among Dunbar's most accomplished poems, and his most frequently anthologized—"anthologized" in print and by memorization, by word of mouth, by speakers.

Dunbar's reputation suffered from what we might think of as a "poetics of respectability," an embarrassment with, and a shying away from, dialect poetry, which was a fundamental tenet of Harlem Renaissance aesthetics at least since James Weldon Johnson argued in 1922 that dialect had but "two stops, pathos and humor." What's more, its centrality to the racist stage genres of minstrelsy and vaudeville had corrupted its poetic potential hopelessly, or so the argument went. Even the quickest glance backward from 1922 would have led directly to the towering figure of Dunbar, whose dominance in the history of the tradition—especially in the period immediately preceding the Renaissance—had to be transcended, undermined, or circumvented if Renaissance poetry was to find its voice. No, Dunbar as a poetic model just would not do. And despite the publication of several biographies and editions of his work, Dunbar has never regained the dominant position within the tradition that he held at the turn of the last century. Nevertheless, no poet in the tradition was more crucial in the shaping of a distinct African-American poetic diction or voice than he.

Put simply, Paul Laurence Dunbar during his lifetime was the most famous black writer in the world. This fact is all the more astonishing given his extremely humble origins, and given his short career as a writer, a professional career that spanned barely fourteen years. Perhaps because of the brevity of his career, few scholars have realized how prolific Dunbar was, and how prolific he was in such a wide range of genres. A well-edited edition of Dunbar's collected and uncollected works and a sophisticated biography would go far toward enabling a complete revaluation of Dunbar's place in the canon of American and African-American literature. More than any other single author, Paul Laurence Dunbar gave African-American literature its resplendent vernacular voice.

HENRY LOUIS GATES, JR.

Paul Laurence Dunbar, author, was born in Dayton, Ohio, the son of Joshua Dunbar, a plasterer, and Matilda Burton Murphy, a laundry worker. His literary career began at age twelve, when he wrote an Easter poem and recited it in church. He served as editor in chief of his high school's student newspaper and presided over its debating society. While still in school, he contributed poems and sketches to the *Dayton Herald* and the *West Side News*, a

Frontispiece from the 1905 edition of *Lyrics of Sunshine and Shadow*, by Paul Laurence Dunbar. *(Library of Congress)*

local paper published by Orville Wright of Kitty Hawk fame, and briefly edited the *Tattler*, a newspaper for blacks that Wright published and printed. He graduated in 1891 with the hope of becoming a lawyer, but, lacking the funds to pursue a college education, he went instead to work as an elevator operator.

Dunbar wrote and submitted poetry and short stories in his spare time. His first break came in 1892, when the Western Association of Writers held its annual meeting in Dayton. One of Dunbar's former teachers arranged to have him deliver the welcoming address, and his rhyming greeting pleased the conventioneers so much that they voted him into the association. One of the attendees, poet James Newton Matthews, wrote an article about Dayton's young black poet that received wide publication in the Midwest, and soon Dunbar was receiving invitations from newspaper editors to submit his poems for publication. Encouraged by this success, he published *Oak and Ivy* (1893), a slender volume of fifty-six poems that sold well, particularly after Dunbar, an excellent public speaker, read selections from the book before evening club and church meetings throughout Ohio and Indiana.

In 1893 Dunbar traveled to Chicago, Illinois, to write an article for the *Herald* about the World's Columbian Exposition. He decided to stay in the Windy City and found employment as a latrine attendant. He eventually obtained a position as clerk to Frederick Douglass, the former abolitionist who was overseeing the Haitian Pavilion, as well as a temporary assignment from the Chicago *Record* to cover the exposition. After a rousing Douglass speech, the highlight of the exposition's Negro American Day, Dunbar read one of his poems, "The Colored Soldiers," to an appreciative audience of thousands. Sadly, when the exposition closed, Chicago offered Dunbar no better opportunity for full-time employment than his old job as elevator boy, and so he reluctantly returned to Dayton. However, he did so with Douglass's praise ringing in his ears: "One of the sweetest songsters his race has produced and a man of whom I hope great things."

Dunbar's determination to become a great writer was almost derailed by a chance to pursue his old dream of becoming a lawyer. In 1894 a Dayton attorney hired him as a law clerk with the understanding that Dunbar would have the opportunity to study law on the side. However, Dunbar discovered that law no longer enthralled him as it once had; moreover, he found that working and studying left him no time to write, and so he returned to the elevator and his poetry. He soon had enough new poems for a second volume, *Majors and Minors* (1895), which was published privately with the financial backing of H. A. Tobey of Toledo, Ohio. This work contains poems in both standard English ("majors") and black dialect ("minors"), many of which are regarded as among his best. In 1896 William Dean Howells, at the time America's most prominent literary critic, wrote a lengthy and enthusiastic review of *Majors and Minors*'s dialect poems for *Harper's Weekly*, a highly regarded literary magazine with a wide circulation. The review gave Dunbar's career as a poet a tremendous boost. Sales of *Majors and Minors* skyrocketed, and Dunbar, now under the management of Major James Burton Pond's lecture bureau, embarked on a national reading tour. Pond also arranged for Dodd, Mead and Company to publish *Lyrics of Lowly Life* (1896), a republication of ninety-seven poems from his first two volumes and eight new poems. Howells, in the introduction to this volume, described Dunbar as "the only man of pure African blood and of American civilization to feel the negro life aesthetically and express it lyrically." The combination of Howells's endorsement and Dunbar's skill soon led the latter to become one of America's most popular writers.

After the publication of *Lyrics of Lowly Life*, Dunbar went on a reading tour of England. When he returned to the United States in 1897, he accepted a position as a library assistant at the Library of Congress in Washington, D.C. Meanwhile, several national literary magazines were vying with one another for anything he wrote, and in 1898 Dunbar seemed to have developed the golden touch. *Lippincott's Monthly Magazine* published his first novel, *The Uncalled*, which appeared in book form later that year; *Folks from Dixie*, a collection of twelve short stories that had been published individually in various magazines, also came out in book form; and he collaborated with Will Marion Cook to write a hit Broadway musical, *Clorindy*. At this time he developed a nagging cough, perhaps the result of an abundance of heavy lifting in the dusty, drafty library combined with skimping on sleep while pursuing deadlines. Partly because of his success and partly because of ill health, he resigned from the library at the end of 1898 to devote himself full time to his writing.

In 1899 Dunbar published two collections of poems, *Lyrics of the Hearthside* and *Poems of Cabin and Field*, and embarked on a third reading tour. However, his health deteriorated so rapidly that the tour was cut short. The official diagnosis was pneumonia, but his doctor suspected that Dunbar was in the early stages of tuberculosis. To help ease the pain in his lungs, he turned to strong drink, which did little more than make him a near-alcoholic. He gave up his much-beloved speaking tours but continued to write at the same breakneck pace. While convalescing in Denver, Colorado, he wrote a western novel, *The Love of Landry* (1900), and published *The Strength of Gideon and Other Stories* (1900), another collection of short stories. He also wrote two plays, neither of which was ever published, as well as some lyrics and sketches. In the last five years of his life, he published two novels, *The Fanatics* (1901) and *The Sport of the Gods* (1901, in *Lippincott's*; 1902, in book form); two short story collections, *In Old Plantation Days* (1903) and *The Heart of Happy Hollow* (1904); eight collections of poetry, *Candle-Lightin' Time* (1901), *Lyrics of Love and Laughter* (1903), *When Malindy Sings* (1903), *Li'l Gal* (1904), *Chris'mus Is A-comin' and Other Poems* (1905), *Howdy, Honey, Howdy* (1905), *Lyrics of Sunshine and Shadow* (1905), and *Joggin' Erlong* (1906); and collaborated with Cook on another musical, *In Dahomey* (1902).

Dunbar had married Alice Ruth Moore in 1898; they had no children. In 1902 the couple separated, largely because of Dunbar's drinking, and never reconciled. After the breakup Dunbar lived in Chicago for a while, then in 1903 returned to live with his mother in Dayton, where he died of tuberculosis.

Dunbar's goal was "to interpret my own people through song and story, and to prove to the many that after all we are more human than African." In so doing, he portrayed the lives of blacks as being filled with joy and humor as well as misery and difficulty. Dunbar is best known for his dialect poems that, intended for a predominantly white audience, often depict slaves as dancing, singing, carefree residents of "Happy Hollow." On the other hand, a great deal of his lesser-known prose work speaks out forcefully against racial injustice, both before and after emancipation, as in "The Lynching of Jube Benson," a powerful short story about the guilt that haunts a

white man who once participated in the hanging of an innocent black. Perhaps his two most eloquent expressions of the
reality of the black experience in America are "We Wear the
Mask," in which he declares, "We wear the mask that grins and
lies, . . . / We smile, but, O great Christ, our cries / To thee from
tortured souls arise," and "Sympathy," wherein he states that "I
know why the caged bird sings, . . . it is not a carol of joy or
glee, / But a prayer that he sends . . . upward to Heaven."

Dunbar was the first black American author to be able to
support himself solely as a result of his writing. His success
inspired the next generation of black writers, including James
Weldon Johnson, Langston Hughes, and Claude McKay, to
dream of and achieve literary success during the Harlem
Renaissance of the 1920s. Because Dunbar had no white
ancestors, he was celebrated and scrutinized by the national
media as a representative of his race. His charm and wit, his
grace under pressure, and his ability as a speaker and author
did much to give the lie to turn-of-the-century misconcep-
tions about the racial inferiority of blacks.

C.W.C.

John England

[23 SEPTEMBER 1786–11 APRIL 1842]

John England, the first Catholic bishop of Charleston, is the invisible giant of the Catholic Church in the United States because he was able, almost two centuries before the fact, to anticipate the changes that Vatican Council II enacted for the whole Church. England's conviction that Catholicism was compatible with American democracy, while a minority opinion in his own time, demonstrates that there was an element in the Catholic heritage that was capable of embracing progress, growth, and freedom and of engaging in friendly conversation with those who were not Catholic.

The documents of Vatican II on religious freedom, ecumenism, and collegiality in the church often sound like an echo of John England. They represent that strain of Catholic thought which lay dormant for a long time but which finally emerged in the late twentieth century. His sister, incidentally, was not only the editor of the first Catholic paper in this country but also the first woman editor.

He was a churchman who was far ahead of his time, perhaps in his openness and optimism even ahead of the present time. Yet the changes in the Catholic Church after 1960 vindicated what he believed. He should be hailed not because he influenced further developments in the Catholic Church in the United States—alas he did not—but because his life and work were a prophecy of what would come.

ANDREW GREELEY

John England, the first Catholic bishop of Charleston, South Carolina, was born in Cork, Ireland, the son of Thomas England, a successful tobacco merchant, and Honora Lordan. From 1792 to 1800, during the early years of the relaxation of the penal laws against Irish Catholics, England received his primary education in the Cork Protestant schools, where the more prosperous members of Cork society sent their children. Two years after his early classical education, he apprenticed himself to a Cork lawyer, intending to enter the bar, a profession open to Irish Catholics after 1793. He abandoned the study of law, however, in 1802 and went to St. Patrick's College in Carlow, Ireland, where he studied for the priesthood.

After ordination in 1808, England returned to the Diocese of Cork to assume a number of pastoral functions in the city. From 1808 to 1812 he was a preacher and lecturer at the cathedral, a chaplain to the Presentation Sisters, an inspector of schools, and a writer of school textbooks. He also followed the Quaker educational reformer Joseph Lancaster (1778–1838) in establishing in Cork schools for the poor, enlisting older pupils to instruct younger ones, using the pupils themselves to maintain discipline, and fostering a Christian education that was open to all denominations. He became president of Cork's newly established College of St. Mary in 1812 and remained in that position until 1817. From 1814 to 1818, moreover, he was editor and contributor to the *Cork Mercantile Chronicle*, a leading newspaper that during England's trusteeship became a strong defender of Irish civil and political rights and an opponent of British attempts to veto the nomination of Catholic bishops in the British Isles. In 1817, after the so-called veto controversy, which put him in the national limelight along with Daniel O'Connell, England was appointed pastor of Bandon, Ireland, where he remained until he was ordained as bishop of Charleston, South Carolina, in 1820.

As a young priest in Ireland and as a bishop in the United States, England represented the side of late-eighteenth- and early-nineteenth-century Catholicism that was open to and accommodating toward an Enlightenment mentality prizing reason, democracy, religious liberty, voluntaryism in religion, and separation of church and state. In Ireland he fostered clerical nominations of bishops, and in his diocese of Charleston he established a constitution that incorporated laity and clergy in the management and supervision of parish and diocesan affairs. Like many Gallican-influenced clergy and bishops of his day, he emphasized the rights, dignity, and integrity of the national church, pressuring the archbishops of Baltimore to convoke national councils of bishops to symbolize the unity of the church and to provide a forum for an efficient and effective episcopal governance of the American church.

From 1820 until his death England became something of a national spokesman and apologist for the compatibility of Catholicism and American democratic traditions. He repeatedly argued, for example, that republican constitutionalism had its origins in the Middle Ages, could be found in the governmental forms of the mendicant religious orders, and was part of the general conciliar experience of Catholicism throughout the ages. In his own diocese he developed a written constitution that outlined the rights and duties of all in the church and that provided for yearly meetings of a house of lay representatives elected by the parishes and a house of representative clergy. The annual conventions, presided over by the bishop, not only discussed matters of spiritual concern, but also voted on matters of temporal concern in the diocese. This constitutional form of government was considered too democratic by many of the other American bishops and did not endure beyond England's death. He was frequently called upon to preach in Protestant as well as Catholic churches in his own diocese, which comprised both Carolinas and Georgia, and in numerous other churches from Boston to New Orleans. In 1822 he established the first national Catholic newspaper, the *U.S. Catholic Miscellany*, to provide information, to defend the church, and to give Catholics a voice in national affairs. His national prominence was acknowledged early in his episcopacy when he was invited in 1826 to address the U.S. Congress, the first Catholic clergyman to do so. The address presented Catholic claims on the church's infallibility and simultaneously demonstrated the constitutional limits of the church's authority, thereby showing the Catholic Church's compatibility with religious liberty and separation of church and state. The Vatican, too, acknowledged his skills when it appointed him apostolic delegate (1833–1837) to negotiate a concordat with the Haitian government of President Jean-Pierre Boyer. Under Boyer's absolute control of Haiti, England tried to secure an indispensable minimum of internal freedom for the church, but his negotiations failed to produce a Vatican and Haitian agreement. In 1860, though, a concordat was signed between Haiti and the Vatican that contained substantially the same terms as England's mid-1830s document.

In his own diocese, England erected a seminary for the education of a clergy who would have American sensitivities and ideas (1825), a philosophical and classical school for Charleston's white students (1822), and a school for blacks (1835) that was forced to close because of resistance from prominent Charleston city fathers. He founded a religious order for women, the Sisters of Our Lady of Mercy, in Charleston (1829). He established the Brotherhood of San Marino, the first Catholic society for working men in the United States, organized the Anti-Duelling Society of Charleston, edited catechisms, and prepared a new edition of the missal. Although he considered southern slavery personally repugnant, he defended the institution itself as compatible with Scripture and the Christian tradition. His ideological support of slavery and his view of the compatibility of Catholicism and American democracy won him many friends in the city of Charleston but also demonstrated clearly the difficulties inherent in his accommodationist stance toward the world in which he lived. He died in Charleston.

P.W.C.

Oliver Evans

[13 SEPTEMBER 1755–15 APRIL 1819]

*A*sk anyone if they know who put the first automotive vehicle on an American road. Or who was it that invented and manufactured the first amphibious craft? Or who invented the high-pressure steam engine that powered the early American factories? And who dreamed up the basic design for air-conditioning? Or who was it that devised and ran the first automatic production line? The questions might reasonably be answered by five names. In fact, only one name is needed: Oliver Evans. What is amazing about Evans is that he did all these things right in the turmoil of the American Revolution and in the early years of the United States in the late eighteenth century. He was, in fact, the new nation's first notable inventor at a time when manufacturing was primitive, machine tools and steel had yet to be developed, technical education did not exist, and he could call only on his genius for invention and determined improvisation. It is extraordinary that he is such a neglected figure. He was a prophet as well, envisaging the age of railways and steamboats. Of course, like so many innovators, he attracted the scorn of the traditionalists and the envy of inferiors, all the more reason why our generation owes him his due.

HAROLD EVANS

O liver Evans, inventor and engineer, was born in Newport, Delaware, the son of Charles Evans, a cordwainer and farmer, and Ann Stalcop, the daughter of a prosperous miller. Little is known of his early years, including whether he had any formal schooling before being apprenticed to a wheelwright in 1771. Self-taught or not, he learned to read and to write passable prose.

In 1777, just as Evans was completing his apprenticeship, he proved that he had an inventive turn of mind by designing a device to cut and bend iron wire for insertion as teeth in wool or cotton cards. He also found a way to mechanically punch holes and insert the cut wire into the leather of such cards. As he later told it, he had turned his attention to the possibilities of steam locomotion on land and water even earlier, in 1773. He did not pursue steam navigation until many years after that and consequently did not contest John Fitch's tenuous claim to "originality," even though Fitch's experiments came a full decade after his own first ruminations. Evans's interest in steam locomotion on land caused him to approach the Pennsylvania legislature for a patent in 1783. With no working model to prove feasibility, he failed and experienced the frustration that would dog him throughout his career: it was one thing to envision a new device; it was quite another to see that idea take practical form as an invention and then press on to see that invention adopted as a profitable technological innovation. Evans would frequently lament, as had Benjamin Franklin a generation before, that it was an inventor's plight to be misunderstood and unappreciated.

By the end of the War of Independence Evans was living in Tuckahoe, Maryland, where he and a brother owned a small store. In 1783 he married Sarah Tomlinson, the daughter of a Delaware farmer; they would have seven children. That same year Evans began experiments leading to a fully automated flour mill. Water-driven grinding stones had long been common; Evans connected all the mill machinery to the water-wheel by a system of shafts, gears, and leather belts. Included in his new system were the "elevator" (leather or wooden cups attached to belts) to move grain vertically, the "conveyor" (a screwlike rod) to push grain horizontally, and a "hopper-boy" (a rake that swept in a revolving motion) to sift and dry flour. The hopper-boy was original to Evans; most of the other devices were not. True originality came from Evans's creation of an integrated, fully mechanized operation, which produced fine flour that was drier and less likely to spoil in a bag or barrel.

Excited about his prospects, in 1785 Evans, with two of his brothers as partners, erected a water-powered mill on Red Clay Creek in the heart of Delaware's wheat country. He gradually adapted that mill to fit his designs, which he continued to improve. Within two years Evans had obtained patents from the state legislatures of Maryland and Pennsylvania for fourteen years, and for fifteen years in Delaware. New Hampshire followed in 1788 with a patent for seven years. Not long after that Evans sold his interest in the Tuckahoe store because he assumed that he would make a comfortable living selling licenses to millers wanting to use his inventions. He was wrong. Even local millers were slow to convert. Some doubted that Evans's new system would really work; others felt threatened by the "progress" of automation that could put men—often family members and friends—out of a job. Although George Washington had his Dogue Run mill converted to the Evans method in 1791, many of Evans's own neighbors remained reluctant to change. Still others made the changes, but without paying any fees, causing Evans to sue for patent infringement. Evans had secured a fourteen-year federal patent in December 1790 for his mill machinery, a patent that superseded the old state monopolies and in theory protected him nationwide. By the turn of the century the Evans method had become widely adopted, and yet Evans ultimately spent almost as much money on lawsuits as he made in selling licenses. Small wonder that he was never happy with either state or federal patent laws, feeling that inventors were not allowed enough time to reap the rewards of their genius.

In 1792 Evans sold his share in the Red Clay Creek flour mill, moved to Philadelphia, and opened a combination mercantile firm and machine shop. There, in the national capital, he hoped to benefit from the greater availability of financing, the large number of skilled craftsmen, and a vigorous scientific community. After a long struggle he finally persuaded Congress in 1808 to renew most of his milling patents for another fourteen years, but by then he had shifted his attention to steam power. Even as he pursued his milling experiments he had not entirely put aside his interest in steam. When he applied for state patents for his automated mill back in the 1780s he had also sought monopolies for steam-powered land carriages. Only Maryland granted him one, the same year that it awarded him a patent for his mill machinery.

After 1800 Evans concentrated on the design and construction of high-pressure steam engines, machines that could be used for milling operations as well as for propulsion. He considered his work here more important and potentially even more lucrative than his flour-milling experiments. In England, Richard Trevithick moved in the same direction, but with no knowledge of Evans—nor did Evans know of him, proof of the old adage about the simultaneity of much invention. Trevithick focused on land locomotion, Evans on water. Both proved the superiority of their designs. Direct, high-pressure engines generated more horsepower than the older Watt condenser-equipped models, but they demanded metallurgical knowledge and machine skills that pressed Evans and his associates to the limit. Evans used a small engine to grind plaster in his machine shop before he designed an engine in 1803 that could be used with his type of mill machinery and another engine that he planned to install on a Mississippi riverboat—but it ended up in a sawmill instead. The next year Evans took out a federal patent (which Congress extended for an additional seven years in 1817) for his high-pressure steam engines; he also tried to interest a turnpike company in his proposed steam wagon to haul freight between Philadelphia and Lancaster.

Failing there, Evans took advantage of a contract with the Philadelphia Board of Health for a dredge to build his *Orukter Amphibolos*. Completed in July 1805, this steam-driven scow was some thirty feet long and twelve feet wide and weighed more than fifteen tons. No contemporary drawing of it survives. Presumably, by shifting belts the pilot could either drive wheels to move the vehicle on land or turn a rear-mounted paddlewheel to propel it in water. The *Orukter Amphibolos* was in no sense a prototype for a land carriage. Evans wanted it to serve a twofold purpose: to satisfy his contractual requirements to the city and to show skeptics the potential of his dreamed-of locomotion by steam. Few skeptics changed their minds and the public did not make the imaginative leap Evans hoped it would. The *Orukter Amphibolos* worked well enough as a dredge, but it survived only a few years before it fell into disrepair with the expiration of Evans's contract.

Before then, in 1806, Evans had opened his Mars Works where, during the next decade, he supervised the construction of more than one hundred steam engines and boilers. The iron foundry and machine shop at the works also made mill machinery and sundry other devices. Evans profited from the enterprise and left a modest estate when he died, in large part because of the business generated at the Mars Works. He even opened a smaller foundry in Pittsburgh. Evans-made machines drove steamboats that plied the Delaware River, and, by the end of the War of 1812, a steam engine from the Pittsburgh shop had been installed on a boat that paddled down the Ohio River to the Mississippi.

In 1816 Evans's wife died and his own health began to fail. The aging inventor rallied enough to marry Hetty Ward of New York City in 1818. It was while on a visit to New York a year later that Evans was stricken with a fatal "inflammation" of the lungs. He learned that the Mars Works had burned to the ground on 11 April 1819, just four days before he died. Initially buried in the Zion Episcopal Church yard, his remains were eventually moved to an unmarked plot in the Trinity Cemetery at Broadway and 157th Street.

Evans was arguably the leading inventor of his generation. He knew how to combine his ideas with those of inventors who had gone before, proof that "originality" is more complicated than sometimes realized. His flour-milling techniques became the American standard for several generations. Likewise, his type of high-pressure steam engine became the motive force for steamboats from the Mississippi to the Hudson and drove machines in factories around the nation. Evans could be a levelheaded businessman who understood that new ideas had to be marketed to a seemingly unresponsive public. Nonetheless, he became so despondent at what he took to be public ignorance that in 1809 he burned some of his papers and vowed to discontinue his experiments. It was a vow he could not keep. Both realist and visionary, in 1813 he predicted—correctly—that "the time will come, when people will travel in stages moved by steam engines from one city to another almost as fast as birds can fly" (Bathe and Bathe, p. 112).

N.L.Y.

Dorothy Fields

[15 JULY 1905–28 MARCH 1974]

*S*ometimes overlooked in discussions of great American lyricists,
Dorothy Fields would deserve posthumous applause if she had
only written the words of "On the Sunny Side of the Street." That
song enchants us into leaving our worries on the doorstep: "I used to
walk in the shade / With those blues on parade / But I'm not afraid
/ Because this rover / Crossed over." The statement that you can be
broke yet "rich as Rockefeller" is a clever variant on the Depres-
sion-era theme that "The Best Things in Life Are Free" and as powerful an affirmation of American optimism as Irving Berlin's "Blue
Skies." With her brother Herbert, Dorothy collaborated on the book
of Annie Get Your Gun *and several musicals with Cole Porter.
Among her standards are "I'm in the Mood for Love," "I Can't Give
You Anything but Love," "A Fine Romance," and "The Way You
Look Tonight."*

*Fields's best songs are witty, subtle, and feminine. Think of "You
Couldn't Be Cuter," as sung ideally by Ella Fitzgerald ("You couldn't
be keener, / You look so fresh from the cleaner"). Or listen to Billie
Holiday's jubilant version of "A Fine Romance," which sounds like a
feminine counterpart to male seduction poems: "A fine romance, / My
good fellow, / You take romance, / I'll take jello. / You're calmer than
the seals in the Arctic Ocean. / At least they flap their fins to express
emotion." Some February or March days when I grab my coat and
get my hat and head for the side of the street that's sunny, humming
that happy tune with maybe Sinatra's voice in my head or maybe
Nat King Cole's, I think with a wink of Dorothy Fields.*

DAVID LEHMAN

Dorothy Fields, lyricist for stage and screen, was born in
Allenhurst, New Jersey, the daughter of Lew Fields, a
renowned theatrical comedian-producer, and Rose

84

Dorothy Fields and Arthur Schwartz at work on the score of *A Tree Grows in Brooklyn*, 1951. *(Library of Congress)*

Harris. Fields grew up in New York City, where she was educated at the Benjamin School for Girls. In 1925 she married Dr. Jack J. Wiener; they had no children.

Having written poems during her youth, she developed an interest in song lyrics. Songwriter J. Fred Coots introduced her to his colleague Jimmy McHugh, and in 1926 Fields and McHugh wrote songs for Harlem's famous Cotton Club revues. This led to the revues *Delmar's Revels* and *Blackbirds of 1928*; the latter show featured "I Can't Give You Anything but Love," which sold three million copies of sheet music. Fields and McHugh went on to contribute songs for six shows in the following two years: *Hello Daddy*, *The International Revue*, *The Vanderbilt Revue*, *Rhapsody in Black*, *Shoot the Works*, and *Singin' the Blues*. In 1929 the team began writing songs for several movies as well, most notably *Dancing Lady* (1933), which featured the debut of Fred Astaire. Fields's style had matured into an often deceptively informal, colloquial use of words that gave a song a lighthearted air, but it took traditional ballads into a more worldly, more direct, and less sentimental realm. Her lyrics were wryly mature in tone, and her pithy wit became rapidly recognized in the highest echelons of the songwriting profession.

In 1935 Fields wrote lyrics to additional music Jerome Kern had composed for the film adaptation of his Broadway show, *Roberta*. The result was "Lovely to Look At," which so impressed Kern that he asked Fields to work on his next project, *I Dream Too Much*. Then came the score for the Fred Astaire–Ginger Rogers musical *Swingtime*, for which "The Way You Look Tonight" won an Academy Award as best song of 1936.

During the course of her career, Fields's two brothers worked with her. Herbert teamed frequently with her on both stage and film projects, and Joseph was a producer and playwright. In 1936 Fields wrote three screenplays with Herbert: *Riviera*, *Love before Breakfast*, and *The King Steps Out*. *Fools for Scandal* and *The Joy of Living* followed in 1938. Fields's first marriage had ended in 1932, and in 1938 she married businessman Eli D. Lahm, with whom she would have a son and a daughter.

In 1939 Fields collaborated with Arthur Schwartz on the Broadway show *Stars in Your Eyes* and then returned to work with Kern on the film *One Night in the Tropics* (1940). Thereafter came another productive period with Herbert. They wrote the screenplay for the film *Father Takes a Wife* (1941), and for Broadway they collaborated on three Cole Porter shows: *Let's Face It* (1943), *Something for the Boys* (1944) and *Mexican Hayride*. Another successful Broadway show the two wrote was *Up in Central Park*, for which Sigmund Romberg composed the music.

A key inspiration for Fields was her idea of Ethel Merman as frontier sharpshooter Annie Oakley. She and Herbert wrote the book, and Irving Berlin wrote the words and music, for one of the greatest Broadway musicals, *Annie Get Your Gun* (1946), which ran for 1,147 performances. Dorothy and Herbert Fields also wrote the screenplay for the 1950 film version, for which they earned the Screen Writers' Guild Award. The pair's next Broadway show, *Arms and the Girl* (1950), proved a rare failure. More popular the following year was *A Tree Grows in Brooklyn*, with music by Schwartz. A subsequent reteaming with Schwartz, *By the Beautiful Sea* (1954), had a brief run.

Fields continued to write lyrics for films, including a remake of *Roberta* called *Lovely to Look At* (1952). She was coauthor and lyricist for *Mr. Imperium* (1951) and wrote the lyrics for *The Farmer Takes a Wife* (1953) and *Excuse My Dust* (1953). In 1957 Fields turned to television and wrote the lyrics for the CBS special "Junior Miss." This time her brother Joseph wrote the script.

In 1958 both Fields's husband and her brother Herbert died. At the time of his death, Herbert was co-writing the book for her latest Broadway show, *Redhead* (1959). The show was a success and won a Tony Award for its book.

After working on several unrealized projects, Fields achieved a major hit with *Sweet Charity* (1966). Her collaborator was Cy Coleman, and their songs included "Hey, Big Spender" and "If My Friends Could See Me Now." The 1969 film version featured two additional songs by them. In 1973 Fields and Coleman reteamed on *See-Saw*.

Fields died in her Manhattan apartment. In addition to her professional accomplishments, she was remembered for having been active in charity work, especially in connection with the Federation of Jewish Philanthropies. Some of her earliest songs were revived after her death in the Broadway shows *Ain't Misbehavin'* (1978) and *Sugar Babies* (1979).

The diversity and quality of Fields's work as a lyricist were exceptional, as evidenced by her collaborations with Max Steiner, Fritz Kreisler, Oscar Levant, Harold Arlen, Burton Lane, Morton Gould, Albert Hague, and Harry Warren. Fields collaborated with the most prominent songwriters of her day on nearly 400 songs, including "I'm in the Mood for Love," "On the Sunny Side of the Street," and "A Fine Romance."

She was the first woman to win the Academy Award for best song, and she was the first woman elected to the Songwriters Hall of Fame.

In his book *Words with Music* (1972), Lehman Engel counted Fields as one of an innovative generation of lyricists who were "native, talented, original, stylish and literate. They allow their characters to sing as three-dimensional human beings." Fields's skill as a lyricist put her at the forefront of the maturing of the American musical tradition.

B.R.

Charles Grandison Finney

[29 AUGUST 1792–16 AUGUST 1875]

Charles Grandison Finney probably affected the daily lives of more Americans in the nineteenth century than any other single individual. His evangelical preaching of moral perfection reached hundreds of thousands and sparked the movement that led to the abolition of slavery.

EDMUND S. MORGAN

Charles Grandison Finney, evangelist and president of Oberlin College, was born in Warren, Connecticut, the son of Sylvester Finney and Rebecca Rice, farmers. The family moved to the town of Kirkland, Oneida County, New York, when he was two and in 1808 to Henderson, Jefferson County, near Lake Ontario. Finney attended common school and perhaps Hamilton-Oneida Academy in Clinton, and he taught school as an older teen in Henderson. At age twenty he enrolled at Warren Academy in Connecticut, decided against going on to Yale, and taught in New Jersey from 1814 to 1818, when he returned to Jefferson County to apprentice at law. Practicing in an Adams, New York, law firm and directing the local Presbyterian church choir, he began to study the Bible. Having grown up during the Second Great Awakening, Finney was aware of the strengths and weaknesses of every Protestant denomination's evangelistic style. During an 1821 revival, at age twenty-nine, he experienced a religious crisis. He promised God, as he recalled in his *Memoirs*, "If I am ever converted, I will preach the gospel." His conversion entailed anguish for his sinfulness followed by a submission to "the righteousness of God through Christ."

Finney was licensed to preach by the Presbytery of St. Lawrence in December 1823 after a period of theological

Charles Grandison Finney and his second wife, Elizabeth. "A revival is not a miracle," Finney argued. "It is a purely philosophical result of the right use of the constituted means." *(Library of Congress)*

study, in lieu of seminary training, with his pastor, George W. Gale. Even though Finney severely criticized him for his apparent acceptance of Calvinism's emphasis on human moral and spiritual incapacity, Gale was instrumental in Finney's conversion and rushed him into the ministry. In March 1824 the Female Missionary Society of the Western District of New York commissioned Finney as an evangelist; on 1 July 1824 the presbytery ordained him. Finney's "plain and pointed" sermons impressed crowds with their directness. He preached without notes, looked listeners in the eye and addressed them as "you," and presented the case for the gospel as if he were a lawyer before a jury. He warned of hell in vivid language and used illustrations from daily life. Like Methodist and Baptist revivalists, he called for an immediate decision for Christ. His early revivals shared the enthusiasm of the radical evangelical groups, with men and women alike weeping, crying out, falling down "in the Spirit," and testifying. He believed in "prevailing prayer," that specific prayers made in faith would be efficacious. In October 1824 he married Lydia Root Andrews, with whom he was to have six children. His wife assisted him by establishing women's prayer groups and missionary and social reform organizations.

Finney began the Oneida County phase of his career in late 1825 at the invitation of Gale, who had moved there. Finney's great appeal was not in the countryside or on the frontier but among the commercial and professional classes in America's booming urban centers. Revivals in the new cities of Utica and Rome on the just-completed Erie Canal spread his reputation as an evangelist. After a revival in Auburn, the site of a Presbyterian seminary, Finney moved east to Troy. His preaching drew the attention of New England Congregational leaders Lyman Beecher and Asahel Nettleton, who objected to several features of the "western revivals," which they termed "new measures"—female testimony in mixed congregations, prayer for sinners by name, immediate decisions for Christ, and emotionalism. Finney defended his evangelism by attacking his enemies as worldly and spiritually dead in *A Sermon Preached in the Presbyterian Church at Troy, March 4, 1827*. Based on the text "Can two walk together except they be agreed?" (Amos 3:3), the sermon was his first publication. This salvo prompted Beecher to organize a conference of New England and Mohawk Valley clergy at New Lebanon, New York, in July 1827. Many issues were deadlocked or decided by compromise, but Finney emerged the winner by gaining national stature.

Finney led revivals in 1828 in Wilmington, Delaware, and Philadelphia, Pennsylvania, the heart of the Presbyterian New School–Old School conflict. In 1829 he preached at a "Free Presbyterian Church" organized by an "association of gentlemen" in New York City; these evangelical businessmen became his financial supporters. His signature sermon exhorted, "Make you a new heart and a new spirit, for why will you die?" (Ezek. 18:31), published in his *Sermons on Various Subjects* (1835) as "Sinners Bound to Change Their Own Hearts."

Echoing the New Divinity of Samuel Hopkins and progressive Yale professor Nathaniel William Taylor, Finney espoused an understanding of the Atonement whereby Christ's death satisfied "public justice," enabling God to offer salvation to all of sinful humanity. He argued that individuals are responsible for their own sinfulness, defined sin as selfishness and godliness as "disinterested benevolence," and preached that each person is a free moral agent able to choose good or evil. Calvinist defenders of the Westminster Confession excoriated Finney for Arminian or Pelagian elevation of human ability, but he defended his orthodoxy by insisting that the sinner "never does, and never will turn, unless God indures him to do it; so that although the act is the sinner's own, yet the glory belongs to God, inasmuch as he caused him to act."

Finney's greatest revival was in Rochester, New York, from September 1830 to June 1831. There he developed the "new measures" of the "anxious seat" and "protracted meetings," or four- and five-day revivals in nearby villages. He had employed "inquiry meetings" for penitents, but in Rochester he began calling them forward immediately at the end of the sermon to designated seats for special prayer. Influenced by his associate Theodore Dwight Weld, he also linked conversion to social reform by advancing the temperance cause. Community and business leaders in Presbyterian, Baptist, Methodist, and Episcopal churches endorsed the revival as a means of civic improvement.

Finney's success brought new invitations, but his 1831–1832 Boston campaign, headquartered at Park Street Church, produced only modest results. In 1832 philanthropists such as Arthur Tappan and Lewis Tappan established Finney at his own church in New York City at the Chatham Street Theater; in 1836 he moved to Broadway Tabernacle, which was constructed to his specifications. Finney was cautious on racial issues (continuing to seat blacks in the gallery) but embraced the abolition movement, preaching against slavery and refusing to serve communion to slaveholders. Because the Antislavery Society convened there, antiabolitionist mobs vandalized his church. Conservative Congregationalists and Old School Presbyterians led by Princeton's Charles Hodge also stepped up their attack on his theology in print. After a voyage to the Mediterranean Sea to complete his recovery from cholera, and a vocational crisis and spiritual renewal, Finney in 1835 delivered and published *Lectures on Revivals of Religion*, which extended his reputation to Great Britain. "A revival is not a miracle," he argued. "It is a purely philosophical result of the right use of the constituted means." Frustrated with Presbyterianism and anticipating heresy charges, Finney became a Congregationalist in 1836.

The newly established Oberlin Collegiate Institute in 1835 brought Finney to Ohio as a professor of theology, with the concession that he could preach at Broadway Tabernacle each winter. Abolitionist students and faculty expelled from Cincinnati's Lane Seminary transferred to Oberlin on the condition that Finney would join the faculty. Finney also stipulated that students be admitted to the pioneering coeducational school without regard to race and that the faculty (not trustees) govern academic affairs. Resigning his New York City pulpit in 1837, he assumed the pastorate of First Church in Oberlin.

Finney, with Asa Mahan, the president, and other Oberlin faculty, developed the doctrine of sanctification in ways that sparked further controversy. Essentially concerned with nurturing believers in a "higher Christian life," Finney adopted the Wesleyan language of entire sanctification, holiness, and Christian perfection, while remaining within the Reformed tradition. He advanced his ideas in the *Oberlin Evangelist*, publishing some of his articles as *Lectures to Professing Christians* (1837) and *Views of Sanctification* (1840). Building on his understanding of moral agency and Jesus' injunction "be ye perfect" (Matt. 5:48), he defined entire sanctification as "the consecration of the whole being to God." God "created us moral beings in his own image, capable of conforming to the same rule with himself . . . to love impartially, with as perfect love — to seek the good of others with as single an eye as he does." Because he used the term "perfection" — which was tainted by the Oneida Community and other eccentric groups — and claimed that it was possible "in this life," many New School Presbyterian and Congregationalist friends abandoned him. For Finney, obedi-

ence to God meant both personal holiness (including abstinence from alcohol, tobacco, caffeine, and other stimulants as
well as moderation in dress and diet) and a commitment to
abolitionism; consequently, Oberlin became a prominent station on the Underground Railroad. He published his teachings in volume one of *Skeletons of a Course of Theological Lectures* (1840) and volumes two and three of *Lectures on Systematic
Theology* (1846, 1847).

During the winters of the 1840s, Finney preached in Boston,
Providence, Rochester, Detroit, and New York City while serving as professor and pastor at Oberlin. His wife's illness provoked a new spiritual crisis and a "fresh baptism of the Holy
Spirit." She died in December 1847, and in November 1848 he
married a Rochester widow, Elizabeth Ford Atkinson, who
became an energetic partner and promoter of his evangelistic
work; they had no children. The couple undertook an ambitious tour of England from November 1849 to April 1851, which
culminated in a ten-month London campaign.

In August 1851 Finney became the president of Oberlin.
Finney's presidency was largely symbolic as he continued to
arrange four- and five-month revival campaigns every winter
in major northeastern cities, including Boston, where he was a
leader in the "Businessmen's Revival" of 1857–1858. His second
British tour, from January 1859 to August 1860, included joint
prayer meetings with English Congregationalists and Meth-
odists and engagements in Edinburgh, Scotland, through the
Evangelical Union, a breakaway group from the national
church. During the Civil War, Finney devoted himself to teaching and preaching at Oberlin. His second wife died in November 1863, and in October 1865 he married Rebecca Allen Rayl,
a widow who was assistant principal of the Oberlin College
female department; they had no children. In the late 1860s he
worked on his *Memoirs* (published posthumously in 1876),
which were widely read well into the twentieth century, and
wrote a series of anti-Masonic articles for the *New York Inde-*

pendent, published as *Freemasonry: Its Character, Claims, and Practical Workings* (1869). He retired from the college presidency in August 1865 and as pastor of the church in May 1872, although he continued to teach and preach as his health permitted. He died in Oberlin.

Finney contributed to the development of an evangelical style of preaching and church life in nineteenth-century America. For him, ecclesiastical tradition diverted people from true religion, which consisted of an experience of being born again through a personal decision for Christ and obedience to God's law of benevolence. He mediated Calvinist and Wesleyan expressions of Protestant Christianity by teaching freedom of the will and holiness of life under the power of the Holy Spirit. As an evangelist he modified earlier revival traditions to promote church growth in the Jacksonian-era market economy. His methods of urban evangelism influenced later revivalists such as Dwight L. Moody and Billy Graham. His emphasis on the baptism of the Holy Spirit and entire sanctification helped foster the holiness movement and pentecostalism. His academic career illustrates the role of evangelicals in the development of higher education. Evangelicalism's relationship with social reform is reflected in Finney's involvement with temperance, women's rights, and abolitionism. Yet he insisted that any reform movement must be secondary to evangelistic work for the conversion of sinners.

C.E.H.-S.

Arthur J. Goldberg

[8 AUGUST 1908–19 JANUARY 1990]

A rthur Goldberg, though no longer a household name, reached the highest echelons of our government and had an enormous and continuing influence on American life. Raised in the humblest of circumstances, he was the first in his family to receive a formal education. By dint of his incredible intelligence and energy, he became America's first great labor lawyer. Eventually, he was appointed as U.S. secretary of labor, transforming that role, and then as an associate justice of the Supreme Court. He served on the High Court for only three years; for one of those years, I was honored to be his law clerk. During his brief tenure on the bench, he helped shape the legacy of the Warren Court in civil rights and civil liberties. Though he intended to remain on the Supreme Court for the rest of his life, he patriotically accepted President Lyndon Johnson's call for him to replace Adlai Stevenson as our representative to the United Nations, hoping thereby to help bring about peace in Vietnam. Leaving the High Court entailed an enormous personal sacrifice, one of many that Goldberg made in his lifelong quest for peace and justice.

ALAN M. DERSHOWITZ

A rthur Joseph Goldberg, lawyer, jurist, and diplomat, was born in Chicago, Illinois, the son of Rebecca (maiden name unknown) and Joseph Goldberg, a peddler. Goldberg grew up in an immigrant slum on Chicago's West Side, where he led a life filled with hard work. Thanks to extraordinary intelligence and drive, he managed to graduate from Benjamin Harrison Public High School in 1924, the first member of his family ever to get that much schooling. He then attended Crane Junior College, from which he soon made his way into Northwestern Law School. During his three years there, Goldberg compiled the best academic record in the school's history up to that point and served as editor of the law review, while continuing to work part-time. He earned his bachelor of law degree in 1928 and his doctor of science in law degree one year later. He then joined the Chicago firm of Pritzger and Pritzger. In 1931 he married Dorothy Kurgans, an art student he had met at Northwestern; they were to have two children.

After serving as secretary of labor, Supreme Court justice, and U.S. ambassador to the United Nations, Arthur Goldberg ran unsuccessfully for governor of New York in 1970. *(Collection of the Supreme Court of the United States)*

Unhappy with the bankruptcy work he was obliged to do and wanting to become his own boss, Goldberg established his own practice in 1933. His reputation as a skilled lawyer friendly to the left encouraged leaders of the Chicago branch of the Congress of Industrial Organizations (CIO) to approach him for help during a newspaper strike in 1938. Goldberg agreed to represent the strikers and to take other labor work that the CIO began steering his way. His acceptance of such cases stemmed from his own working-class origin and the sympathy it gave him for workers trying to unionize during the Great Depression. As Goldberg later explained this key change in his life and career, "I got attached to the CIO in Chicago because they were the down-and-outers at that time" (Stebenne, p. 15).

The country's entry into World War II interrupted Goldberg's career as a labor lawyer. Eager to join the fight against fascism, he volunteered to serve in the Office of Strategic Services (OSS), the wartime intelligence agency. There he organized a labor branch, which gathered information from union members on the Continent for use in resisting the Axis advance and eventually aiding the Anglo-American invasion in Normandy. In the fall of 1944 Goldberg, convinced that the war was over and having exhausted his savings, returned to Chicago and resumed his law practice.

After the war ended, tensions within the CIO between its social democratic and more radical factions intensified, a division that led early in 1948 to the ouster of the CIO's top lawyer, the radical Lee Pressman. In Pressman's place, CIO president Philip Murray appointed Goldberg on 5 March 1948 as general counsel for the CIO and the Steelworkers. For the next thirteen years Goldberg served as a leading Washington lobbyist for the American labor movement and the top contract negotiator for the Steelworkers, one of the country's largest and most influential unions. Among his most important achievements, he helped to expel the CIO's radical-led affiliates in 1949; he negotiated that same year a pension plan for the Steelworkers that became a model for many other unions; he brokered the 1955 merger between the American Federation of Labor (AFL) and the CIO, which reunited the American labor movement for the first time since the mid-1930s; and he guided the Steelworkers union during its influential rounds of contract negotiations. Goldberg also played a major part in trying to rid the AFL-CIO of corruption, work that led him in the late 1950s to collaborate closely with Massachusetts senator John F. Kennedy. Serving in effect as Kennedy's tutor in the labor-management field, Goldberg became increasingly involved with Kennedy's successful bid for the presidency in 1960. Following the election, Kennedy named Goldberg secretary of labor. During his twenty months as labor secretary, Goldberg worked hard to settle strikes that imperiled American industry's long-term economic health and to provide federal support for the growth of public-employee unionism and for the growth of labor unions in Latin America.

Goldberg's tenure as labor secretary came to an early close in September 1962 when Kennedy appointed him to the Supreme Court, thereby producing a major change in its orientation. Like Chief Justice Earl Warren and Associate Justice William Brennan, whose views on the Court's role he essentially shared, Goldberg consistently supported efforts to expand legal protections for criminal defendants and suspects; to require state and local legislative bodies to reapportion themselves on the basis of one person, one vote; and to protect the civil rights of blacks menaced by segregationists.

Although he had intended to remain on the Supreme Court for the rest of his career, Goldberg reluctantly agreed to resign in July 1965 to become U.S. ambassador to the United Nations. Moved by President Lyndon Johnson's request that he go to the UN to help negotiate a Vietnam peace settlement, confident that he could persuade Johnson to seek such a peace, and unwilling to antagonize the president by refusing, Goldberg took the new post. Johnson, however, ignored Goldberg's advice to halt the escalation of the war effort until the unworkability of that policy became clear in the spring of 1968. Goldberg left the administration shortly afterward. Two years later he ran unsuccessfully as the Democratic candidate for governor of New York. After his defeat, Goldberg returned to Washington, D.C., where he practiced law until his death there in 1990.

An organization man and aide to others for most of his life, Goldberg enjoyed an influence in the American labor movement and the postwar political and economic system greater than many of his contemporaries realized. As CIO and Steelworkers general counsel, he played a leading role in negotiating labor's post–World War II social contract or "New Deal" with management, and in sustaining it into the early 1960s.

Goldberg is noteworthy, too, because he served in three high public offices, an unprecedented attainment for an American trade unionist. A prototypical New Deal liberal, he reflected in his life and career both the rise of American-style social democracy from the 1930s through the 1950s and its subsequent decline.

D.L.S.

Emma Goldman

[27 JUNE 1869–14 MAY 1940]

I first discovered Emma Goldman during the 1960s, when I was myself becoming politically radicalized. Her life and her writings spoke dramatically to many of the central concerns then beginning to dominate my life, and she quickly became an iconic figure for me. I was enormously taken with this rash, courageous, difficult, and incorruptible woman whose passionate concern for the world's unfortunates made her an implacable foe of privilege and traditional authority.

Denouncing capitalism and nationalism, Goldman used her oratorical skill and personal charisma to proselytize for an alternate—an anarchist—vision of the good society, one based on voluntary association and mutual aid, and freed from the traditional pieties of religion and allegiance to the power of the state. A figure of high-pitched, operatic intensity, Goldman challenged orthodoxy in all its forms and suffered the consequences—from jail to deportation to ostracism within left-wing circles for her early, daring denunciation of Lenin as a "betrayer of the revolution."

I became so smitten with Emma Goldman that in the early 1970s I wrote a teleplay about her life. But the New York PBS executives who commissioned the script changed their minds about producing it after they saw the finished product and realized just how radical a figure Goldman was. Happily, the play was later published as a short book, Mother Earth, *and—as I write this in 2001—it is about to be produced on the stage. I like to think that Emma Goldman's vision of a free society will find in the future a comparable resurrection.*

MARTIN DUBERMAN

Emma Goldman, anarchist and feminist activist, was born in Kovno, Lithuania, the daughter of Abraham Goldman and Taube Zodikoff, innkeepers and, later, small shopkeepers. Emma's lonely childhood was shaped by her parents' precarious social status and the contradictory influences of czarist anti-Semitism, the first stirrings of Russian feminism, and a growing revolutionary movement whose young members, especially the women, became Goldman's lifelong inspiration. After attending a *Realschule* in Königsberg, she entered a Russian high school in St. Petersburg, where her family moved in 1881, but straitened financial circumstances forced her to leave school after a year to work in a garment factory. In 1885 she immigrated with her sister Helena to Rochester, New York, where the rest of the family soon joined her.

In Rochester, Goldman met a fellow Russian immigrant, Jacob Kersner, to whom she was briefly married. Making shirtwaists in a sweatshop, she lived in an imaginary world of political intrigue, her mind filled with stories about the heroic Russian revolutionists who had been driven underground following the assassination of Czar Alexander II. She began following the trial and execution of the Chicago anarchists accused of setting off a bomb in Haymarket Square in the spring of 1886. A speech by Johanna Greie, a German anarchist, persuaded Goldman of the innocence of the accused men and perhaps also offered her a model of female activism that helped inspire her own flight from Rochester. Hungry for wider horizons and increasingly alienated from her husband, Goldman left for New York City, where she immediately became involved with the anarchist group around the flamboyant German agitator Johann Most. Within a few years Emma Goldman became one of the most controversial and charismatic figures in the international anarchist movement.

From the first, Goldman's life was entangled with that of Alexander Berkman, another Russian Jewish immigrant whose youthful belief in "propaganda by the deed" inspired his 1892 assassination attempt against Henry Clay Frick, manager of the Carnegie Steel Mills at Homestead, Pennsylvania. Goldman assisted in this attempt, though her complicity was never proven or acknowledged until the publication of her autobiography, *Living My Life*, in 1931. Berkman alone went to prison for fourteen years. However, the disastrous aftermath of his attempt, which neither killed Frick nor aroused the masses, convinced Goldman to relinquish her support for acts of violent individual protest, though not her admiration for those who were willing to sacrifice their lives for an ideal. She retained her belief in "direct action" as opposed to "political action" to effect revolutionary change but increasingly defined such action in terms of strikes, boycotts, acts of civil disobedience, and propaganda aimed at raising political consciousness.

At the time Goldman entered the anarchist movement, it was composed predominantly of small circles of German-, Russian-, Yiddish-, Italian-, and Spanish-speaking immigrants, most of them skilled workers and craftsmen. The Yiddish-speaking Jewish anarchists who increasingly made up the bulk of the movement after the turn of the century drew heavily on the ideas of Peter Kropotkin with his emphasis on ethics and his vision of a decentralized, stateless, communist society based on voluntary cooperation and mutual aid. Goldman tried to combine the anarchist communism of Kropotkin with the individualism of Max Stirner, Nietzsche, Ibsen, and the American individualist anarchists and midwestern free lovers, with whom she had considerable contact. As she explained in *Anarchism and Other Essays* (1911), anarchism meant "direct action, the open defiance of, and resistance to, all laws and restrictions, economic, social and moral." But it also meant a vision of society organized around "the freest possible expression of all the latent powers of the individual."

For Goldman, that individual was a woman as well as a man.

The originality of her anarchist vision lay in her critique of gender inequality within anarchist theory and practice as well as within capitalist society, and her insistence on claiming for women the freedoms anarchists demanded for men. Though she remained aloof from the movement for woman suffrage, which she criticized as too puritanical and middle-class, she spoke out strongly against the economic and social inequality of women, which made prostitution and marriage equivalent institutions. In Goldman's words, it was "merely a question of degree whether she sells herself to one man, in or out of marriage, or to many men." Criticizing the inadequacies of merely legal reform, Goldman emphasized that the emancipation of women required freedom from the "internal tyrants" of repressive social convention as well as from "external tyrannies" of political and economic inequality. Although Goldman extolled the glories of heterosexual love, she also urged tolerance for what she called "the intermediate sex," linking her very definition of anarchism to her defense of sexual minorities. "To me anarchism was not a theory for a distant future," she wrote in *Living My Life*. "It was a living influence to free us from inhibitions, internal no less than external, and from the destructive barriers that separate man from man."

By the turn of the century, Goldman had become a media star, a demonic figure to some, an inspiration to others. She had already served a year in Blackwell's Island Penitentiary in New York, for allegedly "inciting to riot" during a hunger demonstration in 1893. She was arrested on charges of inspiring the assassination of President William McKinley in 1901 but was released for lack of evidence. "Her name was enough in those days to produce a shudder," recalled her friend Margaret Anderson, editor of the avant-garde *Little Review*, in her autobiography, *My Thirty Years' War* (1930). "She was considered a monster, an exponent of free love and bombs." An electrifying presence on the lecture platform, Goldman began making annual coast-to-coast tours, speaking out on a wide variety of subjects, from anarchism, anarchosyndicalism, and trade unionism to birth control and sex as an element of "creative work." She supported herself by working as a midwife, masseuse, and nurse—skills she had learned during a year of study at the Vienna General Hospital in 1895–1896. Her lectures in English attracted not only anarchists and other radicals but many liberals as well. She maintained ties with the radical wing of the labor movement, particularly the Industrial Workers of the World, whose strikes and free speech fights she often supported.

Upon Alexander Berkman's release from prison in 1906, the two comrades began publishing an anarchist monthly magazine, *Mother Earth*, combining cultural criticism and social analysis. With the emergence of bohemian communities in Greenwich Village and in cities around the country, Goldman began courting the intellectual avant-garde, who in turn embraced her as a heroine and inspiration. Emphasizing the need for a transformation of consciousness, she helped create libertarian schools through the "modern school" movement. She also lectured widely on literature, especially on the work of dramatists such as Ibsen, Hauptmann, Strindberg, Shaw, and others whose plays dramatized contemporary social evils. Her *Social Significance of the Modern Drama* (1914) offered one of the first political analyses of modern theater in English. Friendly with many actors and directors, she supported the "little theater" movement that created experimental regional theaters around the country.

Harassed by police and political officials, Goldman turned persecution into triumph as she organized free speech groups around the country to defend the rights of persecuted radicals and act as a support group for her own campaigns. Though she had long defended the right of women to control their own bodies, the arrest of Margaret Sanger in 1915 mobilized Goldman to more direct involvement in the campaign to legalize birth control. She spent two weeks in jail in 1916 for explaining birth control methods from the lecture platform and giving out free information.

World War I brought Progressivism to a halt in the United States, and Goldman and many of her comrades turned to antiwar activity. Arrested in 1917 for opposing the draft, Goldman and Berkman spent two years in prison. They were released at the height of the postwar Red Scare in 1919 and were promptly deported along with several hundred other immigrant radicals to the newly created Soviet Union. Although Goldman and Berkman had defended the Russian revolution and the fight against czarism, the Bolshevik vision of a highly centralized socialist state remained anathema to them and to most anarchists. Within a few months Goldman had grown alienated from the Bolshevik regime, particularly disgusted by the increasing persecution of anarchist and other left-wing dissidents from Bolshevism. In December 1921 Goldman, Berkman, and other anarchists left Soviet Russia for the West. In Stockholm, Berlin, Paris, London, St. Tropez, and Toronto, Goldman carried on an anti-Soviet campaign, condemning what she considered the Bolshevik betrayal of the masses and calling international attention to the plight of political prisoners in the jails and prison camps.

Finding herself increasingly isolated from all segments of the Left, not only the Communists but also the anti-Soviet socialists and even some anarchists, Goldman spent two years in a beautiful little house in St. Tropez where she wrote *Living My Life*. The autobiography used a conventional chronological narrative form to show how a lifelong commitment to anarchism opened new worlds of politics and love. Despite criticism from her comrades, she frankly described her tumultuous nine-year passion for a flamboyant Chicago physician, Ben L. Reitman, the only man who knew how "to love the woman in me and yet who would also be able to share my work."

Following publication of the autobiography, Goldman secured a ninety-day visa to lecture in the United States. But the Roosevelt administration feared alienating support for a more liberal immigration policy and denied her a permanent visa. In exile once again, she briefly realized her dreams in Barcelona in the fall of 1936, shortly after the start of the anarchist revolution and the civil war. The Spanish anarchosyndicalist organization the Confederacion Nacional del Trabajo–Federacion Anarquista Iberica (CNT-FAI) appointed her as its agent in London, where she campaigned for aid for her beleaguered comrades. With the small international anarchist movement badly split over the decision of Spanish comrades to enter the wartime government, Goldman attempted to reconcile factions while also criticizing CNT-FAI strategy. After the defeat of the anarchists by the Communists in 1937, and the fall of the republic in 1939, a grief-stricken Goldman traveled to Toronto to work on behalf of all refugees from European fascism. She died in Toronto and was buried in Chicago, in the country she always considered her home.

Emma Goldman's legacy within the anarchist movement remains controversial. Widely admired for her courage and tenacity in the face of persecution, she was also criticized as dominating and dictatorial. She remained like most immigrant radicals relatively blind to racism. For all her championing of the avant-garde, she preferred nineteenth-century realism and naturalism to twentieth-century modernism. She never succeeded in building an English-speaking movement, as she had hoped, though anarchist ideas had considerable influence within the Industrial Workers of the World and the Jewish trade union movement, as well as among middle-class intellectuals and artists. After 1921 Goldman's wholesale opposition to Marxism as well as her anti-Communism isolated her, not only from most of the western Left, including the anti-Soviet socialists, but also from much of the cultural avant-garde as well.

No other figure, however, so skillfully dramatized the rebellious social and cultural currents of Gilded Age and Progressive America. Certainly no other woman of her generation used her public persona so effectively to flout bourgeois conventions and taboos, using her own body on stage as a lightning rod for rebellion. Goldman brought keen theatrical gifts to the performance of protest, exploiting the controversy she created while lecturing in cities and towns across the country to educate and mobilize public opinion around a diverse array of progressive causes. Although more an activist than a theorist, she subjected anarchist ideas to a feminist critique, identifying the gender blindness in much anarchist theory and opening the way to the anarcho-feminism of the 1960s. She introduced a more sophisticated notion of psychology into anarchist thought, pointing out the subjective, often unconscious forces that helped maintain authoritarian or submissive attitudes even in those consciously opposed to all authority. *Living My Life* remains a compelling anarchist critique of America, as well as the record of a woman's lifelong resistance. Perhaps Emma Goldman's very originality conspired against the creation of a lasting anarchist movement, for to build such a movement she would have had to sacrifice the iconoclasm that remains her most enduring legacy.

A.R.W.

Adolphus Washington Greely

[27 MARCH 1844–20 OCTOBER 1935]

*A*dolphus Washington Greely has been my personal American hero since I first discovered his remarkable life story, hidden away in a cabin trunk in his granddaughter's summer cottage in North Conway, New Hampshire, in 1973. I hope that by including this Giant among these Invisibles I will bring him entirely out of the shadows and bring Adolphus Washington Greely due regard for being one of the more extraordinary figures from recent American history that, for the past thirty years, I have steadfastly believed him to be.

The Greely girls used to babysit for my then very young children, when we were neighbors in Chevy Chase, Maryland; their mother kindly loaned us the family cottage; and one summer, while looking in the attic for yet more old copies of Life magazine, I found the long-forgotten trunk. The story held in the papers and diaries piled hap-hazardly inside—and which began with a failed High Arctic expedition, its members marooned in desperate circumstances, ignored by officials, abandoned to their fate, and yet with some, Greely included, surviving against all odds—has captivated me ever since.

Adolphus Greely's is the kind of life by which I am endlessly fas-cinated: a man whose career followed a trajectory that was initially mired in tragedy and yet which eventually soared to the greatest peaks of achievement; a figure whose contribution to society is now regarded as inestimable; a man whose life is very little known to those outside his own specialization. In Greely's case, there were so many specializations—exploration, electronics, aerial warfare, languages, American Indians, military strategy, communications, publishing—that he is more widely known than some, and yet until now, not to the wider audience that I believe his life properly deserves.

SIMON WINCHESTER

General A. W. Greely, c.1900. "I know of no law," he wrote in response to charges of cannibalism on his Arctic expedition, "human or divine, which was broken at Sabine." *(Library of Congress)*

A dolphus Washington Greely, soldier and arctic explorer, was born in Newburyport, Massachusetts, the son of John Balch Greely, a shoemaker, and Frances D. Cobb, a cotton mill weaver. Greely graduated from Brown High School, Newburyport, in 1860, and in the following year, at the age of seventeen, he joined the Nineteenth Massachusetts Volunteer Infantry. He served as a private, corporal, and first sergeant and was hospitalized for wounds sustained at Antietam, including a facial injury, which he covered with a beard for the remainder of his life. On furlough in 1863 he accepted a commission as a second lieutenant in the Fourth U.S. Volunteers (later Eighty-first U.S. Colored Infantry), stationed in Louisiana.

After the war, Greely assisted in the organization of the Thirty-ninth Infantry and Ninth Cavalry, mustered out as captain and brevet major, and accepted a commission as second lieutenant, Thirty-sixth Regular Infantry, serving in Wyoming and Utah. In 1869 he joined the U.S. Signal Corps, in which service he served the bulk of his army career. For the next twelve years he inspected telegraph lines, surveyed flood lines, directed the construction of military telegraph lines in Montana, Dakota, Texas, and the Southwest, and engaged in weather prediction. He met Henrietta H. C. Nesmith while on assignment in San Diego; they married in 1878 and eventually had six children.

In March 1881 Greely volunteered for the command of the International Polar expedition to Lady Franklin Bay, Greenland, one of thirteen sent out in a cooperative international effort to establish a ring of scientific stations at high latitudes. The 25-member expedition—including Greely, physician Octavus Pavy, two officers, eighteen enlisted men, and two sledge drivers—established Fort Conger at Discovery Harbor, Ellesmere Island. From this station they mapped the area, gathered scientific information, took regular weather readings, and sent out exploratory parties. In May 1882 one of these sledging parties led by Lieutenant Charles Lockwood successfully reached 83°24', the "farthest north" point yet achieved by explorers. Their expected resupply ship, blocked by ice in the Kane Sea, did not arrive during the summer of 1882. The next summer the relief ship, *Proteus*, also failed to arrive; it had capsized in the ice—its crew, rescued by a naval ship, left only a small cache of supplies for the Greely party.

Now out of contact for two years, Greely and his men, following prearranged instructions, abandoned Fort Conger in August 1883 and made their way by small boats and foot toward Cape Sabine more than 500 miles to the south, picking up some supply caches along the way. They expected to meet a party from the *Proteus* wintering at Littleton Bay but learned instead of the ship's demise. The men spent a hard winter and spring in a makeshift camp on Bedford Pym Island, north of Cape Sabine, subsisting first on limited rations and the meager results of hunting and fishing, then on small crustaceans, moss, lichens, and their leather equipment. Amid heightened public interest in the fate of the expedition and lobbying by Mrs. Greely and others, Congress authorized a naval rescue operation. By the time Commander Winfield S. Schley located the survivors in late June 1884, eighteen men had died—most of starvation, but one had been executed for stealing food, and one had drowned—and one died on the way home.

Greely and the remaining five enlisted men received national publicity and acclaim, but controversy soon surrounded the expedition. Schley reported that pieces of body tissue had been removed from six of the recovered bodies; Greely vehemently denied the newspaper charges of cannibalism. "I know of no law," he wrote in *Three Years of Arctic Service*, his 1886 two-volume account of the expedition, "human or divine, which was broken at Sabine." Greely's leadership and judgment also were questioned. As David Brainard, one of the survivors who remained in touch with Greely until his death, later recalled, Greely's "obstinate nature" and strict adherence to military conduct and orders shaped his command. Other arctic explorers, such as Robert E. Peary, debated whether those attributes also contributed to the expedition's disastrous outcome.

After two years spent recovering from the ordeal and preparing his official report, *Report on the Proceedings of the United States Expedition to Lady Franklin Bay, Grinnell Land* (1888; also issued as U.S. 49th Cong., 1st sess., 1888, House Misc. Doc. 393), Greely received his overdue captain's promotion. He continued to be engaged by and to write extensively on arctic and polar exploration throughout his life, publishing books and articles in popular and scientific magazines. In 1887 Greely was appointed chief signal corps officer with the rank of brigadier general, a post he held until 1906, and through which he pursued his meteorological interests. His official congressional reports on western U.S. climatic conditions (U.S. 50th Cong., 2d sess., 1888, Sen. Exec. Doc. 91; U.S. 51st Cong., 2d sess., 1891, House Exec. Doc. 287) emphasized the diversity of arid regions and argued that no single irrigation plan would be applicable to the West. Under his command the U.S. Signal Corps expanded its weather forecasting service (until those responsibilities were transferred in 1891 to the Department of Agriculture), laid undersea cables and tactical wires during the Spanish-American War, and established the extensive Alaskan telegraph, cable, and wireless system.

At the end of his military career, Greely, promoted to major general, served as a replacement commander of western military divisions. As commander of the Pacific Division he directed the army relief for the San Francisco earthquake in April 1906. And in October 1906, as commander of the Northern Military Division, he sent a show of military force to persuade sojourning Utes to return to Utah from Wyoming. After retirement in 1908, Greely participated actively in numerous scientific organizations, clubs, and civic work, lectured and wrote extensively, and continued to be consulted, as he had been for many years, on all matters arctic. A founding member of the National Geographic Society, he published numerous articles in *National Geographic* magazine. He served as the first president of the Explorers' Club, New York, and represented the United States overseas at various international geographic and telegraph conferences. He received the Congressional Medal of Honor in 1935 and died later that year in Washington, D.C.

K.G.M.

Nathanael Greene

[27 JULY 1742–19 JUNE 1786]

*L*ike most Americans, my knowledge of the American Revolution was intertwined with the saga of George Washington. Then, while watching a PBS documentary on the war, I heard the name of another general about whom I knew little: Nathanael Greene. The program did not dwell much on General Greene—like most histories of the war, it focused on Washington's leadership to the exclusion of his immediate subordinates. Still, the program certainly demonstrated that Greene was everywhere: Bunker Hill, Long Island, the slog through New Jersey, Christmas morning in Trenton, Brandywine, Valley Forge, Monmouth, Morristown.

Then, after Benedict Arnold betrays West Point, Greene disappears from his supporting role. And before you know it, George Washington is astride his horse at Yorktown, directing General Benjamin Lincoln to accept the British surrender. What, I wondered, happened to General Greene? I ordered a couple of ancient biographies of the man, and soon was the proud owner of a complete set of his papers, all eleven volumes (the largest collection of military correspondence from the war, except for Washington's). That's when I learned what happened to Major General Nathanael Greene.

Washington, knowing that defeat was only a lost battle away, sent his trusted friend to the shattered South in 1780 to stop the British rampage through the Carolinas. And there, in a magnificent bit of generalship, Nathanael Greene won the war. An exaggeration? Perhaps, but only a slight one. This Quaker from Rhode Island who educated himself in military science, who joined his local militia despite a knee ailment that left him with a very unmilitary limp, who so impressed Washington that he became the Continental army's de facto second-in-command, was responsible for sending Cornwallis and his battered troops on the road to York-

town. He did it without winning a major battle. He did it by out-thinking, and out-generaling, his enemy.

In an era that produced so many astonishing people, Nathanael Greene was one of the young nation's most selfless patriots. He had more reason than most to stay at home and await events. He was raised a Quaker; he had a substantial business in Rhode Island; he had a wonderfully independent wife and a young family. His letters reveal just how much he longed for peace and the blessings of domestic life. But he could not stand by. He risked all he loved for an ideal. He never gave up, and in the end he found a way to win.

TERRY GOLWAY

Nathanael Greene, general in the American Revolution, was born in Potowomut (now Warwick), Rhode Island, the son of Nathanael Greene, an iron founder, and Mary Mott. Because his Quaker parents believed in manual labor and a minimum of education, he commenced working early in life at his father's forge without an opportunity for schooling. However, he was very bright and early on acquired a love of books. A self-taught reader, he also became a fluent letter writer. During his lifetime he came to possess over 200 volumes on various subjects, especially military history and theory. In 1774 he married Catherine Littlefield; they had five children.

Greene began to show interest in public affairs when tensions between the colonies and Great Britain mounted in the mid-1770s. At that time he rejected the pacifism of his parents and organized the Kentish Guards in preparation for war. When he was rejected as an officer because of a limp caused by a childhood injury, he volunteered as a private in order to prove himself and spent his spare time studying military science. He also served on a committee empowered by the state legislature to prepare Rhode Island's defenses. Thus gaining the attention of the assembly, he received appointment in 1775 as general of the Rhode Island Army of Observation, being promoted over veteran officers of the Seven Years' War because of his likable personality, knowledge of military strategy, and political influence. In the next few weeks he organized three regiments and reported with them to General George Washington at the siege of Boston. The commander in chief was impressed by Greene's acumen and marked the young man for future responsibilities in the Continental army.

During his first year as a soldier Greene's performance was not particularly distinguished. He spent months in Boston and New York in a stalemate with the enemy, during which time he continued his studies of military matters and prepared Long Island's defenses. He was promoted to major general in August 1776, but he was too ill with a "raging Fever" to lead his troops when General William Howe attacked a month later. In November Greene was placed in command of Forts Washington and Lee, north of New York City. Partly because of his decision not to evacuate Fort Washington on Manhattan when it became endangered by the enemy, the British captured the fort, taking 2,800 prisoners. His confidence greatly shaken, Greene momentarily doubted his military acumen, as did others. However, he redeemed himself in December by helping Washington plan and execute the American retreat across New Jersey and the enormously successful attack on Trenton.

Over the next few months Greene made himself indispensable to Washington by taking on numerous tasks, not least of which was helping fend off Howe's attacks in New Jersey during the early summer of 1777. After the British landed at the head of Chesapeake Bay to drive toward Philadelphia from the south, he played a pivotal role in the battle of the Brandywine in September, marching his division four miles to thwart Howe's maneuver against Washington's right flank. A month later, at Germantown, he penetrated enemy lines before being compelled to carry out a masterful retreat, pressed hard by the British general James Grant. In camp at Valley Forge during the following winter, he and Washington were accused of incompetence by several congressmen because of their defeats in Pennsylvania; but neither general was ever in serious danger of losing command, and the grumbling soon faded.

In fact, Greene was in such high standing among Americans that he was soon urged by Congress and Washington to assume the vital post of quartermaster general. In deference to Washington's wishes, Greene accepted the post, but he disliked giving up battlefield command and later asserted that he considered the office "derogatory." In the next two years, despite enormous obstacles, he vastly improved the flow of matériel to the troops. Because inflation required them to pay huge prices for goods, he and his assistants were charged with profiteering, although the accusation was never proven. In August 1780 Greene resigned his post in disgust after a months-long battle with Congress. Throughout his tenure as quartermaster general, Greene had continued to serve Washington as an adviser and occasionally as a commander in the field. At the battle of Monmouth in June 1778 he took charge of Charles Lee's troops after Washington relieved Lee for retreating without orders during the fight. He used his knowledge of his home state to assist John Sullivan in his Rhode Island campaign of 1778, and two years later he commanded at Springfield, New Jersey, when Baron Wilhelm von Knyphausen made a foray out of New York City to test American mettle.

In October 1780 Greene received the greatest opportunity of his military career: independent command in the Southern Department. During the previous summer British troops under Lord Cornwallis had gained control of Georgia and South Carolina and had defeated Horatio Gates at Camden. With North Carolina and Virginia seemingly in peril, Congress granted Washington the right to choose Gates's replacement. He immediately selected Greene, who at once commenced his journey southward. After pausing in Philadelphia to plead successfully for the addition of Henry "Light-Horse Harry" Lee's legion to his command, he proceeded to Virginia, where he appointed Baron Friedrich von Steuben to gather men and supplies. During his journey he studied maps of the South in preparation for his new duties. On 3 December 1780 in Charlotte, North Carolina, he took command from General Gates of his army of 2,200 troops, almost two-thirds of whom were militiamen.

Fully aware that Cornwallis was in Winnsboro, South Carolina, awaiting reinforcements from Virginia before attacking, Greene decided to make a bold stroke against his foe before the reinforcements arrived. Dividing his army, he sent Daniel Morgan westward with 600 men to shadow Cornwallis while he rebuilt his army at Cheraw, South Carolina. After Morgan's tactically brilliant victory over Banastre Tarleton's forces at Cowpens on 17 January 1781, Greene raced north ahead of an angry Cornwallis to rendezvous with Morgan and cross the Dan River to relative safety. Having successfully eluded his foe, he augmented his forces to a total of 4,200 men and recrossed the Dan, challenging Cornwallis to a battle at Guilford Courthouse, North Carolina. On 15 March he was attacked and after a furious fight was driven from the field. Cornwallis, having suffered 30 percent casualties, limped to the coast at Wilmington, where he refitted his army. Deciding to change his field of action to Virginia, he marched his troops northward to Yorktown.

Greene moved southward with 1,500 Continentals, his only remaining troops after militia departures, in an effort to overcome about 8,000 enemy soldiers garrisoned throughout South Carolina and Georgia. Although he was overpowered by the British in confrontations at Hobkirk's Hill and Fort Ninety-six, Greene, aided by partisans such as Francis Marion, Thomas Sumter, and Andrew Pickens, compelled his enemies to fall back from their interior posts. On 8 September he fought a drawn battle with Colonel Andrew Stewart at Eutaw Springs, after which Stewart withdrew to Charleston. A few weeks later Greene learned of Cornwallis's surrender to Washington at Yorktown. However, this American triumph did not bring an end to Greene's struggle in the South; the British still held Charleston and Savannah, and patriots and Loyalists still warred on each other throughout his command. Aided by General Anthony Wayne, he worked to restore peace in the South while continuing to apply pressure against the British in Charleston and Savannah until both cities were evacuated in 1782. His military labors ceased only when the final peace treaty was signed the following year.

After the war, both South Carolina and Georgia granted Greene large estates. Although he returned to the North in late 1783 as a conquering hero, two years later he and his wife settled in Georgia. His last years were plagued by accusations of profiteering in the closing months of the war and by a debt of thousands of dollars after a note that he had cosigned came due. Although he was vindicated of the profiteering charges, his debt woes continued, probably shortening his life. He died of an infection at "Mulberry Grove," his plantation near Savannah, leaving his family in financial straits until his debts were liquidated by Congress ten years later.

The first time Washington met Greene he declared that Greene could be relied upon to assume command of the Continental army should he become incapacitated. Thomas Jefferson asserted long after the war that Greene had no equal as a military thinker among his peers in the officer corps, and Francis Kinloch, a congressman who fought in the war, called him the "military genius" of the American Revolution. These assessments of Greene are borne out by his military record in both the North and the South, and historians today evaluate his military abilities as highly as did his contemporaries. Few would deny that he deserves to be remembered as the "strategist of the Revolution."

P.D.N.

Charles Tomlinson Griffes

[17 SEPEMBER 1884–8 APRIL 1920]

I spent my piano youth immersed in Teutonic composers: Bach, Beethoven, Brahms, Mozart. I never gave a fig for the French, or for Americans. I certainly didn't like forgotten composers. I had time only for titans. Then I grew up, saddened, quit piano. A decade passed. I started to play piano again. This time, acknowledging myself to be a failure, and savoring my own unsuccess, I wanted to concentrate on French composers—Fauré, Ravel. And I wanted to concentrate on minor Americans. I found Charles Tomlinson Griffes, his piano fantasy, titled The White Peacock, *in an old G. Schirmer anthology of staples from the once contemporary repertoire. What enchanted me about Griffes were his novel harmonies (French-derived, and yet entirely his own); his minimalism (no grandiose or overextended gestures); and his continual, unquenched yearning for modernity. His earliest pieces (a Rhapsody in B minor for piano) show a Brahmsian tendency, though also the influence of Rachmaninoff; his middle pieces (*The White Peacock*) are all shimmering Gallicism, with "Orientalist" colorations that would have pleased Puccini; his final works (a piano sonata, some unfinished piano sketches) indicate that he was in the process of forging a condensed, provocative idiom, like Scriabin with a taste for the plains and the prairies.*

The personal aspects of Griffes's life also touched me: his early death; his demanding, only slightly rewarding job, teaching music at the Hackley School for Boys in Tarrytown, New York; his jaunts into Manhattan to promote his music and to pick up men; his homosexuality (he had a long love affair with a policeman); his reticence. He reminded me of my idol Joseph Cornell, an urban soul who lived apart from urbanity, and therefore developed a relationship with a dream metropolis. It would be difficult to found a cult based on Griffes; his music is not bountiful enough to sustain supplicants. But he is, in his way, a perfect composer who was also an ordinary American gay man without a particularly satisfying life. I am moved by his failure, as well as by his success: without wishing to make a monument of him, I want to draw attention to the offbeat sublimity of his compositions, and to his earnest, stalwart tempera- ment, a poor fellow struggling to compose on the train from Tarry- town to New York, until failing health and onerous pedagogic responsibilities broke him down.

WAYNE KOESTENBAUM

Charles Tomlinson Griffes, composer, was born in Elmi- ra, New York, the son of Wilbur Griffes, a manufacturer, and Clara Tomlinson. He was a precocious student, showing great flair and love for art and literature as well as for music. First bent upon a career as a pianist, Griffes, like most American music students of the day, studied in Europe (1903- 1907). Among his teachers was the composer Engelbert Humperdinck. In Europe he perfected his pianistic technique and learned the crafts of harmony and composition. In course, Griffes discovered composition to be his true musical calling.

In 1907 Griffes returned to the United States and secured a position on the faculty at the Hackley School, a boys' prepara- tory academy in Tarrytown, New York. The post gave him a steady income and ready access to the publishers and general culture of New York City, but some critics have since felt that the drudgery of preparatory school life undermined his com- posing career, causing his genius to go underutilized and unappreciated. Most composers do spend much time teach- ing, however. Griffes's pupils were younger than those of many music teachers, but they ran the gamut of aptitudes that most composers face as teachers.

During school breaks and even while teaching, Griffes devoted his energies to composing. His early works exhibited a decided Germanic Romanticism, which appeared a bit old- fashioned. But by 1911 Griffes had turned away from this approach. At times he favored leaner musical textures and more dissonant harmonies, as exemplified by his *Piano Sonata* (1919). The sonata, which many critics regard as his greatest work, indicated the composer's potential for exploring the stark avant-garde aesthetics of the day.

A brilliant orchestrator, Griffes underscored the translucence of his music by the employment of exotic programmatic topics in many pieces. His orchestral transcription *The Pleasure Dome of Kubla Khan* (1912) musically depicted imagery both of medieval China and of the poetry of Samuel Taylor Coleridge. His *Sho-jo* (1917), an ensemble piece inspired by Japanese pantomime drama, and the five orchestral *Poems of Ancient China and Japan* (1917), in which he wove scales, harmonies, and instrumental colors of those Eastern cultures, were a thematic and harmonic revelation to his early twentieth-century American audiences.

It was in the impressionistic style of his French contemporaries Claude Debussy and Maurice Ravel that Griffes seemed to hit his stride and begin to gain professional recognition. Like other impressionists, Griffes possessed a keen sense of the lyrical qualities of each orchestral instrument and layered his music with rich and colorful orchestral textures. Griffes's harmonies and scales stretched listeners just beyond the bounds of traditional major/minor modality, as if to elevate them onto slightly unfamiliar pathways of emotions. The *Poem for Flute and Orchestra* (1918) holds the listener in a suspension of seamless melody, as the solo and orchestral accompaniment gently flow, with little perceptible cadence, in a kind of tense intoxication. Many critics applauded, and innovative conductors like Frederick Stock and Leopold Stokowski sought out Griffes and performed his works.

To what musical ends Griffes's considerable gifts would have led him is but sad conjecture. In December 1919 he came down with pleurisy complicated by pneumonia. As Griffes was convalescing at the Hackley School, some students and staff, fresh from the scares of the influenza epidemic, grew anxious to the point of hysteria. False rumors raged that Griffes was infectious with tuberculosis. Hackley's officials cowardly caved in, and Griffes had to be removed to a mountaintop sanitorium for consumptive patients. He did not belong there, and the banishment greatly depressed and weakened him. As he lay in his room he watched workmen digging about a water main and grew obsessed with the image that they were symbolically digging his grave. Surgeons drained a quantity of fluid from his lungs, but a second operation revealed that they had left a small metal piece in his chest, causing him even greater pain. Further emaciated and depressed, Griffes suffered a hemorrhage and died. He was only thirty-five and had written music for but thirteen years. The wealth of his short creative life and the portent of so much more led one critic to eulogize that his death "seems so unfair."

A. L.

John Hoskins Griscom
[14 AUGUST 1809–28 APRIL 1874]

*I*n 1842, John H. Griscom, a learned and pious Quaker physician, issued a scorching report on sanitary conditions in the city. Griscom had seen the effects of living in cellars and tenements close up during his years of service at the New York Dispensary and New York Hospital, and when he was appointed to the post of city inspector in 1842, he embarked on a comprehensive survey of city health.

Among Griscom's many striking departures from conventional middle class wisdom was his refusal to blame the poor for their wretched housing. He knew that lack of fresh water and adequate sanitation made it impossible for residents to keep clean and pious homes, even if they wanted to, and he even declined to blame laboring men for escaping from such hovels to the grog shops. For Griscom, dirt was a symptom of poverty, not its cause.

On the other hand he didn't blame the rich, as the land reformers did. Rather he appealed to them to provide decent housing, not just as "a measure of humanity, of justice to the poor," but as a matter of self-interest. Bad housing meant sick workers, and sick workers meant lower profits, higher relief outlays, and higher taxes. Ultimately, too, slums fostered the growth of "a class in the community more difficult to govern, more disposed to robbery, mobs, and other lawless acts, and less accessible to the influence of religious and moral instruction." Griscom was convinced that such rational appeals would have weight because the problem seemed to stem from lack of understanding: "one half of the world does not know how the other half lives."

The comfortable half didn't pay much attention to Griscom, however, until rudely reminded of the costs of inaction by the cholera epidemic of 1849 which claimed over 5000 lives. Bodies lay in the streets for days. Eventually they were rowed over to Ran-

dall's Island and dumped in an open trench, at which point a grue-some public health device came into play as thousands of rats swam over and gnawed the flesh from the carcasses before they rotted.

As in 1832, many declared the cholera God's retribution for sin, but this time many others riposted that moralizing was no longer a sufficient response to social crisis. Instead the city had to take an active response to reforming the environment. It would take a long time for the new attitude to influence municipal institutions. But Griscom kept hammering at the need for a sanitary police force throughout the 1850s, and was joined by other activist physicians, civic-minded businessmen, and reformers who pointed out that a series of violent upheavals which culminated in the great draft riots of 1863 were themselves a function of a degraded environment.

Finally, with a cholera epidemic approaching, the state legisla-ture, in 1866, created a Metropolitan Board of Health and gave it extraordinary powers to fight the scourge. The ensuing mobiliza-tion helped keep New York's death toll under 500 — one-tenth the fatalities of an 1849 epidemic, despite a one-third increase popula-tion since then. Thanks in considerable measure to John Griscom — an unsung civic hero — New York City had erected a milestone in the history of public health.

MIKE WALLACE

John Hoskins Griscom, physician and sanitarian, was born in New York, New York, the son of John Griscom, an edu-cator and chemist, and Abigail Hoskins. He attended the Collegiate School of Friends and the New York High School, a school owned and run by his father, where he absorbed the elder Griscom's Quaker, philanthropic, and scientific outlook. After studying with anatomist John D. Godman and surgeon Valentine Mott and attending medical lectures at Rutgers Medical College, Griscom transferred to the University of Pennsylvania, where he received his M.D. in 1832. Appointed assistant physician to the New York Dispensary in 1833, he was promoted to physician a year later. He married Henrietta

Peale, daughter of painter Rembrandt Peale, in 1835; they had eight children. He purchased the goodwill of a retiring New York City physician in 1837, acquiring a practice that he maintained until his death.

In addition to his private practice, Griscom held scientific and medical posts throughout his life, including professor of chemistry at the College of Pharmacy in New York from 1836 to 1838 and physician to the New York Hospital from 1843 to 1870. In 1840 he published *Animal Mechanism and Physiology*, which ran through several editions. His participation in the founding of the New York Academy of Medicine in 1846, his service as its vice president in 1854, and his work with the American Medical Association demonstrated his commitment to improving the status of the medical profession.

Griscom believed that, through the analysis of vital statistics, humankind could understand nature's laws and thereby design appropriate sanitary reforms to prevent illness and premature death. During his tenure as city inspector and as head of the New York City Health Department (1842), Griscom improved the reliability of the city's mortality statistics. He accomplished this by successfully promoting an ordinance requiring a city inspector's permit before the dead could be transported beyond the city limits. Although he was removed from these posts after a year because of his plans for reorganizing the structure of the city health department, he used the information gathered during these municipal appointments to form the basis of his most important work, *The Sanitary Condition of the Laboring Population of New York* (1845). Modeled on Edwin Chadwick's work on Great Britain, this report correlated the higher morbidity rate among the laboring class with their overcrowded, unventilated tenement living conditions. For Griscom, tenement reform required the provision of better ventilation so that the inhabitants might live in accordance with nature's laws. Cramped, unventilated spaces forced people to live in close quarters and breathe vitiated air, leading to a progression from declining morals to depression, illness, and unemployment.

Griscom's solution to this problem reveals his pietistic education and utilitarian outlook; for him, improving the physical health and moral sensibilities of the poor through education and legislation would benefit society as a whole. The poor, once freed from the ills of tenement living, would become useful and productive members of society. In *The Uses and Abuses of Air* (1850), he again stressed the importance of proper ventilation and offered concrete solutions for achieving it. Griscom's belief that immigrants and prisoners would benefit from these reforms is shown in the medical and sanitary rules he developed for the Emigrant Refuge and Hospital on Ward's Island while serving as Commissioner of Emigration (1848–1851) and in his well-known report *Prison Hygiene* (1868) for the New York Prison Association.

Griscom's influence extended beyond the confines of New York City. He corresponded with Massachusetts sanitarians Lemuel Shattuck and Edward Jarvis. In 1859 he presided over the Third National Quarantine Convention, confirming his national reputation. Griscom remained active in New York sanitary reform until his death. His tireless letter campaign contributed to the success of the Metropolitan Health Act of 1866, which established a Board of Health for New York City and served as a model for cities nationwide. Through his writings, lectures, and public service, John Hoskins Griscom helped lay the foundation for mid-nineteenth-century urban public health reform in the United States. His ideas came to fruition in the late nineteenth century with tenement reform laws and in the writings of later reformers including those of Jacob Riis. He died in New York City.

C.G.S.

William Halsted

[23 SEPTEMBER 1852–7 SEPTEMBER 1922]

*E*very time I or any other American surgeon perform an operation, our technique is guided by principles first elucidated by William Halsted. Over a period of about twenty-five years, he introduced an entirely new approach to surgery, characterized by meticulous attention to detail and a profound knowledge of human biology. Halsted's work abolished the old smash-and-grab methods of his predecessors and taught generations of us that surgery is an aesthetic and intellectual undertaking. It is because of his teachings that I chose it as my life's work.*

Paradoxically, I admire him most for what many would believe to be a profound weakness: his contributions were made by a man secretly addicted to cocaine and later to morphine. He managed to soldier on, year after year, so successfully fighting the ravages of his addiction that he left a body of work unsurpassed by any surgeon of his or other time.

Unfortunately, the general public nowadays most commonly associates Halsted's name with his radical mastectomy, the first operation to successfully treat breast cancer. Though it is today known that this extensive and mutilating procedure is rarely if ever justified, self-righteous critics seem unaware that Halsted's innovation was at one time the only hope for hundreds of thousands of women: a disease previously thought incurable would now respond to surgery. Ironically, he would no doubt have been among the first to abandon it once the value of less drastic procedures became appreciated, long after his death.

SHERWIN NULAND

William Stewart Halsted, surgeon, was born in New York City, the son of William Mills Halsted, the president of Halsted, Haines and Co., a textile-importing

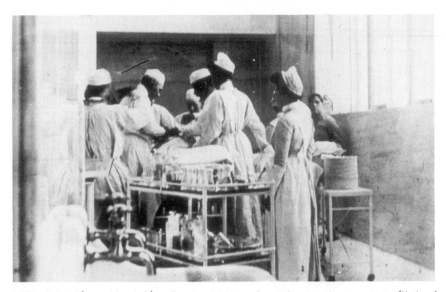

William Halsted (second from left) performs surgery in an observation operating room, 1903. *(National Library of Medicine)*

firm, and Mary Louisa Haines. Privately educated as a child, he graduated from Andover in 1869 and after a further year of preparation entered Yale University in 1870. There he had an undistinguished academic career and was known for his sporting prowess; he served as captain of the football team. He attributed his interest in medicine to the purchase of *Gray's Anatomy* and John C. Dalton's *Physiology* textbooks in his senior year at Yale. After his graduation from Yale (A.B., 1874), Halsted began medical studies at the College of Physicians and Surgeons in New York City. There he became the assistant of the professor of physiology, John C. Dalton—the author of the textbook that had led him to a medical career. An outstanding medical student, Halsted won a place for himself as an intern at Bellevue Hospital, where he met William H. Welch, who was to become a founding member of the Johns Hopkins Medical School.

Halsted received an M.D. in 1877 with honors. He then took a position as house physician to the New York Hospital. During the visit of English surgeon Joseph Lister that same year to New York, Halsted became convinced of the utility of antiseptic surgical techniques. In 1878 Halsted went for two years to Europe, where he studied embryology, histology, and surgery, mainly in German-speaking medical centers, spending the largest amount of time in Vienna. On his return to New York in 1880 Halsted took charge of the Roosevelt Hospital outpatient surgical department. In addition he taught medical students, was an anatomy demonstrator at the College of Physicians and Surgeons, and during these years in New York became associated with five other New York hospitals (the Charity, Emigrant, Bellevue, Presbyterian, and Chambers Street hospitals). It was a period of intense work: he spent his mornings at the Roosevelt, his afternoons and evenings at the other hospitals as he was needed, and he was also teaching.

Interested in transfusions, Halsted intervened in 1881 when his sister almost died from a postpartum hemorrhage. By his own account, according to Samuel James Crowe, "After checking the hemorrhage, I transfused my sister with blood drawn into a syringe from one of my veins and injected immediately into hers" (p. 21). His sister survived. A year later Halsted saved his mother by operating on her to remove gallstones.

Around 1884, Halsted was at the height of his career as a New York surgeon. In September of that year Carl Koller announced at the Ophthalmological Congress in Heidelberg his discovery that injections of cocaine could be used to anesthetize the conjunctiva and cornea of the eye. Hearing of this Halsted (along with some colleagues) began experimenting on the anesthetic properties of cocaine. He used himself as an experimental subject and became addicted first to cocaine and then to morphine. He was apparently unable to shake the morphine addiction for the rest of his life. Through these experiments Halsted found that if cocaine was injected into the trunk of a sensory nerve, all of its branches were numbed to pain. So by using a small amount of cocaine carefully injected, a portion of the body, such as they jaw, could be anesthetized. Halsted had discovered neuro-regional anesthesia, or nerve-blocking, which was particularly important for the development of oral and dental surgery. This research gained Halsted in 1922, shortly before his death, the gold medal of the American Dental Association. At the time of his experiments, however, his addictions resulted in a noticeable deterioration in Halsted's ability to work, and by 1886 he was forced to leave New York, his once promising career in ruins.

In early 1886 Halsted appealed to his old friend Welch for assistance. Welch tried to cure him and got Halsted a position in his own laboratory at Johns Hopkins. Although it was generally believed that Halsted had been entirely cured—and it does seem that he overcame his cocaine addiction—his once outgoing personality had been permanently altered. He remained rather withdrawn for the rest of his life.

In 1889, the first year of the Johns Hopkins Hospital, Halsted was appointed acting surgeon to the hospital, head of the dispensary (Outpatient Department), and associate professor of surgery. Halsted had been the second choice of the committee (which included Welch and the famous clinician William Osler) and was appointed for only a year at first because of worries about his performance. Halsted's appointment was made permanent: in 1890 he became surgeon-in-chief to the hospital, and in 1892, professor of surgery. Thus he was the founding professor of surgery at the Johns Hopkins Medical School, which opened in 1893.

During his time at Johns Hopkins, Halsted made the contributions to surgery for which he is famous. He was noted first for the development of an organized system of training surgeons, thereby replacing the former apprenticeship method, and one of his most famous articles is "The Training of the Surgeon," reprinted in the *Johns Hopkins Hospital Bulletin* ([1904]: 267–75). Second, he was credited with changing the surgical philosophy in America from an aggressive and somewhat unsafe approach to a more conservative one that depended heavily on a knowledge of anatomy and physiology.

Where previously speed had been the essence of good surgery, Halsted was known for operating slowly and deliberately, controlling blood loss and minimizing the damage to tissues. In so doing, Halsted was an originator of modern surgical practice. He had many prominent students, including John M. T. Finney, Hugh Young, and the pioneering neurosurgeons Harvey Cushing and Walter Dandy.

Halsted also discovered numerous new surgical techniques. He was known for his surgery of the blood vessels, particularly related to aneurysms, and was the first to routinely produce successful results when operating on hernia of the groin. He also introduced methods for treating goiters and for operating on the gallbladder and its ducts. He is famous, or perhaps infamous, as the man who developed techniques of radical mastectomy for breast cancer. Although it was largely superseded in the 1960s in favor of the modified mastectomy, Halsted's procedure, despite its mutilating effect, was viewed at the time as an advance that provided hope for otherwise terminal breast cancer patients.

In late 1889 or early 1890 Halsted played a role in the introduction of surgical gloves, an important step in the move away from antiseptic surgery toward aseptic surgery. His head nurse at Johns Hopkins had complained about the dermatitis from which she suffered as a result of the use of antiseptic mercuric bichloride during surgery. Halsted asked the Goodyear Rubber Company to make thin rubber gloves for use by the surgical staff. In June 1890 he married the nurse in question, Caroline Hampton; they had no children.

Halsted died in Baltimore, his reputation restored, and his addiction still a secret. One of the first surgeons to grasp the implications of anesthesia and antisepsis (later asepsis) for surgery, he made clean, slow, careful, and controlled techniques his trademark and passed these along to a new generation of surgeons.

T.M.R.

Fannie Lou Hamer

[6 OCTOBER 1917–14 MARCH 1977]

*F*annie Lou Hamer was a civil rights leader from rural Mississippi who helped to change the face of electoral politics in
this country. She is not recognized enough for that work, but she
is recognized even less for her feminist work on behalf of all
women. This may be because issues that affect only females are
still taken less seriously than those, like racism, that also affect
males; yet, as a black woman, she suffered from both forms of
oppression.

Even in many excellent biographies and works of reference, her
entries do not include such crucial facts as her courage in going
public about her sterilization, without her knowledge, in a southern
hospital. Though this was not taken up as an issue by the Student
Nonviolent Coordinating Committee, the organization to which she
first exposed it, her public acknowledgment of it later became a
landmark in the feminist struggle for reproductive freedom.

GLORIA STEINEM

Fannie Lou Townsend Hamer, civil rights activist, was
born in Montgomery County, Mississippi, the twentieth
child of Lou Ella (birth name unknown) and Jim
Townsend, sharecroppers. When Fannie Lou was two the family moved to Sunflower County, where they lived in abject
poverty. Even when they were able to rent land and buy live-
stock, a jealous white neighbor poisoned the animals, forcing
the family back into sharecropping. Fannie Lou began picking
cotton when she was six; she eventually was able to pick 300 to
400 pounds a day, earning a penny a pound. Because of poverty she was forced to leave school at age twelve, barely able to
read and write. She married Perry ("Pap") Hamer in 1944. The
couple adopted two daughters. For the next eighteen years

133

In 1965 Fannie Lou Hamer ran as a Mississippi Freedom Democratic Party candidate for Congress, saying she was "sick and tired of being sick and tired." *(Library of Congress)*

Fannie Lou Hamer worked first as a sharecropper and then as a timekeeper on the plantation of B. D. Marlowe.

Hamer appeared destined for a routine life of poverty, but two events in the early 1960s led her to become a political activist. When she was hospitalized for the removal of a uterine tumor in 1961, the surgeons performed a hysterectomy without her consent. In August 1962, still angry and bitter over the surgery, she went to a meeting in her hometown of Ruleville to hear James Forman of the Student Nonviolent Coordinating Committee (SNCC) and James Bevel of the Southern Christian Leadership Conference (SCLC). After hearing their speeches on the importance of voting, she and seventeen others went to the courthouse in Indianola to try to register. They were told they could only enter the courthouse two at a time to be given the (purposely difficult) literacy test, which they all failed. On the trip back to Ruleville the group was stopped by the police and fined $100 for driving a bus that was the wrong color. Hamer subsequently became the group's leader. B. D. Marlowe called on her that evening and told her she had to withdraw her name. Hamer refused and was ordered to leave the plantation. (Because Marlowe threatened to confiscate their belongings, Pap was compelled to work on the plantation until the harvest season was finished.) For a time, Hamer stayed with various friends and relatives, and segregationist night riders shot into some of the homes where she was staying. Nevertheless, she remained active in the civil rights movement, serving as a field secretary for SNCC, working for voter registration, advocating welfare programs, and teaching citizenship classes.

Hamer gained national attention when she appeared before the credentials committee of the 1964 Democratic National Convention in Atlantic City, New Jersey, on behalf of the Mississippi Freedom Democratic Party (MFDP), an organization attempting to unseat the state's regular, all-white delegation. Speaking as a delegate and co-chair of the MFDP, she described atrocities inflicted on blacks seeking the right to vote and other civil rights, including the abuse she had suffered at the Montgomery County Jail, where white Mississippi law enforcement officers forced black inmates to beat her so badly that she had no feeling in her arms. (Hamer and several others had been arrested for attempting to integrate the "white only" section of the bus station in Winona, Mississippi, during the return trip from a voter registration training session in South Carolina.) After giving her dramatic testimony, she wept before the committee. Although her emotional appeal generated sympathy for the plight of blacks in Mississippi among the millions watching on television, the committee rejected the MFDP's challenge.

That same year Hamer traveled to Ghana, Guinea, Nigeria, and several other African nations at the request and expense of those governments. Still, her primary interest was in helping the people of the Mississippi Delta. She lectured across the country, raising money and organizing. In 1965 she ran as an MFDP candidate for Congress, saying she was "sick and tired of being sick and tired." While many civil rights leaders abandoned grassroots efforts, she remained committed to organizing what she called "everyday" people in her community, frequently saying she preferred to face problems at home rather than run from them. In 1969 she launched the Freedom Farm Cooperative to provide homes and food for deprived families, white as well as black, in Sunflower County. The cooperative eventually acquired 680 acres. She remained active, however, at the national level. In 1971 she helped to found and was elected to the steering committee of the National Women's Political Caucus, the first national electoral organization of modern feminism, and the following year she spoke on national TV in support of the nomination of Sissy Farenthold as vice president in an address to the Democratic National Convention in Miami.

After a long battle with breast cancer, Hamer died at the all-black Mound Bayou Hospital, thirty miles from Ruleville. Civil rights leaders and feminists attended her funeral, including Andrew Young, Julian Bond, and Eleanor Holmes Norton.

M.E.L.

Handsome Lake

[1735–10 AUGUST 1815]

*Handsome Lake, a Seneca chief and prophet known as the
Peacemaker, brought a message of peace to the Haudenosaunee (Iroquois) in the late eighteenth and early nineteenth
centuries and helped the Haudenosaunee figure out a way to live
with the new Americans. Handsome Lake said he had been visited
by four spiritual messengers who gave him instructions on how the
people were supposed to live — to be thankful and continue the
thanksgiving ceremonies, to respect other humans and everything in
the natural world, to honor the family and refrain from abuse of
spouses, the children, or the elderly. Even into the twenty-first century, almost two hundred years after his death, the good words of
Handsome Lake are still used extensively by the Haudenosaunee.*

WILMA MANKILLER

Handsome Lake, Seneca prophet, was born probably in
what is now western New York State. He was the half
brother of Cornplanter and the nephew of Guyasuta.
Although he served as a warrior against the Cherokees in the
1760s and aided the British during the Revolution, he does not
seem to have particularly distinguished himself. Apparently
during the 1790s he received the title Handsome Lake
(Ganeodiyo, the name traditionally borne by one of the
sachems chosen to represent the Seneca at the national Iroquois council), and in that capacity he signed the treaty of Big
Tree (1797), by which the Iroquois of New York were left with
eleven reservations. The name used by Handsome Lake before
acquiring his title is not known. In 1799 he was living an
intemperate life in Cornplanter's town on the Allegheny River
in one of the Iroquois reservations.

Handsome Lake's reforms were rooted in the wretched conditions of the Iroquois communities. Their populations had been reduced by war and disease, and their economies were faltering. As white settlement around the reservations grew, the hunting declined and the Indians became overdependent on the horticulture performed by the women and on inadequate treaty annuities. Morale was also low. The retreat of the hunting and warrior life, and with it traditional paths by which many men achieved fulfillment or prestige, created indolence and alienation. Alcoholism, violence, depression, and accusations of witchcraft were common problems.

These difficulties provoked several somewhat contradictory responses. From 1798 onward, Quakers were at work in Cornplanter's town, not so much to proselytize as to develop the Indian economy, to intensify agriculture, and to teach stock raising, spinning, weaving, and the fencing of land. They also attacked social problems such as drunkenness. But while this program, involving the reformation of the local economy, was under way, a simultaneous nativist movement began. A Mohawk claimed that the Creator (Tarachiawagon) was displeased with the Iroquois for neglecting such ceremonies as the worship dance. This prophet was mainly influential among the Oneidas of New York and the Canadian Iroquois, but in February 1799 a Seneca in Cornplanter's town declared that he had visited hell and witnessed the torments of drunkards and other sinners. Thus, native prophets ascribed the misfortunes of the Iroquois to the anger of the Creator at the decline of traditional observances and the assimilation of undesirable white influences. Handsome Lake distilled both the Quaker and the nativist impulses for his own reforms.

Between June 1799 and February 1800 Handsome Lake experienced three visions, recorded in the contemporary Quaker diaries. According to Henry Simmons, on 15 June, Cornplanter was told that his brother was dying and found him "laying breathless for the space of half an hour, but in about two hours after he came to himself again," and related that angels had visited and instructed him. The following August the prophet "fainted or fell into a trance in which posture he remained 7 hours; his legs and arms were cold; his body warm but breathless." When he recovered, Handsome Lake claimed to have visited heaven, and after a third vision he reported a further visit of the angels. From these incidents Handsome Lake professed himself the medium of the Creator and the bringer of the Gaiwiio or Good Word.

The message was apocalyptic, declaring that unless the Indians reformed, they would suffer sickness, drought, and flood, while the sinful would be excluded from heaven. The proscribed sins were largely those already condemned by nativist preachers and the Quakers—drunkenness; the practice of witchcraft, which the Indians blamed for disease and strife; violence; the neglect of old ceremonies; and even the riotous "frolics and dancing" condemned by the Quakers. Subsequently Handsome Lake broadened his message to sanction the economic development promoted by the Quakers, but he insisted that farming should be for subsistence and that surpluses be made available to the native community rather than for commercial sale.

Not unnaturally, the Quakers and President Thomas Jefferson, whom Handsome Lake, as a member of an Iroquois land and agriculture delegation, visited in 1802, endorsed Handsome Lake's campaign, which was neither anti-American nor excessively nativist. Yet his was not a servile doctrine. Handsome Lake recognized the need to raise the material standards of the Iroquois and to adjust to the existence of a dominant white society, and he backed economic development and peace with the United States. But he offered the Indians a religion distinct from Christianity, one that preserved native ritual and the aboriginal emphasis upon community life. Such Christian influences as it embraced were integrated into traditional Indian beliefs. For example, the notion of God and the Devil directing the forces of good and evil and competing for souls was blended into the Iroquois creation story of the good and bad twins. Handsome Lake also opposed the further sale of land to the United States. His religion facilitated Iroquois adjustment to reservation life but protected their culture and identity. It was partly for this reason that Handsome Lake's religion, while more localized than that of his contemporary Tenskwatawa, the Shawnee prophet, enjoyed greater longevity. Handsome Lake's preaching was compatible with living alongside the European-American farming frontier; Tenskwatawa's, espousing a return to more traditional Indian ways of life, was rooted in an ultimately disappearing Indian world.

Handsome Lake's influence was strongest among the Senecas, Onondagas, and Oneidas of New York, although it spread to the Wyandots and Iroquois of the Sandusky in Ohio, whom he visited in 1806. By then Handsome Lake, the Quakers, and others had done much to reduce Iroquois drunkenness and spur economic development. Some Iroquois men were beginning to reappraise their traditional contempt for husbandry. In 1801 the prophet was briefly elevated to the unprecedented position of premier sachem of the New York Iroquois. However, he abused his power with overzealous accusations of witchcraft, and consequent executions threatened to create blood-feud conflicts. In 1801 the Senecas and Delawares of Cattaraugus were brought to the brink of hostilities on account of Handsome Lake's activities, and he divided the Senecas, denouncing his political enemy, Red Jacket, for witchcraft. After the execution of a woman in 1809, Cornplanter admitted, "I hope we shall be careful in future how we take the lives of any for witchcraft, without being sure that they were guilty." In 1803 Handsome Lake's relations with his brother had so deteriorated that the prophet had left Cornplanter's town and established a new settlement at nearby Cold Spring.

Handsome Lake died on a visit to Onondaga, but his teaching survived, reworked and codified by individual preachers, and remains a significant force in Iroquois life, offering a distinctly Indian alternative to Christianity.

J.S.

Herman Haupt

[26 MARCH 1817–14 DECEMBER 1905]

Herman Haupt, hardly a household name even to informed people (except Civil War historians), is one of the genuine giants in the history of American engineering and railroading. Perhaps his chief claim to fame was his eighteen-month stint as chief of construction and transportation on the U.S. Military Railroads, 1862–1863. In this post he managed what became the largest railroad in the world at that time, consisting of the patchwork of captured southern railroads in conquered Confederate territory. Haupt transformed these lines into an efficient network of logistics and transportation that was an important factor in Union military success. A graduate of West Point (class of 1835), he spent most of his antebellum and postwar career as chief engineer for various railroads. In 1851 he wrote a treatise on bridge construction that became the Bible for such projects, and he superintended the drilling of the Hoosac Tunnel, inventing a new type of pneumatic drill in 1858 that vastly improved the safety and accuracy of tunneling. During the Civil War he developed techniques for the rebuilding of railroad bridges and trestles destroyed by the enemy that enabled the U.S. Military Railroads to keep trains running over trestles that appeared to be, as Lincoln lightheartedly expressed, "nothing but bean-poles and corn-stalks." Born in 1817, Haupt lived a long and productive life, dying in 1905 of a heart attack suffered, appropriately enough, while he was riding a train in New Jersey.

JAMES M. MCPHERSON

Herman Haupt, railway engineer, inventor, author, and administrator, was born in Philadelphia, Pennsylvania, the son of Jacob Haupt, a businessman of modest attainments, and Anna Margaretta Wiall, the proprietor of a small dry goods store. Herman attended several private schools

A stereograph portrait of General Herman Haupt taken by Mathew Brady during the Civil War. *(National Archives and Records Administration)*

in Philadelphia, but in 1827 his father, suffering from poor health, gave up the grocery store he then owned and moved to Woodville, New Jersey. Jacob Haupt died the next year, leaving his widow in straitened circumstances; Herman, the eldest of six children, was only eleven years of age. Two years later Herman Haupt's congressman, John B. Sterigere, offered to help the boy gain admission to the U.S. Military Academy at West Point. He received a presidential appointment in 1830, but his entry was deferred for a year because of his youth. Unhappy with the strict upbringing he had received from his father, he was very uncertain about subjecting himself to the hard discipline of the academy, but his mother prevailed.

Haupt graduated thirty-first in his class of fifty-six men in 1835, after which he became a brevet second lieutenant of infantry. His military career was short; he resigned at the end of September 1835 and worked briefly as a draftsman and transitman for several Pennsylvania railroads. In January 1836, at only nineteen years of age, he was appointed an assistant engineer for a railroad running from Gettysburg, Pennsylvania, to Hagerstown, Maryland.

In 1838 Haupt married Ann Cecilia Keller of Gettysburg. Their first home, Oakridge, was built on several acres of land on Seminary Ridge, west of the town, near where Haupt would support Union troops twenty-five years later. The couple had eleven children, eight of whom lived to adulthood. One son, Lewis, was to graduate from West Point and become a professor of civil engineering at the University of Pennsylvania.

In 1840 Haupt helped construct the York and Wrightsville Railroad in Pennsylvania. In so doing he discovered that no American railway engineer had previously assessed the strength of railway trusses in bridge construction. He therefore completed some technical experiments, and he was later recognized as having devised a means of "representing strains of geometrical solids; deflections by parabolic areas; and the variable pressures at various parts of beams by the corresponding ordinates of plane curves" (Lord, p. 24). He continued with this work and in 1841 published an anonymous booklet, *Hints on Bridge Construction*. Ten years later a revised and expanded version, *The General Theory of Bridge Construction*, appeared under his authorship. This pioneering study became a respected text in the field.

Haupt was an unpaid instructor in civil engineering and architecture at Pennsylvania College in Gettysburg from 1837 to 1839. He was granted an honorary M.A. by the college in lieu of salary in the latter year. He also operated a private school in Gettysburg from 1837 to 1845, which was then taken over by the college. For two years (1845–1847) Haupt served as a half-time professor of mathematics at Pennsylvania College while operating the Female Seminary of Gettysburg.

In 1847 Haupt joined the Pennsylvania Railroad as assistant to the chief engineer. When the first division of that line was completed in 1849, he became its superintendent. Within a few years he had become general superintendent of the company, in charge of construction, passenger, and freight operations. Much of Haupt's time was spent in controversies with the state canal commission, which owned the main line the company had to use until its own network had been completed. Haupt also battled the Pennsylvania's trustees over a variety of issues and finally resigned late in 1852. He accepted the post of chief engineer for the Southern Railroad of Mississippi, but six months later a reconstituted Pennsylvania Railroad board asked him to return. While working with the Pennsylvania, he demonstrated that the company could make money by encouraging the development of local industries along its right of way. Haupt was sometimes abrupt and less than tactful with his superiors, and ill feelings frequently resulted. During his final year with the Pennsylvania, Haupt was elected to the line's board to represent the city of Philadelphia's interests in the company.

In 1856 Haupt accepted a new post as chief engineer and contractor for the Troy and Greenfield Railroad and Hoosac Tunnel in Massachusetts. This association, which continued on and off for nearly thirty years, would prove the most frustrating, costly, and vexatious venture of his life. Haupt invested heavily in the company, in which he held a controlling interest for some time. Although he was able to resolve the many technical challenges that arose, Haupt's progress was continually undercut by executives of the rival Western Railway Company and their political allies in the Massachusetts state government. In addition, he had to deal with a byzantine series of organizational and fiscal complications, resulting in frequent interruptions in construction. The financial panic of 1857 nearly drove Haupt out of business. Owing to disagreements with state officials about his handling of the contract, state authorities held up reimbursement of several hundred thousand dollars he had spent on wages, supplies, and equipment. In the spring of 1862 state authorities terminated his railroad construction contract and took control of the incomplete line pending an investigation.

With the coming of the Civil War in 1861, Haupt sought the newly created post of assistant secretary of war, for which an experienced railway man was needed. As a member of the West Point Board of Visitors, however, he had earlier antagonized Secretary of War Simon Cameron when the latter proposed a weakening of standards at West Point, and the job went to another man. In April 1862, however, Edwin M. Stanton, Cameron's successor, asked Haupt to come to Washington. Stanton recognized that civilian railroad men were better prepared to construct and maintain railroads than the military engineers, who had more experience with field fortifications and coastal defenses. Haupt was initially appointed to the post of aide-de-camp to Major General Irvin McDowell with the nominal rank of colonel, even though he had accepted with the understanding that he might work in civilian clothes. He declined any salary, asking only that his expenses be paid.

For nearly seventeen months, until September 1863, Haupt designed, built, and repaired critically important railway lines and bridges. President Abraham Lincoln inspected one bridge project Haupt had completed and characterized it as "the most remarkable structure that human eyes ever rested upon. That man Haupt has built a bridge across Potomac Creek, about 400 feet long and nearly 100 feet high, over which loaded trains are running every hour, and upon my word . . . there is nothing in it but bean poles and corn stalks" (Lord, p. 77). Haupt had to cope with conflicting lines of authority, appealing to the War Department when more senior officers attempted to take over his lines for the movement of their own troops and equipment. At no time, despite Haupt's strong urging, was any one individual given overall authority over military railroads. Historians have generally agreed that he coped brilliantly with most logistical challenges, moving troops to the front, wounded to the rear, and equipment to where it was most needed with efficiency and dispatch. Haupt's unflagging efforts to assist in Major General John Pope's withdrawal from the battle of Second Bull Run (Second Manassas) in August and September 1862 won him a promotion to brigadier general of volunteers. He never formally accepted his new commission, however, because he wanted to be free to cope with the ongoing railroad imbroglio in Massachusetts. He designated himself as Chief of Construction and Transportation, U.S. Military Railroads, although his authority never extended beyond ground held by the Army of the Potomac.

At odd moments between his railroad duties with the Union army and return trips to Massachusetts to attempt some resolution of his continuing difficulties there, Haupt turned his mind to the possible solution of other military needs. These included ideas about coastal defenses and the propulsion of boats by water jets for the Union navy. He also developed a torpedo for destroying railroads and bridges, endorsed and utilized a subordinate's effective portable track-wrecking device, and proposed new methods of destroying locomotives and rolling stock. He also put forward proposals for a more effective military intelligence system. Save for the track-wrecking project, few of his ideas were adopted. Some of his suggestions for change and reform got him into difficulties with Stanton and with Secretary of the Treasury Salmon P. Chase of and Secretary of the Navy Gideon Welles. Haupt was particularly caustic toward Welles. Early in 1863 he found time to draft another book, this one an instructional text, *Military Bridges: With Suggestions of New Expedients and Constructions for Crossing Streams and Chasms*, which was published in 1864.

Haupt anticipated and met most of the army's demanding logistical requirements before and during the battle of Gettysburg. Within a three-day period at the beginning of July 1863, for example, his work crews had reconstructed nineteen destroyed bridges between Hanover and Harrisburg, Pennsylvania. For the balance of his time with the army, his people were engaged primarily in guarding existing railway lines.

In September 1863 Haupt's military work came to an abrupt

end when Massachusetts governor John Andrew, who had opposed Haupt on the Troy and Greenfield matter, pressed Stanton to insist that Haupt formally accept his brigadier general's commission. Andrew, a staunch administration supporter, reasoned that with Haupt in uniform, his military obligations would prevent him from returning to Massachusetts to press his claims for financial restitution against the state. Stanton insisted that Haupt sign his commission, which Haupt declined to do, and Stanton angrily relieved him of all responsibilities with the army. When the final report of military railroad operations was submitted by Haupt's successor after the war, Haupt's name was not mentioned—an unfortunate omission.

Haupt's long disputes with the state of Massachusetts were not resolved for twenty years. In 1868 his construction firm was awarded $53,000—Haupt had claimed nearly $400,000—for losses and expenses while building the Troy and Greenfield Railroad. Haupt received less than $22,000; the remainder went to former partners and retired old debts. Not until 1884 did the state agree to pay Haupt and his former partners $150,000, or eight cents on the dollar, for the shares they held in the railroad company. All told, Haupt's personal loss in the Troy and Greenfield Railroad exceeded $400,000.

From 1863 until the time of his death, Haupt attempted a number of other business ventures, most with little or only short-term success. He began a farm in Virginia and later tried creating a resort in a remote western part of that state. He developed an effective rock drill, but turned the project over to a son, who could not market it effectively. In many joint enterprises with others, he was saddled with partners less than straightforward in their financial dealings with him, which got him into financial difficulties. From late 1872 until the end of 1875 he was superintendent of the Richmond and Danville Railroad, a subsidiary of the Pennsylvania Railroad, but he was discharged after the Pennsylvania pulled out of the project.

In 1878 Haupt was named superintendent of the Tide Water

Pipe Company, which successfully built an oil pipeline between Coryville and Williamsport, Pennsylvania. Following a rate war with the competing Standard Oil Company, however, Tide Water was obliged to enter an oil traffic pool in 1880, which gave it less than 20 percent of the business in the state. Named general manager of the Northern Pacific Railroad in 1881, Haupt completed its construction two years later, despite formidable obstacles. A successful company union he formed was still operating well into the twentieth century. Operating costs were too high to satisfy investors, however, and Haupt resigned. His efforts to complete the Dakota and Great Southern Railroad foundered, owing to poor financial conditions following the panic of 1883.

Haupt invested time and money on the use of compressed air in urban transportation systems and in the National White Cross Milk Company, which was engaged in the manufacture of condensed and powdered milk. For years, the stock in this firm had little value, but when it was taken over by the Borden Company after Haupt's death, it earned income for his heirs until the patents expired in 1930. Books and articles published by Haupt during his later years reflected the wide range of his interests. They included *Tunneling by Machinery* (1867); *Herman's Wooing: A Parody on Hiawatha* (1881); *Street Railway Motors* (1893); *Compressed Air and Electricity for City, Suburban, and Rapid Transit Service* (1895); *The Presidential Election of 1900 and Its Probable Consequences* (1901); and *Reminiscences of General Herman Haupt* (1901).

Haupt's financial position was often precarious, and his last ten years were spent living on borrowed money. At the age of eighty-seven he suffered a heart attack following an unproductive meeting with the owners of the National White Cross Milk Company in New York; he died on a train returning to his home in Washington.

K.B.S.

DuBose Heyward

[31 AUGUST 1885–16 JUNE 1940]

*D*uBose Heyward has gone largely unrecognized as the author *of the finest set of lyrics in the history of the American musical theater — namely, those of* Porgy *and* Bess. *There are two reasons for this, and they are connected. First, he was primarily a poet and novelist, and his only song lyrics were those that he wrote for* Porgy. *Second, some of them were written in collaboration with Ira Gershwin, a full-time lyricist, whose reputation in the musical theater was firmly established before the opera was written. But most of the lyrics in* Porgy — *and all of the distinguished ones — are by Heyward. I admire his theater songs for their deeply felt poetic style and their insight into character. It's a pity he didn't write any others. His work is sung, but he is unsung.*

STEPHEN SONDHEIM

*D*uBose Heyward, novelist, dramatist, and poet, was born Edwin DuBose Heyward in Charleston, South Carolina, the son of Edwin Watkins Heyward, a mill hand from an old and distinguished southern family ruined after the Civil War, and Jane Screven DuBose, also descended from once-prosperous plantation owners. His father died when Heyward was two, and his mother was reduced to taking in sewing to support the family. He attended a private school until he was nine and entered public school in the fourth grade but was, as he later described himself, "a miserable student," uninterested in schoolwork. He dropped out in his first year of high school, at the age of fourteen, to work as a clerk in a hardware store and later worked among African-American stevedores as a checker for a steamship company. Often sick as a child, he got polio when he was eighteen; two years later he contracted typhoid fever and the next year pleurisy. At twenty-one, Heyward and his friend Henry T. O'Neill organized a real estate and insurance company. A skilled salesman of great personal charm, he succeeded in making himself financially independent.

Always interested in literature, the young Heyward had passed the time in his sickbed writing verses and stories. In 1913 he wrote a one-act play, *An Artistic Triumph*, which was produced in a local theater. A derivative farce about mistaken identity, it showed little promise, but its success sharpened the young author's appetite for a literary career. Heyward never fully recovered from the illnesses of his youth. In 1917, while convalescing, he began to devote himself seriously to writing fiction and poetry. In 1918 his first published short story, "The Brute," appeared in *Pagan, a Magazine for Eudaemonists*. The next year he met Hervey Allen, then teaching at the nearby Porter Military Academy. The two became close friends and together formed the Poetry Society of South Carolina, which helped spark a revival of southern literature. Heyward edited the society's yearbooks until 1924 and contributed a good deal of their content. His poetry was well received, earning him a Contemporary Verse award in 1921. With Allen he published a collection, *Carolina Chansons: Legends of the Low Country*, in 1922. That same year the two edited a southern issue of *Poetry* magazine.

While spending the summer at the MacDowell Colony in New Hampshire, Heyward met Dorothy Hartzell Kuhns, a student in George Pierce Baker's playwriting workshop at Harvard. They were married in 1923 and had one child. In 1924 his first independent book, a volume of poems titled *Skylines and Horizons*, appeared. Largely based on themes from Charleston history, it established his local reputation as a poet. With the encouragement of his wife, Heyward determined to make a living by writing. In 1924 he gave up the business that had supported him for eighteen years, resigned as president of the Poetry Society, and moved with his wife to the Great Smokies to work on a novel. Between stints of writing, he supported himself by lecturing on southern literature at college campuses.

Porgy, published in 1925, was a powerful story of a crippled African-American beggar, set in a black waterfront neighborhood of Charleston called Catfish Row. A poignant picture of a culture seldom before depicted without quaintness or condescension, *Porgy* was an immediate success, described in the *New York Times Book Review* (7 Sept. 1925) as "a noteworthy achievement in the sympathetic interpretation of negro life by a member of an 'outside' race," and conveying "an intimate and authentic sense of the dignity, the pathos . . . the very essence of his chosen community."

Heyward's next novel, *Angel* (1926), dealt with mountaineers in North Carolina. It was not a popular success, but the following year he renewed his large audience with a dramatization of *Porgy* done in collaboration with his wife. The first major Broadway play with an all African-American cast, it was a great hit, running for a total of 367 performances in 1927–1928 and earning the Heywards a Pulitzer Prize. The play was later turned into an opera, titled *Porgy and Bess* (1935), with music by George Gershwin and libretto by Heyward and Ira Gershwin. Hailed as the first great American folk opera, it was influential in opening the American theater to African-American musical forms and was made into a successful motion picture in 1959.

"The Half Pint Flask," a short story dealing with the conflict between white science and supernatural forces in the African-American community, appeared as a separate volume in 1929. Later that year Heyward returned to Catfish Row as a setting for *Mamba's Daughters*, his longest novel, which chronicled the social elevation of an African-American girl in white society as an opera singer. In 1931 he published *Jasbo Brown and Selected Poems*. A play, *Brass Ankle*, dealing with the problems of a mulatto in small-town white society, was produced that same year but was a commercial failure. Abandoning the theme of race in 1932, Heyward published *Peter Ashley*, a romantic novel set in pre–Civil War Charleston. The next year he answered the siren call to Hollywood, where he wrote screenplays for Eugene O'Neill's *The Emperor Jones* (1933) and Pearl Buck's *The Good Earth* (1934). In 1936 he published the novel *Lost Morning*. Set in the Piedmont region, the story is about the competing values of business and the artistic life. In the year before his death of a heart attack in Tryon, North Carolina, he published *Star-Spangled Virgin*, a novelette about a society of blacks whose harmony with nature in the Virgin Islands is disrupted by the effects of the New Deal. That year the Heywards' dramatization of *Mamba's Daughters*, starring Ethel Waters, was produced on Broadway; he also published a children's book written for his nine-year-old daughter Jenifer.

A slight, graceful figure with courtly manners, Heyward was personally popular and widely admired. He was a member of the Poetry Society of America and the National Institute of Arts and Letters. Although his poetry has been largely dismissed as fragmentary and conventional and the plots of his fiction criticized as melodramatic, his sensitivity to the rhythms of African-American life has retained its vitality and given him, and the society he so keenly observed and so sympathetically celebrated, a lasting place in American fiction.

D.W.

Henry Hornbostel

[15 AUGUST 1867–13 DECEMBER 1961]

*H*enry Hornbostel was a Pittsburgh-based architect and Beaux-
Arts exponent who has, unfairly, been little recognized outside
his immediate circle, or beyond the time of his practice, which
spanned the first four decades of the last century. Despite receiving
an Honorable Mention in the prestigious Chicago Tribune Competition and being selected to design the Pennsylvania Pavilion for the
1915 Panama-Pacific Exposition in San Francisco, Hornbostel has
remained an architect known chiefly to the cognoscenti. I first came
upon his works at Emory University in Atlanta, Georgia, for whose
new campus he had completed a master plan in 1915, ultimately con-
structing only a few palazzo-like Florentine buildings of his total
vision. To me, the quadrangle that Hornbostel was able to realize
approaches in quality Thomas Jefferson's much lauded and appreciated designs for the University of Virginia in Charlottesville.

Though it is difficult now to find many examples of Hornbostel's
work extant, in converting his 1916 Law School building at Emory to
the current Michael C. Carlos Museum of Art and Archaeology I
came to know this building and Hornbostel's other work on that
campus quite well. I find his architectural design in general to have
the mixture of history, character, and finesse that also characterizes
that of Sir Edwin Lutyens, who was practicing at approximately the
same time. Hornbostel shared with Lutyens that wonderful ability to
give variety to his work by the rather liberal use of historical prece-
dent used as type. In Hornbostel's case, one can look, for example, at
the drawings and photographs of the now-demolished West View
Cemetery funerary chapel for the Rodef Shalom Congregation of
1917, where there is clearly a debt to the Basilica of Maxentius in
Rome, albeit here brought to a scale that is appropriate to its purpose and setting.

One understands also that Hornbostel had an enormous facility *with drawing, and that his colleagues would marvel at his rapid development of schemes which portrayed with ease the character of his intentions. That sense of drawing can be seen in the incredibly original floor delineation found in the Carnegie Institute of Technology's School of Architecture building designed by Hornbostel. Here, the architect depicted in drawing form the plans of significant monuments of Western architecture, so that the students coming to daily classes would, for a moment, walk across the plans of such great buildings as St. Peter's Basilica or Palladio's villas. With this idea, Hornbostel put into the mind of the student the aspirations that every architect must have to understand the significance of the language of architecture.*

Michael Graves

Henry Fred Hornbostel, architect, was born in Brooklyn, New York, the son of Edward Hornbostel, a stockbroker, and Johanna Cassebeer. Although Hornbostel's father steered him toward the silk trade, a high school teacher observed his drawing talents and encouraged him to study architecture at Columbia University. He graduated at the head of his class with a bachelor of philosophy degree in 1891. Hornbostel then went to work for New York architects Wood and Palmer (a firm whose later iterations were Wood, Palmer and Hornbostel; Palmer and Hornbostel; and Palmer, Hornbostel and Jones). Beginning in 1893 he studied architecture for four years at the Ecole des Beaux-Arts in Paris. In addition to his studies, he sought out sculptors and painters, as well as other artisans and workmen, to develop skills that would serve his architectural designs. Hornbostel's colleagues dubbed him "l'homme perspectif" for his dramatic perspective drawings, works that contrasted with the traditional Beaux-Arts plans, sections, and elevations. During this period Hornbostel also began wearing the red silk ties that became his trademark.

Hornbostel returned to New York in 1897 to take up a variety of architectural activities. As a freelance delineator, he worked

Henry Hornbostel (seated at left) with fellow members of the Independent Bicycle Club, Prospect Park, Brooklyn, 1886. *(Library of Congress)*

for some of the preeminent American firms of the period: McKim, Mead and White; Carrère and Hastings; and George B. Post. He also produced renderings for some architects of the Paris Exposition of 1900. Between 1903 and 1917, working for the Board of Estimate and Apportionment in New York, he designed the Queensborough, Manhattan, Pelham Park, and Hell Gate bridges and earned considerable professional acclaim for his renderings of them. Hornbostel also taught architecture at Columbia, first as an assistant, then as a lecturer. In 1899 he married Martha Armitage; they had two children.

In a period when design competitions enjoyed widespread popularity among prestigious clients, Hornbostel excelled in them. In temporary association with Howells and Stokes, he designed the well-received second-place entry in the 1899 Phoebe Hearst competition for the buildings of the University of California. More important, as a partner in Palmer and Hornbostel, he won the competition to design a new campus for Pittsburgh's Carnegie Institute of Technology in 1903. Although his scheme was steeped in the Beaux-Arts tradition of Roman, Renaissance, and French architecture, Hornbostel gave it clarity and personality. His plan deftly reconciles a complex program with difficult topography, while his details allude to technology with pragmatism and wit. The Paris-trained Hornbostel even convinced industrialist and patron Andrew Carnegie to include a department of fine arts in the new engineering school. For his efforts, he became the first head of Carnegie Tech's School of Architecture.

Palmer and Hornbostel moved their practice to Pittsburgh, even as the firm maintained its national profile. With Hornbostel as chief designer, the firm produced monumental works in the Beaux-Arts style, including city halls for Oakland, California (1910), Wilmington, Delaware (1910), and Hartford, Connecticut (1911). Hornbostel continued to be a presence on university campuses as well, designing buildings for Emory and Northwestern Universities. Meanwhile, the construction of his bridges in New York reached completion, culminating with the Hell Gate Bridge of 1917.

At the same time, Hornbostel's buildings made a profound mark on Pittsburgh. In the city's Oakland area alone, he designed the Rodef Shalom synagogue, the Schenley Hotel, the University Club, and the Upper Campus of the University of Pittsburgh. He also won the competition to design the Soldiers and Sailors Memorial (1910). The urbanity of these designs, separately and severally, helped transform a collection of foundling and relocated institutions into the city's center of culture and higher learning. Nationally known as a competition-winning pillar of Beaux-Arts architecture, Hornbostel became a Pittsburgh personality, adding a dash of refined color to the architecture and the social scene of what was then a grim industrial city. He also matched his design output with a visible professional profile. He was active as a member of the American Institute of Architects, the National Sculpture Society, the Architectural League of New York, and the Society of Beaux-Arts Architects, of which he was the president in 1916.

During World War I Hornbostel was commissioned as a major and served as first assistant gas officer in the Twenty-sixth Division of the U.S. Army in France. Although his sophisticated manners and Van Dyke beard clashed with military custom, he discharged his duties successfully and with notorious good humor before his safe return to the United States. With his postwar return to architecture, Hornbostel dissolved his partnership with Palmer and embarked upon increasingly modern designs. His Smithfield Street Congregational Church in Pittsburgh is an early and innovative use of architectural aluminum, while his Grant Building is an Art Deco essay of unapologetic abstraction.

The Great Depression brought Hornbostel personal and professional turmoil. In 1932, his first marriage having ended, he was married to Maybelle Weston. During this period, he saw a drastic reduction in commissions brought about by the economic decline. Hornbostel was, however, able to secure a position as director of Allegheny County Parks beginning in 1935. In 1939 he retired, first to Connecticut, then to Melbourne, Florida, where he lived in a modern house of his own design until his death.

Hornbostel, who was best known for his Beaux-Arts work, had the misfortune to die when the style was at a low point in popularity, eclipsed by Modernism. The professional press, which had once adored him, barely noted his passing. Subsequently, the historical curiosity that accompanied postmodern architecture helped revive Hornbostel in the professional consciousness. Later twentieth-century devotees rediscovered, in addition to the monumentality and historical pedigree that they expected in Beaux-Arts buildings, a technologically and artistically progressive oeuvre with far-reaching affinities.

C.R.

James Gibbons Huneker

[31 JANUARY 1857–9 FEBRUARY 1921]

*I*t is astonishing that James Gibbons Huneker has become the forgotten man of American letters; none of his nearly two dozen
volumes of essays, fiction, biography, travel, parodies, memoirs, and
letters is presently offered by a commercial publisher. Yet he dominated American arts criticism between 1890 and 1920 to a degree
unmatched before or since. An impressionistic polymath of extraordinary zeal and perspicacity, he focused on music but also introduced a broad range of European culture to the New World—
including Vermeer, Chopin, Liszt, Wagner, R. Strauss, Ibsen,
Strindberg, and Conrad, who wrote of him, "What mental agility!
What a flexible liveliness of style!"

Yet it was his style—jaunty, volatile, occasionally purple, always
sensuous—that dated him when a new generation of writers, as
represented by H. L. Mencken and Edmund Wilson, both of whom
idolized Huneker, introduced a more tempered, economical, and
sober prose. Still, his writing offers plenary delights to the modern
reader, not least in his once-controversial fiction, including the neglected masterpiece, "Dusk of the Gods," and the most Wildean of
American novels, Painted Veils.

GARY GIDDINS

James Gibbons Hunecker, critic, essayist, and musician,
was born in Philadelphia, Pennsylvania, the son of John
Joseph Huneker, a prosperous housepainter and decorator, and Mary Gibbons, a schoolteacher. Huneker was introduced to the world of music, drama, and art by his father, who
owned one of the largest private collections of prints in the
United States; his interest in literature was fostered by his
mother, the daughter of the Irish printer and poet James Gibbons. After attending Philadelphia's Broad Street Academy

(1865–1872), Huneker began a five-year apprenticeship in law before discovering his chief interest, music. In 1875 he started piano lessons with one of Philadelphia's outstanding teachers, Michael Cross, and began writing music critiques and articles for the *Evening Bulletin*, Philadelphia's leading newspaper.

In the fall of 1878 Huneker sailed to France with the intention of studying music at the Paris Conservatoire. Although his audition was unsuccessful, he was permitted to audit the piano classes of Georges Mathias, Chopin's protégé, at the conservatoire, while absorbing French culture and gathering information for articles for the *Bulletin*. He also studied philosophy for a brief time at the Sorbonne. In July 1879 he returned to Philadelphia, where he studied and taught piano. Beginning in 1885, Huneker wrote articles for *Etude* magazine, an activity he continued for some thirty years.

After moving to New York in 1886, Huneker pursued his studies in piano with Edmund Neupert and Rafael Joseffy. In 1888, owing to his vast knowledge of piano literature and considerable pianistic skills, Huneker became Joseffy's assistant and a member of the piano faculty of the prestigious National Conservatory of Music in New York. For the next ten years he taught piano there while simultaneously pursuing his career as a critic and essayist.

In 1887 Huneker began a fifteen-year association with the New York *Musical Courier*, where, primarily as a columnist ("The Raconteur"), he made his reputation as a witty, clever writer of unusual insight, ardent admiration, and frequently passionate expressions. For example, he encapsulated his negative reaction to Richard Wagner's operas by dubbing the composer "Richard of the Footlights" (*Mezzotints*, p. 9). During this period Huneker also worked as a music and drama critic for the New York *Recorder* (1891–1895) and the *Morning Advertiser* (1895–1897), and as a music critic for the weekly magazine *Town Topics* (1897–1902). In 1900 he joined the New York *Sun*, becoming in rapid succession its critic for music (1900–1902), drama (1902–1904), and art and literature (1906–1912), a feat of versatility only paralleled by England's George Bernard Shaw. From 1912 to 1914 Huneker served as a foreign correspondent for the *New York Times*. He then began writing "The Seven Arts," a potpourri column in *Puck* magazine, the oldest humorous weekly in the United States. The column was filled with short stories, humorous sketches, and critiques of literature, art, music, drama, and motion pictures. In 1916 he stopped writing for *Puck* and for a short time rejoined the editorial staff of the *Sun*, primarily as a book reviewer, before becoming a music critic for the *Philadelphia Press* (1917–1918), the *New York Times* (1918–1919), and the *New York World* (1919–1921).

Most of Huneker's twenty-two books consist of reprints of criticisms, essays, and short stories previously published in newspapers and magazines. Hailed by music critic Henry T. Finck as "one of the most readable and at the same time useful books on music ever issued in this country" (*Nation*, 4 May 1899, p. 338), Huneker's first book, *Mezzotints in Modern Music* (1899), successfully established Huneker's writing career in the United States and Europe. In 1900 he published what he called his "magnum opus," *Chopin: The Man and His Music*, a critically acclaimed biography and scholarly analysis of the composer's works. A less successful biography of Franz Liszt followed in 1911.

Other significant books by Huneker that deal with music and musicians include *Melomaniacs* (1902), *Visionaries* (1905), and *Bedouins* (1920). He also edited and published collections of the songs of Brahms, Tchaikovsky, and Richard Strauss and of the piano music of Chopin. Huneker's *Iconoclasts: A Book of Dramatists* (1905) deals with drama criticism; *Egoists* (1910), with literary criticism; and *Promenades of an Impressionist* (1910), with art criticism. He wrote one novel, *Painted Veils* (1920), and two autobiographies, *Old Fogy* (1913) and *Steeplejack* (1920). His widow, Josephine Huneker, compiled much correspondence by him in two posthumous collections, *Letters of James Gibbons*

Huneker (1922) and *Intimate Letters of James Gibbons Huneker* (1924).

Because of his ingratiating manner, Huneker, who according to literary critic Alfred Kazin "almost singlehandedly brought the new currents of European art and thought to America and made them fashionable" (*Saturday Review of Literature*, 3 Feb. 1940, p. 11), was able to acquaint more Americans with European composers, artists, and writers than any other critic of his time. He became a crusader for new and neglected artists: in 1899 he touted Brahms as the "last of the immortals" and "our most modern music maker" (*Mezzotints*, pp. 1, 16); he vehemently supported Richard Strauss, naming him "the greatest living musician and the greatest master of orchestration in the history of music" (*Musical Courier*, 25 Dec. 1901, pp. 23–24), and described Strauss's *Also Sprach Zarathustra* (1896) as "a cathedral . . . dangerously sublime . . . with grotesque gargoyles, hideous flying abutments, exquisite traceries, fantastic arches half gothic, half infernal . . . a mighty structure" (*Mezzotints*, p. 153). After hearing one of the first performances of Arnold Schoenberg's *Pierrot Lunaire* (1912) in Berlin, Huneker concluded that "a man who could portray in tone sheer ugliness with such crystal clearness is to be reckoned with in these topsyturvy times. . . . Perhaps he is a superman and the world doesn't know it" (*Ivory, Apes, and Peacocks* [1915; repr., 1957], p. 97).

Huneker similarly championed controversial writers and artists. A proponent of Nietzsche, he noted that the philosopher preached "egoism, individualism, personal freedom, and selfhood" (*Musical Courier*, 6 May 1896, p. 20). Huneker was the first American to write a detailed criticism of the work of Henrik Ibsen and to publish an interview with Joseph Conrad. After designating the Salle Cézanne in Paris as "the very hub of the Independents' universe," he wrote in 1906 the first study of Paul Cézanne to be printed in an American newspaper.

Huneker also vigorously applauded American artists of all

types, such as the opera singer Mary Garden; writers Walt Whitman, Edgar Allan Poe, and Henry James; composers Edward MacDowell and Victor Herbert; and a group of painters known as "The Eight": Robert Henri, George Luks, John Sloan, Ernest Lawson, Arthur Davies, Maurice Prendergast, William Glackens, and Everett Shinn. Moreover, Huneker's position as a progressive, crusading critic established a new school of American criticism, whose members included H. L. Mencken, George Jean Nathan, and Benjamin De Casseres.

The French government made Huneker an officer of the Legion of Honor in 1910 in recognition of his service to French literature and art. In addition, he was elected to membership in the Authors' Club of London, the Academy of Natural Sciences of Philadelphia, and the National Institute of Arts and Letters (1918).

Huneker married Elizabeth Holmes in 1878; they divorced in 1891. The couple had two children, both of whom died in infancy. In 1892 he married the sculptor Clio Hinton; they had one child. This marriage ended in divorce in 1899. In 1899 he married Josephine Ahrensdorf Laski, a young widow, and remained with her for the last twenty-two years of his life.

Huneker died at his home in Brooklyn, New York. Four days later, on 13 February 1921, more than 1,200 people representative of the musical and artistic life of New York filled the auditorium of the new Town Hall, while hundreds more stood outside, for Huneker's funeral service, where he was eulogized for his credo of criticism. Believing that criticism was "the adventures of the soul among masterpieces" (*New York Times*, 10 Feb. 1921), Huneker said he "never preached aught but the beauty of art; I didn't even spell beauty with a big B. Not that I don't love art, but because I love life the more" (*New York World*, 10 Oct. 1920).

Even though Huneker's highly impressionistic literary style did not remain in favor and his books went out of print, his writings are among the most significant sources for information about the cultural life of the United States and Europe from the 1880s to the 1920s, and his influence on that cultural life is inestimable. According to journalist and poet De Casseres, "He is the greatest of patriots who raises the intellectual levels of his country; and James Huneker is therefore, to me, the greatest of twentieth century Americans. James Huneker was the end of the nineteenth century and the beginning of the twentieth in America" (pp. 17, 20).

S.V.M.

Blind Lemon Jefferson

[JULY 1897–DECEMBER 1929]

*F*irst of all, there's his name—Blind Lemon Jefferson. Growing up in Buffalo as I did, I'd never heard a name even close to "Blind Lemon Jefferson." I loved saying it. The sound was so much like a lick on a fat blues guitar. And it also evoked the South and the history of old men scratching out improvised versions of songs passed on from man to woman to man.

I first heard Blind Lemon Jefferson when I was in college. My next-door neighbor had the odd Bennington-like major in Economics and The Blues. He played records all night long while tap-tap-tapping term papers on his portable. Blind Lemon Jefferson was the blues singer who opened up music and drums for me. There were hardly any studio recordings of him—just happenstance traces of an outdoor festival or a jam session on someone's porch. The recordings were full of static and noise, but his singular style came through. What I learned from him was that music could convey more than one emotion at a time—and that you could convey intimate messages and contradictions. For instance, he picked away at a tune called "See That My Grave Is Kept Clean." The lyrics went, "There's one kind favor I ask of you, see that my grave is kept clean."

This was as dark as I'd ever heard. But the guitar was dancing along in this almost gleeful waltz, and the picking was peppy. It seemed to be coming from the fingers of a spirit. Blind Lemon Jefferson's voice was a doomsday voice telling a joke. The total effect was so eerie that the performance seemed a little mad. Later, I realized that it was irony I'd been experiencing, but illusive and subtle irony—jokes of another time and place. I've heard many folk singers, theater singers, and rock and roll stars, but I've never experienced the theatricality and the mystery of Blind Lemon Jefferson's

blues. Few composers can come up with the layers of color his play-
ing produced. There were definitely African drums beneath his
rhythms. His calling voice was devilish. His laugh was dirty.

As I began to learn more about the bluesman, I was fascinated to
find out that he spent his days riding around on trains. He'd take a
seat in the back, pull out his guitar and his cup. If guys wanted to
join him, they'd have to ride with him. You can hear the wail and
the wheels of the train in his strumming. His stubborn yearning for
freedom exists in the dissonance between his chords and melody.
Blind Lemon Jefferson's musical genius went virtually unrecog-
nized. He is part of a generation of blues singers that is now extinct.
They were dirt poor and ignored or exploited by the formal music
world. They knew things about human nature, death, craving, and
love that we'll never know again.

Elizabeth Swados

Blind Lemon Jefferson, blues singer-guitarist, was born on a small farm near Wortham, Texas, the son of Alec Jefferson and Classie Banks, farmers. Because Jefferson was a poor, rural African American, few official documents exist to verify biographical details. Some researchers speculate that Jefferson, one of seven children, was born as early as 1880 (based on a studio portrait circa 1926 that reveals graying hair) and question the legend that he was blind from birth (printed in 1927 in *The Paramount Book of Blues*). Indeed, he may never have been totally blind, given stories about his ability to travel independently and to identify the denomination of paper money by its "feel."

One account dates Jefferson's performing career from around 1912, at parties and picnics and on the streets in Wortham, but he had moved to the streets, barrelhouses, and brothels of Waco and of the "Deep Ellum" area of Dallas by 1913. Around this time he may have worked as a wrestler and met singer-guitarist Huddie Ledbetter before Lead Belly, as the latter came to be known, went to prison in 1915. From that time into the 1920s, Jefferson remained the itinerant blues singer, hopping freights and traveling extensively, especially in many southern states, and playing at various social functions and, eventually, at house rent parties in Chicago. Around 1922 Jefferson married a woman named Roberta (last name unknown), later fathering a son, Miles, who also became a musician.

Jefferson's big career break came in 1925 when either Dallas dealer R. J. Ashford or pianist Sammy Price alerted J. Mayo Williams, manager of the "Race Artist Series" for Paramount Records, to Jefferson's talent. The peak years of the female vaudeville-blues artists were coming to an end by then. Paramount, seeking a follow-up to their success marketing male blues artist Papa Charlie Jackson, reaching the rural audience through their strong mail-order business, recorded Jefferson in Chicago in 1925. Though Jefferson was known as a blues performer, his first two recordings were spirituals, "Pure Religion" and "I Want to Be Like Jesus in My Heart." These were not issued until Jefferson had had four releases, and then under the thinly disguised pseudonym L. J. Bates. The name was also used for the 1928 release of his two other recorded religious songs, presumably because of Christians' antipathy to singers of what they sometimes termed Devil's music, the blues.

Jefferson's second session, circa March 1926, yielded his first two Paramount releases, the second of which, "Got the Blues" / "Long Lonesome Blues," garnered six-figure sales. Altogether Jefferson had eight Paramount releases in 1926, recording every few months for the next four years, and was the company's premier blues artist for the rest of the decade. During those years Jefferson's ninety-four released sides (seven were unissued) on forty-three records reportedly sold in excess of one million copies. In 1927 his records were released at the rate of about one a month, and a special yellow and black label and photograph graced Paramount 12650, captioned "Blind Lemon's Birthday Record."

Jefferson's records enjoyed continuing popularity until and beyond the time of his death, despite his narrowing vocal range and the repetition of basic instrumental arrangements on many of his final recordings. Jefferson was officially listed as a porter living at Forty-fifth and State Streets in Chicago in 1928–1929, despite his continued popularity recording and performing. For example, he sang with a medicine show and with performer Rubin Lacy in Mississippi, where Jefferson reportedly refused $20 to play a blues song because it was Sunday.

Jefferson died in Chicago under mysterious circumstances sometime in December 1929, possibly of a heart attack or exposure, or both, and perhaps abandoned by his chauffeur. There are various accounts left by various blues musicians. One story has an unknown woman cleaning out Jefferson's bank account and shipping his body to Mexia, Texas, while another has pianist Will Ezell accompanying his body for burial in the Wortham Negro Cemetery on New Year's Day 1930. A grave marker was finally placed in the cemetery and dedicated on 15 October 1967.

Jefferson is indisputably one of the most influential American musicians of the twentieth century. The primary catalyst for the recording of male blues performers, he provided a vocal and instrumental model for generations of blues, country, jazz, rhythm and blues, and rock performers. Emerging from the same milieu as Texas Alexander and Henry Thomas, two probably older performers who reflected the field holler and folk song traditions of Texas, Jefferson melded traditional songs and themes with a highly original, idiosyncratic style that galvanized his listeners. He combined high vocals with a percussive and complex polyrhythmic guitar style consisting of interspersed bass runs and single-string treble riffs and arpeggios. His vast knowledge of traditional lyrics, increasingly modified by an original, poetic turn of mind, was so widely disseminated through recordings and appearances that his influence turns up in the work of blues performers of all styles and eras.

So great was Jefferson's popularity that many performers claim it a badge of honor to have seen, played with, or led him around on the streets. One who apparently did lead him, T-Bone Walker, adapted Jefferson's guitar style to an urbanized, large-band format that made Walker a seminal blues figure in the 1940s and shaped the guitar playing of B. B. King. King recorded Jefferson's "Bad Luck Blues" and in turn became a major blues figure who influenced countless musicians. One of Jefferson's compositions, "Match Box Blues," has been recorded by blues artists, country performer Larry Hensely (1934), rockabilly's Carl Perkins (1955), and the Beatles (1964), among many others.

Immediately upon his death, Jefferson became a figure of mythical status. Rev. Emmet Dickinson's 1930 tribute compared him to Christ, while Walter Taylor and John Byrd's flip-side tribute also lamented his death, albeit in less grandiose terms. Roark Bradford's 1931 novel *John Henry* employed Jefferson as the archetypical blues singer/sage. But behind the mythologizing is the reality of his greatness—his originality, virtuosity, and intensity—recognized by literary artists such as Langston Hughes and Sterling Brown, critics, and fans. He has entered the American consciousness to the extent that his face has appeared on T-shirts, sweatshirts, and matchbox covers. Jefferson is a member of the Blues Hall of Fame.

Blues performer Tom Shaw stated it simply: "He was the King."

S.C.T.

Murray Kempton

[16 DECEMBER 1918–5 MAY 1997]

*D*uring the second half of the twentieth century, Murray Kempton gloriously championed two vital American traditions that were on a sad, seemingly inevitable, arc of decline—liberalism and the art of crafting a newspaper column on searing daily deadlines. The fate of liberalism left Kempton writing elegiacally about the inevitable ordeal of political losers from Adlai Stevenson and Hubert Humphrey at the top of the ticket to a rogue's roster of now-forgotten New York politicos at the bottom. But it was the 700-word columns, written for tabloid newspapers that Kempton proudly boasted were not quite "respectable," that were his shining epitaph.

At a time when other columnists tended toward the ideological and the didactic, Kempton was discursive and slyly amusing as he trudged off to cover the dramatic set-piece of a trial or press conference. Rereading a random selection of Kempton's columns from late 1988 (alas, most of his earlier work is not available on electronic data bases), I was struck by the small epiphanies that filled his quotidian work. A sample from a column about a Mikhail Gorbachev speech to the United Nations: "The residuary legatee of all the Bolsheviks has at last discovered, as Cosimo de Medici did so long ago, that men cannot be governed by rosary beads."

Kempton should be remembered as an American Samuel Johnson—and we, his devoted readers, did not need the intermediary of a Boswell to treasure the jewels studded in his deadline-driven prose.

Like many peers in the column-writing game, I owe in large measure my career choice to his shimmering example. Yellowing copies of Kempton columns, lovingly clipped from the 1960 New York Post, were tacked to the bulletin board in my childhood room. As a young reporter covering the initial George Bush presidential campaign in New Hampshire in 1980, I met Kempton for the first *time on the fringes of the press pack. For that glorious day, the candidate was ignored as I eagerly signed up as Kempton's Sancho Panza, a role that mostly consisted of fetching his oft-forgotten raincoat and listening to a shambling monologue on political and journalistic history.*

That encounter set the pattern for our chance meetings over the years: He would greet me as a boon companion, well-schooled in the absurdities of life, and pick up the conversation almost where we had left off. During the 1996 New Hampshire primary campaign, when the indefatigable Kempton was nearing eighty, we both found ourselves shut out of a candidate's speech to a local Rotary club. So we repaired to a greasy-spoon dinner across the street for another installment of what I hoped would be an ever-continuing series of chats. That was to be Kempton's last campaign. But every time I venture out on the campaign trail these days, I still vainly look for the columnist who was my boyhood inspiration, hoping once more to be granted the honor of fetching his raincoat.

WALTER SHAPIRO

Murray Kempton, journalist, was born in Baltimore, Maryland, to James Branson Kempton, a stockbroker, and his wife, Sally Ambler Kempton. The senior Kempton died when Murray was three, and he was raised in a shabby genteel household whose atmosphere was dominated by his mother's Virginia relatives. He later recalled that their notions of honor, courtesy, and gentlemanly behavior were derived from the code of the Old South; and though Kempton became a social and political maverick, he never lost his esteem for their values.

Kempton was educated at local schools and at Johns Hopkins University, where he wrote for the student newspaper, flirted with Communism, and became a member of the Socialist Party. After graduating in 1939 with a degree in history and government, he first became a social worker in Baltimore and then was hired as an organizer by the International Ladies

Garment Workers' Union in Peekskill, New York. He subsequently worked as publicity director of the American Labor Party in New York. His career goal, however, was journalism, and in 1942 he was hired by the *New York Post* as a labor reporter. Not long afterward he was drafted by the army and served for the next three years in the Pacific.

After the war ended in 1945, Kempton worked for several years as a reporter for a North Carolina newspaper, the *Wilmington Star*, before returning to the *Post* in 1947. His well-crafted stories about union activities, including the possible link of union officials to organized crime, earned him a promotion to labor editor of the *Post* two years later. While he continued to write about union affairs, he also began doing articles on other subjects, including domestic and foreign politics, and during the 1950s civil rights and civil liberties became the focus of his concern.

This was the so-called McCarthy era, when the search led by Senator Joseph McCarthy of Wisconsin for Communist influence in government had mushroomed into what many feared was a wholesale attack on American democracy. National hysteria, fed by the Cold War, drove alleged Communist sympathizers from their jobs and often from their communities, and loyalty oaths became a requirement for employment. As a columnist at the then-liberal *Post*, Kempton was free to warn against the dangers of McCarthyism, which he did with both wit and eloquence. But he also took Communists to task for what he saw as their naiveté, in particular their blindness to Communism's ultimate betrayal of personal liberty, and he went on to expand his thoughts in his first book, *Part of Our Time: Some Ruins and Monuments of the Thirties* (1955), in which he examined the heyday of the American Communist party in the 1930s. The book was dismissed by conservatives, who felt that Kempton, though disdaining Communism, was still too radical in sentiment. It was also rejected by many on the left, who thought that Kempton had refused to recognize an important role in the radical movement played by these early Communists. However, the book received generous praise from critics who were liberal but staunchly anti-Communist— a category that best described Kempton himself, both as a journalist and as a private individual.

The 1950s also saw the birth of the civil rights movement, and Kempton wrote a number of articles that sympathetically chronicled its early years. He covered the national political conventions of 1952 and 1956 and the subsequent campaigns, ultimately mourning the two-time loss of the Democratic presidential candidate, Adlai Stevenson, his only political hero: Kempton had long since forsworn his allegiance to the Socialist Party and was now a Democrat. He spent much of 1958 in Italy on a Fulbright grant, teaching journalism at the University of Rome. The following year he traveled with Soviet premier Nikita Khrushchev on his American tour, and in 1960 he again covered the American presidential campaign. In the early 1960s he continued to write about the civil rights movement in the South, especially the work of Martin Luther King, Jr., and briefly participated in the Freedom Rides.

Kempton's second book, a collection of his columns titled *America Comes of Middle Age*, was published in 1963 and was reviewed favorably by the critics as a fair assessment of the United States at midcentury. In the spring of that year he moved to Washington, D.C., to become an editor and columnist at the *New Republic*, then a liberal weekly, but remained there for little more than a year. He returned to New York in the fall of 1964 to become a columnist for the *New York World-Telegram and Sun*; and when it stopped publication in the spring of 1966, he returned to the *Post* and resumed writing his old column. Kempton, who had eschewed participation in national politics for more than a decade following the defeat of Adlai Stevenson in 1956, became an active supporter of Democratic presidential hopeful Eugene McCarthy in the spring of 1968, amid growing opposition to the Vietnam War, and served as a delegate from New York to the Democratic National Convention in Chicago that August. Following the nomination of Hubert Humphrey on 29 August, Kempton joined an antiwar demonstration along Chicago's Michigan Avenue and was arrested for disorderly conduct. Although he claimed that he was participating in "a peaceful revolt" against government wrongdoing, he was convicted the following spring and fined $250; an appeal of his conviction was denied in March 1972.

Beginning in the mid-1950s Kempton contributed articles to a number of national magazines, including *Harper's*, the *Atlantic Monthly, Esquire*, and others, and from 1969 on was a frequent reviewer and essayist for the *New York Review of Books*. In 1973 he published his third book, *The Briar Patch: The People of the State of New York vs. Lumumba Shakur, et al.*, an assessment of the Black Panthers. He continued at the *Post* until 1981, when it became a conservative paper, and moved on to *Newsday*, writing a column for that paper until his death; its appearance was sporadic in his final years. His subjects were major and minor events in public life, and his rhetorical stance was invariably on the side of decency, fairness, and support for the underdog. He even found himself coming to Richard Nixon's defense in 1984, when the disgraced ex-president was denied the right to buy a co-op on Manhattan's East Side.

Kempton won a number of professional awards, including a Pulitzer Prize in 1985 for commentary. His last book, a collection of columns, titled *Rebellions, Perversities, and Main Events*, was published in 1994. He died of pancreatic cancer at a nursing home in New York City.

Kempton was married twice. His first wife was Mina Blumenthal, whom he married in 1942; they had four children. They were later divorced and he subsequently married Beverly Gary, with whom he had one son. In his final years he was the companion of Barbara Epstein, coeditor of the *New York Review of Books*.

Kempton's writing style was variously described as pungent, truculent, acerbic, and witty — adjectives that could also be applied to the work of a fellow Baltimorean, journalist H. L. Mencken. But it could also be opaque: unlike the usually terse Mencken, Kempton could generate elaborately constructed thickets of prose whose ultimate meaning often eluded readers and perplexed even admiring critics. In one famous incident he was acquitted in a libel suit brought by the liberal writer Victor Navasky because the court did not understand the meaning of the allegedly offensive article. His syntax aside, Kempton was long considered the conscience of American journalism. Throughout his career he was an outspoken supporter of fairness and decency in public life; and though both his audience and his popularity declined in the last two decades of his life, he was remembered at his death as a tireless champion of the poor and the powerless.

A.T.K.

Walter Lippmann

[23 SEPTEMBER 1889–14 DECEMBER 1974]

*My choice of an American, the memory of whose greatness is
fading, is Walter Lippmann. He is called a journalist but
there is no recognized profession for what he really was: Thinker.
His book* A Preface to Morals, *published in 1929, is better than the
Bible and easier to understand.*

ANDY ROONEY

Walter Lippmann, journalist and author, was born in New York City, the son of Jacob Lippmann, an investor, and Daisy Baum. Born into a family of wealth and leisure, Lippmann traveled yearly to Europe with his art-loving parents, attended private schools in New York City, and entered Harvard in the illustrious class of 1910. Among his classmates were Heywood Broun, T. S. Eliot, and John Reed, who hailed him, to no one's surprise, as a future president of the United States. An idealistic young man, Lippmann worked with the poor of Boston, founded the student Socialist Club, and wrote for college journals pledged to social reform.

At Harvard the brilliant student made a strong impression on three men who influenced him greatly: the philosophers William James and George Santayana, and the British socialist Graham Wallas. From James, Lippmann learned to value experimentation, pluralism, and action; from Santayana, the opposite virtues of detachment, measure, and restraint; and from Wallas, a respect for an unpredictable human nature over the rigidities of political theories and institutions.

Chosen by Santayana as his assistant and expected one day to follow in his footsteps, Lippmann instead left Harvard in May 1910, just a few weeks before receiving his master's degree

The Arsenal and Navy Yard Wage Commission: (from left) Walter Lippmann, Franklin D. Roosevelt, and William Blackmen.

in philosophy, to be a reporter on the *Boston Common*, a socialist newspaper in Boston. At the time journalism was not considered to be a proper profession for gentlemen. But young Lippmann was fired by a need to be a part of the action. This tension between a life of contemplation and a yearning for involvement was a hallmark of his career.

Older men were attracted to Lippmann for his brilliance and he to them for what he could learn. After a few months with the reformist Boston editor Ralph Albertson (who in 1917 became his father-in-law when Lippmann married Albertson's daughter Faye), he won the coveted post of assistant to one of the great muckrakers and political debunkers of the age, Lincoln Steffens. From Steffens he learned irreverence and skepticism, qualities that he took with him in 1912 to Schenectady, New York, where he went to work for the newly elected socialist mayor. But what attracted Lippmann to socialism was less a concern for the poor and downtrodden, as was the case with his friend John Reed, than an impatience with how badly society was organized.

Lippmann's experience with socialists, along with his evenings in Greenwich Village among poets and pamphleteers intent on transforming the world, only intensified his skepticism about romantic reformers. In the summer of 1912 he retreated to the Maine woods and within a few months produced a short, opinionated book bristling with iconoclasm. *A Preface to Politics* was a young man's potpourri, combining James's hymn to experimentation with the Progressives' call to action, and spiced with Henri Bergson and a bit of Sigmund Freud, whose psychoanalytic theories had only begun to cross the Atlantic.

This cheeky tract caught the attention of Lippmann's political idol Theodore Roosevelt and also of Herbert Croly, who was launching a weekly magazine to promote Roosevelt's idea of a "New Nationalism." The 24-year-old Lippmann, talented and self-assured, struck Croly as perfect for an editorship at the *New Republic*. Even before the first issue appeared in November 1914, Lippmann brought out his second book—one sharply at odds with his first. In *Drift and Mastery* he cut his last ties to the socialists and extolled a scientifically managed society run by a public-minded elite. Roosevelt, who hoped to run for president again in 1916, saw this as a description of himself and pronounced Lippmann to be the "most brilliant young man of his age in all the United States."

Although the *New Republic* was meant to be a journal of Bull Moose domestic reform, its launching coincided with the outbreak of war in Europe, and the subject of foreign affairs became unavoidable. Lippmann, who was at the House of Commons when Britain declared war on Germany in 1914 and had cultivated such Fabian socialists as H. G. Wells, George Bernard Shaw, Sidney Webb, and Beatrice Webb, began writing on the issues of the war, and more urgently on whether the United States should be drawn in.

In 1915 he published his first book on foreign policy, *The Stakes of Diplomacy*, and by the following year, convinced that the United States could not allow Britain to be defeated, began a series of editorials designed to bring the United States into the war. Developing close ties with Colonel Edward House, Woodrow Wilson's éminence grise, he gained privileged access to the White House. When the United States entered the war in 1917 Lippmann joined the government as part of a secret team known as the Inquiry. Its assignment was no less than to draw the geographic and political outlines of the postwar world. With Lippmann as coordinator, the group drafted the territorial provisions of Wilson's Fourteen Points.

In the spring of 1918 House sent Lippmann to London to conduct intelligence gathering and disseminate propaganda behind German lines. This experience proved to be critical in his intellectual development. Impressed by how easily public opinion could be molded and distorted, Lippmann returned from the war to examine, in a series of articles and then in the book *Liberty and the News* (1920), the role of the press. This led him to write the far deeper and more sweeping study *Public Opinion* (1922). Behind its bland title lay disturbing conclusions.

If, he argued, the average person's perception of reality was governed by propaganda, prejudice, inattention, and even unconscious stereotypes ingrained by the culture, how could such a person make an informed political decision? Yet the very theory of democracy assumed that ordinary citizens could make intelligent decisions. If they could not, what was the virtue of democracy? Unwilling to give up on democratic government, Lippmann proposed to remedy the problem by training unbiased experts to filter the news and pass on the "truth."

But in *The Phantom Public* (1925), he abandoned even this device. Taking his analysis to its logical conclusion, he decided that the public should leave the experts alone to make decisions. When they made mistakes the public could kick them out and bring in new experts. The public could say "yes" or "no," but "with the substance of the problem it can do nothing but meddle ignorantly or tyrannically." A distressed John Dewey described Lippmann's thesis as "perhaps the most effective indictment of democracy ever penned."

The manipulations of the war and the compromises of the peace had disillusioned Lippmann in more ways than one. He had put his faith in Wilson's idealism and then felt betrayed by the vindictive peace imposed on Germany. The *New Republic*, having urged the United States into the war, now denounced the peace treaty and with it the proposed League of Nations. Lippmann did not join the "lost generation" of Paris, but he shared its disillusion, and for a time he retreated from the ardent internationalism that he had preached.

In 1922 Lippmann left the magazine to join the *World*, New York's leading liberal newspaper. As head of the editorial page he set the paper's position on the leading issues of the day, such as prohibition, disarmament, the financial crash, the Sacco-Vanzetti affair, and the John Scopes trial. At the *World* his stinging editorials reached a far wider audience and established his reputation as a leading opinion maker.

Even while editing the paper and writing daily editorials, Lippmann found time for another book. This one, however, concerned not politics, but ethics and values. *A Preface to Morals* (1929) was meant for those, like himself, who had lost their faith but not their search for meaning in life. Born into a Jewish family, Lippmann rejected this religious and cultural identity. Although (or perhaps because) his analysis was gloomy—he praised the "disinterested" man who would find solace not in revelation but in stoicism—he captured the anxieties of the age, and with it a large new public.

When the *World* shut down in 1931, Lippmann joined its conservative rival, the *New York Herald-Tribune*, as a syndicated columnist. The switch distressed many readers but was not illogical. Lippmann had grown more conservative during the 1920s, and his new post offered not only full independence but also a nationwide audience. At the time there were virtually no

serious political columnists. Yet papers across the nation needed a knowledgeable authority to interpret the news. Writing
simply and directly, but conveying great learning without ideological slant, he became America's guru. Within a short time
his "Today and Tomorrow" column was syndicated to more
than 200 papers with millions of readers. "To read, if not to
comprehend, Lippmann was suddenly the thing to do," sourly
commented an envious rival, Arthur Krock.

Through syndication Lippmann became an international
figure. At least once a year he toured the capitals of Europe,
meeting with heads of state as a matter of course, and pronouncing on the wisdom or folly of their policies. He scrupu-
lously avoided scoops and instead concentrated on the meaning behind the news. As he had demonstrated in *Public Opinion*, facts were not the same as truth. By putting the facts into a
coherent perspective—by telling his readers what to make of
the cacophonous onslaught of news—he made himself virtually indispensable. Even those who disagreed with him had to
know what he had said.

Lippmann owed his success not only to the fact that he was
the first serious political columnist and began in an era long
before television, but also because he wrote with such grace,
clarity, and authority. His audience was the kind of person
who cared about public affairs but did not want to be bom-
barded with details. To read Lippmann was not only the thing
to do, but marked one as a thoughtful person. Oliver Wendell
Holmes captured part of Lippmann's appeal by describing his
prose as being like flypaper, "if I touch it, I am stuck till I finish it."

During his thirty-six years as a newspaper columnist, Lippmann was not always right or universally popular. His rare
gaffes—such as his early dismissal of Franklin D. Roosevelt as
a well-meaning playboy—were memorable. His occasional
enmities—such as his bitter feud with Lyndon Johnson over
the Vietnam War—were monumental. Nor was he invariably

consistent. His views changed with the times and with his own reading of events.

The young man who was a mild socialist in the early years of the century and an ardent interventionist in World War I became in the 1920s and 1930s a skeptic about the wisdom of the average man and an advocate of a hands-off policy toward Europe and Asia, even as the fragile peace began to crack. Although he supported the recovery programs of the early New Deal, once the worst of the economic crisis seemed over he turned against FDR's more ambitious reform programs.

Yet even though his views in the mid-1930s were often closer to Wall Street than to the White House, it would not be correct to label him simply a conservative. His 1934 book *The Method of Freedom* introduced his friend John Maynard Keynes's views on deficit spending to a wide American audience, while his learned study *The Good Society* (1937) was an earnest attempt to find a middle way between laissez-faire conservatism and conformist collectivism. Lippmann labored to show that opposition to collectivism did not make him an enemy of social progress, and he drew up an "agenda of liberalism" that contained heavy components of the welfare state. But the times were not conducive to a nuanced approach, and the book was widely criticized by both the right and the left. Later generations, however, found much of merit in his effort to salvage liberalism without surrendering to a collectivist authoritarianism.

In 1938 Lippmann moved from New York to Washington, D.C., in part because government had become more centralized in the capital. But more importantly it stemmed from the uproar in his social world caused by his 1937 divorce from Faye Albertson and his marriage in 1938 to Helen Byrne, the wife of his close friend and colleague Hamilton Fish Armstrong. Although this double divorce provoked an emotional crisis in Lippmann's life, his second marriage brought him great happiness over the remaining years of his life. Lippmann had no children with either of his wives.

Lippmann's personal crisis coincided almost exactly with the European political crisis at the time of the Munich conference that led to the destruction of Czechoslovakia. All during the 1930s, in the face of the mounting belligerence of the fascist powers, Lippmann had urged a policy of armed neutrality for the United States. But after Munich he became alarmed that Britain and France could not keep Nazi Germany in check. In the fall of 1939, following the German invasion of Poland, he urged the lifting of the arms embargo to the democracies. With the fall of France in June 1940, he pleaded in his column and conspired behind the scenes to supply the British with surplus American destroyers and heavy military equipment under lend-lease. The German onslaught had destroyed his hope that the United States could stand apart. Never again would he put his faith in such Wilsonian notions as disarmament, neutrality, or international forums. Henceforth he would become a hardheaded "realist" concerned with power, alliances, and military balances.

Within a few years, as the German and Japanese armies were being turned back, this view brought Lippmann into conflict with those who believed that the defeat of the aggressors would bring about a peaceful "One World" under the benevolent guidance of the United Nations. To combat what he considered to be dangerous illusions, Lippmann in 1943 wrote a short, argumentative book titled *U.S. Foreign Policy: Shield of the Republic*. Coming at a time when Americans wanted to know what to think about the postwar world over the horizon, it was a bestseller. The core of his argument was that isolation was not possible for the United States, good intentions could not substitute for military force and alliances, and peace in the postwar world required a continuation of the wartime alliance of America and Britain with Russia. "The failure to form an alliance of the victors will mean the formation of alliances between the vanquished and some of the victors," he wrote presciently. A year later he followed this up with another short book, *U.S. War Aims* (1944).

But the wartime alliance did, of course, fall apart. For this Lippmann blamed London and Washington as well as Moscow. Although concerned by Soviet behavior in Eastern Europe, he urged that lines be kept open to Moscow. Lippmann always believed in negotiation, although from positions of strength. For that reason he wrote a series of columns in 1947, also published as a book, *The Cold War* (1947), denouncing the "containment doctrine" as enunciated by George Kennan and pursued by the Harry Truman administration. As the Cold War consensus hardened in Washington, Lippmann remained one of the few skeptics.

But the Moscow-engineered coup in February 1948 by Czech communists and the political disappearance of Czechoslovakia behind the Iron Curtain shattered his lingering hopes that somehow the wartime alliance could be maintained. As the Cold War hardened, Lippmann became an elucidator— always perceptive and authoritative, and often original—rather than a critic of the prevailing foreign policy consensus. Not until the mid-1960s, with the crisis over the Vietnam War, would he move again into the opposition.

In 1955 Lippmann published his last major book, *Essays in the Public Philosophy*. In it he attempted to distill his thinking about politics and come to terms with the weakness of democracies in confronting unpopular social and political problems. Consistent with the skepticism of mass democracy that he had first evidenced in *Public Opinion* more than thirty years earlier, but unwilling to seek refuge in undemocratic methods, he proposed that popular sovereignty be limited according to the tenets of "natural law." To Lippmann's great distress, the book on which he had worked for many years was tepidly received by critics.

For all his eminence and his reputation as the ultimate

insider, Lippmann had a rocky relationship with most presidents. Even those he supported at the beginning, such as both Roosevelts, Wilson, John Kennedy, and Johnson, ultimately disappointed him. This was in part because he tended to idealize strong leaders and thus was inevitably disillusioned when they failed to fulfill his exaggerated expectations. The only exceptions were De Gaulle and Churchill. But of course he never had to live under them. Beyond the waning of infatuations, he had a temperamental need to stand apart. All his life he wavered between the two poles of involvement and detachment, just as he was torn between the active life of writing for newspapers and the more contemplative life of writing books. "It is a fact," Lippmann once wrote of Santayana, "that a man can't see the play and be in it too." Yet Lippmann wanted both: to be spectator and actor, observer and insider. To a remarkable degree he succeeded.

Lippmann's last working years were spent alternately in embrace and opposition. After John F. Kennedy's assassination in 1963 he rallied immediately to Lyndon Johnson and for two years praised his leadership. He once again became the favored insider at the White House, courted by Johnson and awarded the Presidential Medal of Freedom in September 1964. During this period he became a television celebrity, appearing on the CBS network in seven one-hour interviews over a five-year period (1960–1965). This brought him to an entirely new audience, and the programs drew very high ratings.

Had Lippmann retired in 1965 it would have been with every accolade that government could provide. But he kept writing his column for two more years, and they proved to be the most tempestuous of his entire career. In the end he was bitterly estranged from the White House and left Washington with sorrow in his heart.

The cause was that of so many sorrows: the Vietnam War. Lippmann had always tried to draw a distinction between areas of primary concern in foreign policy, like Europe and

Japan, and those he considered to be marginal in the balance of power, like most of the small states of the Third World. For this reason he never was enthusiastic about U.S. aid to South Vietnam and in 1964 supported General de Gaulle's plan for neutralization of Indochina.

But the administration's scornful rejection of this exit plan and its intensification of the war against North Vietnam early in 1965 put Lippmann on a collision course with the White House. As he became convinced that Johnson was intent on a military victory rather than a negotiated peace, and as the casualties of the war mounted, Lippmann moved further into opposition. With mounting frustration over the steadily expanding war, he abandoned his carefully measured prose for the language of combat. The president he had earlier praised as "a man for this season" became a "primitive frontiersman" who had "betrayed and abandoned" the American promise.

Cut off from the administration and denounced as a "defeatist" by those who had so deferentially courted him earlier, Lippmann became an intellectual leader and elder statesman of the antiwar movement. Not since his youth had he thrown himself so passionately into a political struggle. But by the spring of 1967, distressed by the poisonous political climate in Washington and weary of battle after so many fights, he decided to draw an end to the newspaper column he had begun writing nearly thirty-six years earlier. He and his wife returned to New York, which was not the city they remembered from the 1930s, and where they found little peace in their retirement. There Lippmann died.

Although Lippmann is generally described as a journalist, the term does not encompass the full range of his talents and influence. In addition to writing a syndicated column, he was both a magazine and a newspaper editor, a promoter of causes and leaders, and the author of nearly two dozen books on politics, ethics, philosophy, perception, and governance. Considered to be the most influential political writer of his age, his authority rested on his personal relations with statesmen, an intellectual grounding in philosophy and history, an ability to synthesize and explain complex information, and a graceful literary style. Political figures sought him out for the privilege of being interviewed. As a colleague once said, his was "the name that opened every door." During his long career Lippmann had written about nearly every major event that touched Americans. Van Wyck Brooks expressed a widely held view of Lippmann when he wrote that his was the "most brilliant career ever devoted in America to political writing."

But Lippmann would have described his role differently. "Responsibility," he once wrote of a renowned editor, "consists in sharing the burden of men directing what is to be done, or the burden of offering some other course of action in the mood of one who has realized what it would mean to undertake it." This is the task that Lippmann set for himself, and it expresses much of what made him unique.

R.S.

Malcolm X

[19 MAY 1925–21 FEBRUARY 1965]

I never met Malcolm X, but I was aware of his many efforts to secure equality for blacks. Early on, his rhetoric was racist. But there came a time when he recognized that he could not espouse equality for blacks and continue making racist comments about whites when so many whites were part of the civil rights movement and working with Dr. Martin Luther King, Jr., to achieve justice for all.

Before he was brutally murdered, Malcolm X was on the verge of becoming a crossover national leader, very much as Rev. Jesse Jackson ultimately did.

I met his wife, Betty Shabazz, a delightful and highly intelligent woman who was an administrator at Medgar Evers College in Brooklyn. At her request and that of the community residents, I had the privilege of renaming streets in his honor, in Manhattan and Brooklyn.

Both the black and white communities are coming to recognize the huge contributions made by Malcolm X to America's past and future. In my judgment, he was the forerunner to Dr. Martin Luther King, Jr., in the same way that St. John the Baptist was to Jesus.

ED KOCH

Malcolm X, African-American religious and political leader also known as el-Hajj Malik el-Shabazz, was born Malcolm Little in Omaha, Nebraska, the son of Earl Little and Louise (also Louisa) Norton, both activists in the Universal Negro Improvement Association established by Marcus Garvey. Earl Little, a Georgia-born itinerant Baptist preacher, encountered considerable racial harassment because of his black nationalist views. He moved his family several times before settling in Michigan, purchasing a home

Malcolm X speaks at news conference held at a New York hotel in early 1964. *(Library of Congress)*

in 1929 on the outskirts of East Lansing, where Malcolm Little spent his childhood. In 1931 the elder Little was run over by a streetcar and died. Although police concluded that the death was accidental, the victim's friends and relatives suspected that he had been murdered by a local white supremacist group. This incident led to a severe decline in the family's economic fortunes and contributed to Louise Little's mental deterioration. In January 1939 she was declared legally insane and committed to a Michigan mental asylum, where she remained until 1963.

Although Malcolm Little excelled academically in grammar school and was popular among classmates at the predominately white schools, he also became embittered toward white authority figures. In his autobiography he recalled quitting school after a teacher warned that his desire to become a lawyer was not a "realistic goal for a nigger." As his mother's mental health deteriorated and he became increasingly incorrigible, welfare officials intervened, placing him in several reform schools and foster homes. In 1941 he left Michigan to live in Boston with his half sister, Ella Collins.

In Boston and New York during the early 1940s, Malcolm held a variety of railroad jobs while also becoming increasingly involved in criminal activities such as peddling illegal drugs and numbers running. At this time he was often called Detroit Red because of his reddish hair. Arrested in 1946 for larceny as well as breaking and entering, he was sent to prison in February 1946.

While in Concord Reformatory in Massachusetts, Malcolm X responded to the urgings of his brother Reginald and became a follower of Elijah Muhammad (formerly Robert Poole), leader of the Temple of Islam (later Nation of Islam — often called the Black Muslims), a small black nationalist Islamic sect. Attracted to the religious group's racial doctrines, which categorized whites as "devils," he began reading extensively about world history and politics, particularly concerning African slavery and the oppression of black people in America. After he was paroled from prison in August 1952, he became Minister Malcolm X, using the surname assigned to him in place of the African name that had been taken from his slave ancestors.

Malcolm X quickly became Elijah Muhammad's most effective minister, bringing large numbers of new recruits into the group during the 1950s and early 1960s. By 1954 he had become minister of New York Temple No. 7, and he later helped establish Islamic temples in other cities. In 1957 he became the Nation of Islam's national representative, a position of influence second only to that of Elijah Muhammad. In January 1958 he married Betty X (Sanders), also a Muslim; the two had six daughters.

Malcolm's forceful, cogent oratory attracted considerable publicity and a large personal following among discontented African Americans. In his speeches he urged black people to separate from whites and win their freedom "by any means necessary." In 1957, after New York police beat and jailed Nation of Islam member Hinton Johnson, Malcolm X mobilized supporters to confront police officials and secure medical treatment. A 1959 television documentary on the Nation of Islam called *The Hate That Hate Produced* further increased Malcolm's notoriety among whites. In 1959 he traveled to Europe and the Middle East on behalf of Elijah Muhammad, and in 1961 he served as Muhammad's emissary at a secret Atlanta meeting seeking an accommodation with the Ku Klux Klan. The following year he participated in protest meetings prompted by the killing of a black Muslim during a police raid on a Los Angeles mosque. By 1963 he had become a frequent guest on radio and television programs and was the most well known figure in the Nation of Islam.

Malcolm X was particularly harsh in his criticisms of the nonviolent strategy to achieve civil rights reforms advocated by Martin Luther King, Jr. His letters seeking King's participation in public forums were generally ignored by King. During a November 1963 address at the Northern Negro Grass Roots Leadership Conference in Detroit, Malcolm derided the notion that African Americans could achieve freedom nonviolently. "The only revolution in which the goal is loving your enemy is the Negro revolution," he announced. "Revolution is bloody, revolution is hostile, revolution knows no compromise, revolution overturns and destroys everything that gets in its way." Malcolm also charged that King and other leaders of the recently held March on Washington had taken over the event, with the help of white liberals, in order to subvert its militancy. "And as they took it over, it lost its militancy. It ceased to be angry, it ceased to be hot, it ceased to be uncompromising," he insisted. Despite his caustic criticisms of King, however, Malcolm nevertheless identified himself with the grass-roots leaders of the southern civil rights protest movement. His desire to move from rhetorical to political militancy led him to become increasingly dissatisfied with Elijah Muhammad's apolitical stance. As he later explained in his autobiography, "It could be heard increasingly in the Negro communities: 'Those Muslims *talk* tough, but they never *do* anything, unless somebody bothers Muslims.'"

Malcolm's disillusionment with Elijah Muhammad resulted not only from political differences but also his personal dismay when he discovered that the religious leader had fathered illegitimate children. Other members of the Nation of Islam began to resent Malcolm's growing prominence and to suspect that he intended to lay claim to leadership of the group. When Malcolm X remarked that President John Kennedy's assassination in November 1963 was a case of the "chickens coming home to roost," Elijah Muhammad used the opportunity to ban his increasingly popular minister from speaking in public.

Despite this effort to silence him, Malcolm X continued to attract public attention during 1964. He counseled boxer Cassius Clay, who publicly announced, shortly after winning the heavyweight boxing title, that he had become a member of the Nation of Islam and adopted the name Muhammad Ali. In March 1964 Malcolm announced that he was breaking with the Nation of Islam to form his own group, Muslim Mosque, Inc. The theological and ideological gulf between Malcolm and Elijah Muhammad widened during a month-long trip to Africa and the Middle East. During a pilgrimage to Mecca on 20 April 1964 Malcolm reported that seeing Muslims of all colors worshiping together caused him to reject the view that all whites were devils. Repudiating the racial theology of the Nation of Islam, he moved toward orthodox Islam as practiced outside the group. He also traveled to Egypt, Lebanon, Nigeria, Ghana, Senegal, and Morocco, meeting with political activists and national leaders, including Ghanaian president Kwame Nkrumah. After returning to the United States on 21 May, Malcolm announced that he had adopted a Muslim name, el-Hajj Malik el-Shabazz, and that he was forming a new political group, the Organization of Afro-American Unity (OAAU), to bring together all elements of the African-American freedom struggle.

Determined to unify African Americans, Malcolm sought to strengthen his ties with the more militant factions of the civil rights movement. Although he continued to reject King's non-violent, integrationist approach, he had a brief, cordial encounter with King on 26 March 1964 as the latter left a press conference at the U.S. Capitol. The following month, at a Cleveland symposium sponsored by the Congress of Racial Equality, Malcolm X delivered one of his most notable speeches, "The Ballot or the Bullet," in which he urged black people to submerge their differences "and realize that it is best for us to first see that we have the same problem, a common problem — a problem that will make you catch hell whether you're a Baptist, or a Methodist, or a Muslim, or a nationalist."

When he traveled again to Africa during the summer of 1964 to attend the Organization of African Unity Summit Conference, he was able to discuss his unity plans at an impromptu meeting in Nairobi with leaders of the Student Nonviolent Coordinating Committee. After returning to the United States in November, he invited Fannie Lou Hamer and other members of the Mississippi Freedom Democratic Party to be guests of honor at an OAAU meeting held the following month in Harlem. Early in February 1965 he traveled to Alabama to address gatherings of young activists involved in a voting rights campaign. He tried to meet with King during this trip, but the civil rights leader was in jail; instead Malcolm met with Coretta Scott King, telling her that he did not intend to make life more difficult for her husband. "If white people realize what the alternative is, perhaps they will be more willing to hear Dr. King," he explained.

Even as he strengthened his ties with civil rights activists, however, Malcolm acquired many new enemies. The U.S. government saw him as a subversive, and the Federal Bureau of

Investigation initiated efforts to undermine his influence. In addition, some of his former Nation of Islam colleagues, including Louis X (later Louis Farrakhan), condemned him as a traitor for publicly criticizing Elijah Muhammad. The Nation of Islam attempted to evict him from the home he occupied in Queens, New York. On 14 February 1965 Malcolm's home was firebombed; although he and his family escaped unharmed, the perpetrators were never apprehended.

On 21 February 1965 members of the Nation of Islam shot and killed Malcolm as he was beginning a speech at the Audubon Ballroom in New York City. On 27 February more than 1,500 people attended his funeral service held in Harlem. Although three men were later convicted in 1966 and sentenced to life terms, one of those involved, Thomas Hagan, filed an affidavit in 1977 insisting that his actual accomplices were never apprehended.

After his death, Malcolm's views reached an even larger audience than during his life. *The Autobiography of Malcolm X*, written with the assistance of Alex Haley, became a bestselling book following its publication in 1965. During subsequent years other books appeared containing texts of many of his speeches, including *Malcolm X Speaks* (1965), *The End of White World Supremacy: Four Speeches* (1971), and *February 1965: The Final Speeches* (1992). In 1994 Orlando Bagwell and Judy Richardson produced a major documentary, *Malcolm X: Make It Plain*. His words and image also exerted a lasting influence on African-American popular culture, as evidenced in the hip-hop or rap music of the late twentieth century and in director Spike Lee's film biography, *Malcolm X* (1992).

C. C.

Rocky Marciano

[1 SEPTEMBER 1929–31 AUGUST 1969]

*T*he walls of my office are covered with photographs. The one I treasure most is of my grandfather Alfonso Cioffari and the undefeated heavyweight champion boxer Rocky Marciano. I was fifteen years old when Rocky Marciano defeated Jersey Joe Walcott with a knockout punch that would go down in boxing history. I hope people will read about and remember Marciano, not so much for the knockouts but to learn about this Italian-American kid who despite the obstacles (he was "too old, too short, and too light") achieved incredible success due partly to his physical strength and particularly to his human strength. His is an only-in-America story. Like most well-known and successful Italian-Americans, Marciano has not been spared rumored associations with organized crime. Rumors aside, he was a hero, a street-smart, working-class guy with little going for him but a strong right arm and a determination to succeed. I chose Marciano's story because — both in the ring and out — he was a fighter. And, for this son of Italian immigrants, that's something to be remembered.

ALFONSE D'AMATO

Rocky Marciano, heavyweight boxing champion, was born Rocco Francis Marchegiano in Brockton, Massachusetts, the son of Pierino Marchegiano, a shoe-factory worker, and Pasqualena Picciuto. He was considered the roughest kid in the neighborhood, although he was not overly pugnacious. A star athlete who hoped to become a major league baseball catcher, he dropped out of school at age sixteen when the baseball coach barred him from playing on a church team. Marciano then became a manual laborer while playing baseball on local semiprofessional teams. He was drafted into the U.S. Army in 1943 and was honorably discharged in 1946. Marciano kept his baseball dream alive until the spring of 1947, when a tryout with a Chicago Cubs minor league affiliate revealed that he lacked foot speed and a strong throwing arm.

Marciano had begun boxing competitively while in the army, mainly to avoid KP duty. He trained under Gene Caggiano, a local boxing promoter, and they signed an agreement early in 1948 stipulating that Marciano would retain Caggiano as his manager if he turned professional. Once Marciano became a professional boxer, however, he had nothing to do with Caggiano, who then sued Marciano. On 3 November 1950 the Plymouth County Court ruled that their contractual agreement was still valid, which would have entitled Caggiano to one-third of Marciano's earnings. However, on 16 July 1951 the state supreme court reversed the judgment.

Marciano had had one professional fight in 1947, while still an amateur, under the pseudonym Rocky Mack and earned $35 for a three-round knockout. In 1948 Rocky participated in the Golden Gloves and advanced to the All-East championship tournament. He had aspirations to box in the Olympics, but he broke a thumb in winning a New England AAU (Amateur Athletic Union) tournament that served as a trial for the Olympics. He then decided to turn professional and gave up his job as a digger for the gas company. Experts considered Marciano too old, too short, and too light, at 5 feet 10 inches and 190 pounds, to become a successful heavyweight prizefighter.

Later in 1948 Marciano auditioned in New York with fight manager Al Weill and trainer Charley Goldman. They did not consider Marciano ready to be a top contender, but they liked his heart and his strong punch. Goldman found him a defenseless, upright, wild puncher with poor balance; he kept his legs too far apart, overstrode when punching, could not throw combinations, and relied too much on his powerful right fist. Goldman corrected Marciano's poor footwork by tying his laces together, and he taught him how to fight from a crouch, slip punches, and utilize his left hand. Marciano was extremely well trained and took care of his diet. When working out with Goldman in New York he walked four miles just to get to the gymnasium. He was sent home to Brockton to hone his craft while he worked as a highway laborer. There he improved his stamina by running—often more than seven miles a day—and pounding the heavy bag to develop his power, avoiding the speedbag because of awkwardness. Marciano originally followed this regimen with an hour of weightlifting; fearful of becoming muscle bound, however, he stopped lifting and swam laps instead.

Weill's stepson Marty became Marciano's manager of record, although his father was the "undercover manager." Weill was then the matchmaker for the International Boxing Club, and thus holding both positions would have been a conflict of interest. Weill would become Marciano's official manager only in 1952, after he quit the IBC. Rocky's first professional bout under his own name came on 12 July 1948 in Providence, Rhode Island, for which he earned $40 for four rounds. Marciano mostly fought in Providence, where he eventually had twenty-eight matches. His first big break came on 2 December 1949 when he won a second-round knockout over Pat Richards in his first semifinal bout (ten rounds) at Madison Square Garden.

Marciano became a top contender following his sixth-round knockout of Rex Layne at Madison Square Garden on 12 July 1951. His physical style in a very rough bout made him a popular favorite, and the crowd cheered him for twenty minutes after the match. However, Marciano's heavyweight title aspirations were dashed when the number-one contender, Jersey Joe Walcott, won the heavyweight title from Ezzard Charles.

With a Charles-Walcott rematch scheduled, Marciano was matched against former champion Joe Louis, who was making a comeback in order to pay off tax debts. Weill opposed the bout, but Goldman believed Marciano was ready to take on the aging Louis, who was a slight favorite. The fight took place on 26 October, with Louis receiving 45 percent of the purse and Marciano only 15 percent. Marciano won with an eight-round knockout, as youth, power, stamina, and hunger carried the day over experience and reach. With his victory over Louis, Marciano earned a title shot against Walcott, who at age thirty-eight was the oldest champion in boxing history to that time. In preparation for the bout, Marciano tuned up by defeating light heavyweight contender Kid Matthews on 28 July 1952 at Yankee Stadium in New York City; the fight drew a crowd of 31,188 and earned Marciano $50,000.

The Marciano-Walcott championship match took place in Philadelphia on 23 September 1952, with Walcott a 3-1 favorite to win. The fight was attended by more than 40,000 spectators, who paid over $500,000. In addition, the bout was neither on home television nor on radio, but it was televised into fifty theaters in thirty cities, earning a profit of $125,000. The fight began poorly for Marciano, as he was knocked to the canvas for the first time in his career during the first round. In the sixth round the fighters' heads collided, cutting Marciano and blurring his vision; he later claimed that Walcott's manager had rubbed ointment on the champion's gloves. By the thirteenth round Marciano was well behind in points, but he then knocked out Walcott with a short right. Experts have considered this Marciano's defining moment. Having made a total of $100,000 from the bout, Marciano fought in a rematch with Walcott on 15 May 1953 in Chicago Stadium. This time Marciano scored a knockout after just 145 seconds of the first round, earning $166,000 while Walcott earned $250,000. Marciano had trained extraordinarily hard for this defense, sparring a remarkable 225 rounds. Such training was not unusual for Marciano; he typically sparred 40 percent more than the average for a title bout.

On 17 June 1954 Marciano defended his title against the aged former champion Ezzard Charles before 47,585 at Yankee Stadium. Charles put forth a terrific performance, but he wearied after the fifth round and lost a split decision. A rematch on 17 September 1954 drew more than 34,000 to Yankee Stadium and generated a $350,000 gate and $650,000 from ancillary rights. In the rematch Charles completely split Marciano's left nostril in the sixth round, and the doctors considered halting the bout. Marciano responded to the crisis by knocking out Charles in the eighth round. He earned a combined $450,000 for these two fights.

Marciano's final defense came on 20 September 1955 against light heavyweight champion Archie Moore. The fight brought a crowd of 61,574 to Yankee Stadium, with hundreds of thousands attending closed circuit television theaters. The fight grossed $2,248,117, then the second largest gate in boxing history. Marciano was dropped to the canvas in the second round, but he survived to knock out Moore in the ninth round. Moore was to say, "Marciano is far and away the strongest man I've ever encountered in almost twenty years of fighting." For this fight Marciano earned his largest purse of $468,374.

Marciano retired from boxing on 28 April 1956. He had lost his drive, had saved much of the $2 million earned from fights and personal appearances, and did not trust Al Weill, whose contract called for Weill to receive one-half of Marciano's earnings both in and out of the ring. Marciano had long felt that Weill was cheating him. He had also heard that Weill had scalped tickets worth thousands of dollars, without involving Marciano, and that Weill had skimmed $10,000 from the promotional costs of Marciano's title defense against Tom Cockrell on 16 May 1955.

Marciano enjoyed life in the fast lane ("If you want to live a full life then live dangerously"), disliked routine, and was fascinated by the mobsters with whom he socialized and did business, such as Vito Genovese. He was a great hero to Italian Americans. Friends and acquaintances customarily gave him spending money, bought him dinner, and paid for his clothes. Parsimonious, Marciano never picked up checks. However, he was a poor businessman who made several bad decisions, including purchasing Florida swampland, investing substantial sums with loan sharks, and lending money at usurious rates on the street. Such transactions were never written down, and the death of a Cleveland loan shark reputedly cost him $100,000. He was said to have had over $2 million loaned out or stashed away in secret locations that have never been found.

In 1950 Marciano married Barbara Cousins, with whom he had one child and adopted a second. However, their relationship was strained by incompatibility. She was a homebody, while Marciano was constantly traveling, looking for business deals, making personal appearances (he was even paid for stepping into the ring when he attended boxing matches), and meeting beautiful women. He always stayed at friends' homes or hotels that offered him complimentary rooms.

In the mid-1960s Marciano turned down $2 million to fight Muhammad Ali (then known as Cassius Clay) when he could not get into fighting shape. In 1969 he participated in a computer tournament involving former champions that grossed about $1.7 million. For this endeavor he lost nearly 50 pounds, wore a toupee, and sparred eight hours of one-minute rounds with Ali to produce a marketable conclusion. Seven different endings were prepared, with the computer giving the victory to Marciano.

Marciano's professional record was 49-0. He was the victor in all six of his title defenses, and at the end of the twentieth century he was still the only undefeated heavyweight champion in boxing history. He left with a reputation for invincibility and for being particularly dangerous when hurt. A bruising fighter, Marciano was rated as the greatest slugger of all time with an 88 percent knockout record. A member of the International Boxing Hall of Fame, he was Fighter of the Year in 1952 and 1954. Marciano died when a private plane in which he was a passenger crashed near Newton, Iowa.

S.A.R.

Adolf Meyer

[13 SEPTEMBER 1866–17 MARCH 1950]

*T*hough born in Switzerland, Adolf Meyer made the great
American leap that was to distinguish U.S. therapeutic process
from the European models from which it was derived. In this fresh
country of self-invention, he saw that learning to accommodate
one's character was not a sufficient goal for psychodynamics. Here
in America, he saw, one could change one's character. No longer
would you struggle merely to gain tolerance of your flaws; rather,
you would eviscerate them. Meyer believed that man had infinite
adaptive capacities, embodied in the full plasticity of thought. It
was a vision of inspired optimism, in keeping with the brave liber-
alisms of William James and John Dewey, and it changed psychotherapy forever.

Long before others were to do so, Meyer railed against both those
followers of Emil Kraepelin who believed that all mental states
were determined by chemistry and those followers of Sigmund
Freud who believed that all mental states were determined by early
experience and spirit and personality. It was apparent to him that
there was truth in both sets of theories, and that much of what the
theoreticians were spinning out was useless. He deplored the chemi-
cal theories as "neurologizing tautology." Of the psychoanalytic
ones, he said, "My common sense does not permit me to subscribe
uncritically to whole systems of theories of what the human being
must be like and should work like." He believed that neither genetics
nor infantile experience was destiny, and he believed that treatment
had to be based on the individual temperament of a specific patient:
each individual was "an experiment in nature."

Meyer melded science and philosophy to achieve an authentic
humanism, quite possibly the first ever known in psychiatry. To his
discernment, we owe our very understanding of ourselves.

ANDREW SOLOMON

Adolf Meyer in his office at Johns Hopkins Hospital. *(The Alan Mason Chesney Medical Archives of The Johns Hopkins Medical Institutions)*

Adolf Meyer, psychiatrist, was born in Niederweningen, Switzerland, near Zürich, the son of Rudolf Meyer, a minister, and Anna Walder. Meyer completed his medical studies at the University of Zürich in 1892, where he studied under August Forel, who worked on hypnotism and advocated complete abstinence from alcohol. That same year Meyer immigrated to the United States.

Meyer's first position in the United States was as pathologist for the Illinois Eastern Hospital for the Insane at Kankakee (1893–1895). Meyer intended to conduct neurological research by performing autopsies on deceased patients in an attempt to correlate brain lesions with diagnostic categories. He soon realized that such correlations could be valuable only when extensive, accurate, and uniform observations had been made of the behavior, symptoms, and course of the illnesses of the patients when they were still alive. At the time, such observations were made only informally and recorded haphazardly if at all. To change this situation, Meyer educated the staff in the principles of neurology and psychiatry, observation, history taking, and record keeping. As a consequence, Meyer himself became more interested in observing individual mental patients rather than in postmortem brain studies, which did not yield particularly interesting results. Meyer's contacts with Chicago's Hull-House (in particular Julia Lathrop) and John Dewey at the University of Chicago, whose psychological functionalism Meyer found inspiring, reinforced this change of interest.

Subsequently, Meyer was appointed pathologist at the Massachusetts State Lunatic Hospital at Worcester (1895–1901). In this capacity Meyer implemented the ideas he had developed at Kankakee. He emphasized the necessity of integrating patient care and scientific research—no longer merely neurological in character but based on the observation of patients and on their life histories as they were collected through their own accounts and those of their friends and relatives. These ideals required improved methods of record keeping and extensive training for the staff. By integrating research and treatment, Meyer hoped to raise the level of care for mental patients. While at Worcester, Meyer lectured to psychology students at Clark University, who regularly came to the wards for observation. He also maintained contact with neurologists and psychologists in Boston, among them William James and James Jackson Putnam, who were particularly interested in psychotherapy.

In 1902 Meyer married Mary Potter Brooks, a psychiatric social worker; the couple had one daughter. That same year he was appointed director of the Pathological Institute of the New York State Hospitals for the Insane (1902–1909). He transformed the institute from a center for neurological research into a center for coordinating research and training in New York State mental hospitals. The institute offered training, consultation, and continuing education in trends in psychiatric research to all physicians in the state's employ. Meyer introduced standardized methods of record keeping for all

New York State mental hospitals, which made it possible to draw up statewide statistics and to conduct research in psychiatric epidemiology. During his tenure at the New York Pathological Institute, Meyer opened an outpatient clinic to assist former mental patients' transition back to the community and to counsel individuals before commitment to a mental hospital was warranted. Meyer promoted outpatient clinics as the centers of preventative work in psychiatry. In 1904 he was appointed professor of clinical medicine at Cornell University Medical College. Meyer renewed his acquaintance with John Dewey after the latter moved to Columbia University Teachers College and maintained close social contacts with the historian James Harvey Robinson.

During his tenure at the New York State Pathological Institute, Meyer articulated his dynamic psychiatry or psychobiology as a framework and method for studying the life histories of individual patients. Meyer's approach was holistic, pluralistic, and pragmatic; it was inspired by the pragmatism of Charles S. Peirce and William James and the functionalism of John Dewey. Meyer replaced the then-pervasive neurological approach of correlating psychiatric diagnoses with brain lesions with an emphasis on the study of the individual's life history from an evolutionary perspective. According to Meyer, mental problems or maladjustment occurred when an individual lacked the skills for meeting the particular challenges that were facing him or her. Central in Meyer's work was his conceptualization of schizophrenia (or dementia praecox, as it was called at the time). He explained schizophrenia as a progressive disorganization of an individual's habits, as a mental disorder rather than a mental illness, essentially behavioral in nature. According to Meyer, individuals suffering from dementia praecox had shied away from the challenges of life by daydreaming, rationalization, and inaction, thereby becoming increasingly unable to deal with reality.

In Meyer's approach, centered on the concept of maladjustment, the differences between normal functioning, neuroses, and psychoses were only a matter of degree; they all appeared as more or less serious forms of maladjustment. Meyer developed a psychiatry that considered a wide range of human problems, including life problems, asocial behavior, and mental illness, within its domain. Socially disruptive behavior, such as criminality, homelessness, prostitution, alcoholism, and the like, could easily be subsumed under the concept of maladjustment, thereby providing a seemingly medical label for social ills. Psychiatrists used this conception of maladjustment to enlarge the domain of life problems that warranted their professional intervention.

Meyer strongly doubted the usefulness of the extensive nosological and diagnostic systems then common among European psychiatrists. According to him, a diagnostic label in itself did not improve the condition of patients, nor was such a label very informative. Meyer was opposed to those who exclusively emphasized psychological factors, most notably psychoanalysts. In his perspective, mental, physiological, neurological, and behavioral factors were all relevant; consequently, they all had to be taken into account. In his psychobiology Meyer attempted to integrate all these factors.

His subscription to the ideal of prevention made Meyer participate in the organization of the National Committee for Mental Hygiene, which was founded in 1909 by ex-mental patient Clifford W. Beers. This committee set out to develop initiatives aimed at preventing mental disorders though public health education and the establishment of outpatient clinics. Meyer's psychobiology provided the theoretical framework for the mental hygiene movement, which proceeded to increase the domain of psychiatry beyond the mental hospital by including outpatient work, child guidance clinics, industrial psychiatry, and public health education.

In 1909 Meyer was appointed the first professor in psychiatry at the Johns Hopkins Medical School and director of the

Henry Phipps Psychiatric Clinic; he held both positions until his retirement in 1941. The Henry Phipps Psychiatric Clinic integrated research, treatment, and teaching. The career of a great number of leading American psychiatrists began in the Phipps Clinic under Meyer's tutelage.

Meyer's psychobiology emphasized the significance of environmental factors and life events in the development of mental disorders. From the beginning of his career, Meyer emphasized the importance of integrating the mental hospital with the surrounding community. At Johns Hopkins, he partially realized this ideal. The Phipps Clinic had an outpatient clinic where patients were seen after their discharge and where an investigation of their home and work environment could be made. In addition, the clinic treated conditions that were not severe enough to warrant institutionalization. Meyer stimulated the development of psychiatric social work for these new tasks. Ideally, Meyer proposed, the country would be divided into mental health districts organized around mental institutions. The psychiatrists working there would acquire intimate knowledge of the conditions in their district. By coordinating activities promoting mental health in the community, their efforts would become more effective. Psychiatrists and social workers would make mental health insights available to the population, which would aid in the prevention of mental disorders. The Phipps Clinic succeeded in developing relations with a few neighborhoods in Baltimore where school surveys were undertaken and special classes for mentally retarded pupils were organized. In addition, a Child Guidance Clinic was opened.

Throughout his life Meyer attempted to improve the status of psychiatry within the medical curriculum. He was instrumental in establishing standards for training and certification in the field. When he was appointed to Johns Hopkins, very few medical schools offered courses in psychiatry. To change that situation, Meyer was convinced that more psychiatrists needed to be educated who could then be appointed to medical school faculties. In addition, uniform standards for psychiatrists had to be formulated. In his presidential address to the American Psychiatric Association in 1927, Meyer mentioned these issues. In 1931 the National Committee for Mental Hygiene established a Division of Psychiatric Education in order to survey the quality of psychiatric education in American medical schools and to recommend improvements. Meyer and a student of his, Franklin G. Ebaugh, played a central role in these surveys and the subsequent conferences on psychiatric education. In 1934 the American Board of Psychiatry and Neurology was founded to certify members in both professions; Meyer chaired the organizational meeting.

Meyer's influence on the orientation of American psychiatry has been profound. As a practical matter, though, he exerted a direct influence on the profession mostly through his teaching at Johns Hopkins University. His writings are infrequently consulted because they are notoriously obscure and poorly organized; and his psychobiology was overshadowed by the enormous popularity of psychoanalysis after World War II. Meyer died in Baltimore, Maryland.

H.P.

Lindley Murray

[22 APRIL 1745–16 JANUARY 1826]

*B*y the conservative estimate of his most recent biographer
(Charles Monaghan), Lindley Murray was once a blockbuster
author the likes of which the literary world has never again seen.
From 1800 to 1840, some 15.5 million copies of his literacy books sold
in the United States and Great Britain — at a time when the reading
population was a small fraction of what it is today. The most popular was his English Grammar, for which he earned the moniker
"the father of English grammar."

Murray might have become famous for other extraordinary facts
about his life. He was a major landowner in New York City; in fact,
he owned an estate called "Bellevue," where a famous hospital now
operates. He was a prosperous New York lawyer who, after the
American Revolution, was forced into exile for trading with the
British. (The idea that he left for the milder clime in York was, in
Monaghan's words, a "diplomatic white lie.") He bequeathed a substantial sum of money for an American fund to be used in liberating
slaves, educating them and their descendants, and benefiting American Indians; the fund still operates in New York.

But it was as a grammarian that he achieved notoriety. He eclipsed
Noah Webster, the father of American dictionaries, whose ambitions
originally included writing grammar books. After Murray achieved
unquestioned supremacy, Webster largely shifted from grammar to
lexicography. Meanwhile, without any discernible effect, the pugnacious Webster attacked Murray for literary theft. Other critics of Murray pointed out that his prose was far from exemplary. All these criticisms culminated in the publication of an 1869 diatribe-laden book by
George Washington Moon: The Bad English of Lindley Murray
and Other Writers on the English Language. And in what was
perhaps the most notable quip on Murray's deficiencies, his acquaintance John Dalton once said: "Of all the contrivances invented by

human ingenuity for puzzling the brains of the young, Lindley Murray's grammar was the worst." Murray obviously influenced many later generations of grammarians.

By the twentieth century, Murray had retreated into obscurity. In 1996—at a time when writings signed by Samuel Johnson and Noah Webster fetched tens of thousands of dollars—hardly anyone recognized Murray's name. At a bookshop in London, on Charing Cross Road, I found a five-volume 1819 edition of Johnson's great English dictionary. Inside was Lindley Murray's signature, as well as his handwritten will disposing of his most important books. It was dated March 26, 1825. The bookseller said that this beautifully bound set had been sitting on his display table for a couple of months. Here, collecting dust on a display shelf, was the seminal English grammarian's personally inscribed copy of the seminal work of English lexicography. Never having heard of Lindley Murray, the dealer wanted £395. For that modest sum, I decided, Murray's books could have a home, back in America, where their original owner merits more than passing recognition. The books now have such a home.

BRYAN A. GARNER

Lindley Murray, grammarian and Quaker moralist, was born in Swetara, near Lancaster, Pennsylvania, the son of Mary Lindley and Robert Murray. His father's success as a merchant took the family from North Carolina to New York City. Lindley and his brother, John Murray, Jr., were sent to the Friends School in Philadelphia but were then summoned as apprentices in their father's firm, Murray, Sansom & Co., which became the largest New York shipowners. To assert his independence, Lindley ran away to school, to the Quaker Academy in Burlington, New Jersey. Discovered by his uncle John Murray in New York as he delivered a letter, he was prodigally welcomed back by his father, who arranged for him a private tutor in classical and English literature, as well as law studies, alongside John Jay, under noted law counsellor Benjamin Kissam.

Murray joined a debating society and began import trading on his own. His marriage by a clergyman to Hannah Dobson in 1767 caused his "disownment" as a Quaker until he "acknowledged his fault" three months later before the Meeting.

His father's health took his whole family to England in 1771. On their return Lindley prospered both in law and trade until prevented by the beginning of "the Troubles" (the War of Independence) in 1775. In 1774 he was a member

Frontispiece engraving from the 1827 edition of *Memoirs of the Life and Writings of Lindley Murray. (Collection of Bryan A. Garner)*

of the "Patriot" Committee of Sixty to resist British taxation, and he did not resign when asked to so so by the New York Quakers' "Meeting for Sufferings." When the English army landed, his parents stayed in Manhattan, but Lindley retired to a farm at Islip on the Long Island bays, where for four years he produced salt, sailed a boat, and may also have settled black freedmen, until he could return to the city as an importer and lawyer. He was the leader in the setting up of the Friends Seminary in New York and in choosing its headmasters. He felt ready to retire in 1783 to the estate he then bought at Bellevue on the East River, later used by Quaker-led committees on which he served as a Refuge for Juvenile Delinquents and as a New York city hospital.

Before settling at Bellevue he had the first severe attack of a lifelong neurological illness, perhaps myasthenia gravis. When local trips to cooler resorts did not lead to permanent cure, he decided to move with his wife in 1784 to York, England. Two miles away they found a large house, where with only three servants he lived with resolute cheerfulness and piety, as an increasingly helpless invalid for the final forty years of his life. During this period he was eagerly visited by children and scientists such as Benjamin Silliman of Yale and the Quaker John Griscom. Ingenious gadgetry freed him to write, eat, visit, and oversee his famous botanical garden in the years when he could no longer stand. His first book, *The Power of Religion on the Mind, in Retirement, Affliction and the Approach of Death* (1787), reflected his experience by using examples from other men's lives and was given free to fellow citizens of York and by his will to Quaker youth of New York through the Lindley Murray Fund.

The Friends who welcomed the Murrays to York were William and Esther Tuke, whom Murray helped to design and support the first modern mental hospital, The Retreat, which he also persuaded the New York Friends to copy. Murray's second book was *Some Account of the Life and Labours of Sarah [Tuke] Grubb* (1792), the story of a woman who founded a school in Ireland modeled on Esther Tuke's Quaker girls' school at York (later called the Mount). Three teachers there, Ann and Mabel Tuke and Martha Fletcher, came out for long evenings to the Murrays' house to ask how to teach English grammar. The outcome was a third book, *English Grammar, Adapted to the Different Classes of Learners* (1795), which used varied fonts and an appendix to separate lessons and rules for children and principles for their teachers. The popularity of this book led to subsequent new editions.

Murray followed this book with several others, including *English Exercises* and *A Key to the Exercises* (1797), *Abridgement of the English Grammar* (only the children's text, 1797), *English Reader (1799)*, Sequel (1800), and *Introduction to the English Reader* (1801). He went on to publish *English Spelling Book* (1804) and *First Book for Children* (1805), as well as French textbooks for English students, *Lecteur François* and *Introduction au Lecteur François* (1802). Printed with good typefonts (Abraham Lincoln read his *Reader* by firelight) on good paper in leatherbound volumes of 100 to 300 pages (though a revised *English Grammar* ran to two volumes), these books became enormously popular.

The books were first published in York and London (where Darton & Harvey arranged the copyrights), and the Murrays oversaw the printing of American editions by the Quaker printers Isaac Collins in New York and the Johnsons in Philadelphia. Each press reprinted them in annual editions of 10,000, making no effort to stop other printers from "pirating": Harvard Library's roster of 123 editions of the *Abridgement* includes only one of the 132 British or Quaker editions but includes the eighth Baltimore edition, the fifth from Canandaigua, four from Worcester, three from Pittsburgh, the third from Hallowell, Maine, sixteen editions from nine towns in New Hampshire and Vermont, and twenty-four from Boston. His secretary Elizabeth Frank thought a million copies of the *Grammar* were sold. Murray himself was content with receiving fees of £100 to £700 from the printer for all editions of each book, giving the money to Quaker schools and charities, while his brother John handled his investments.

Murray died in York. He made no claims of originality as a grammarian and was told so by outstripped rivals such as Noah Webster. He meant his rules to be memorized, to be understood only by teachers and advanced classes but applied in daily exercises in syntax and parsing sentence structures. Yet his terms were clear and simple (for example, using "noun" for "substantive") and were based on spoken English rather than written Latin. The phrases he quoted to show grammar and his selections for his *Reader*, which were based on his own constant reading, have struck most modern—and many earlier—readers as pedantic, but they appealed for half a century to teachers and parents for their moral tone and style, as well as their examples of virtue and courage.

H.B.

Bronislava Nijinska

[8 JANUARY 1891–21 FEBRUARY 1972]

*B*ronislava Nijinska was one of the premier choreographers of the twentieth century. She and her brother Vaslav Nijinsky were ballet's first two great modernists, but her reputation was occluded by Vaslav's famous story. Also, she did not adapt to emigration as well as other Russian artists: she did not understand Americans, or they her. She was almost deaf by the time she reached the United States, and life (exile, her brother's madness, her son's death) had let her down badly. But her extant works, above all Les Noces (1923), are actually greater than Vaslav's. She should have had a long, glorious career. History is very wasteful.

JOAN ACOCELLA

Bronislava Nijinska, ballet dancer and choreographer, was born in Minsk, Russia, the third child of the Polish dancers Tomasz Nijinski (Russian: Foma Nizhinsky) and Eleonora Bereda. Although Bronislava Nijinska is often identified as the sister of the celebrated Vaslav Nijinsky, she was a major artist in her own right and a key figure in the development of twentieth-century ballet. Most of her work was done in Europe, but she spent more than a third of her life in the United States and obtained citizenship in 1949.

Nijinska made her stage debut when she was just three years old, dancing with her two brothers, Stanislav (born in 1886) and Vaslav (born in 1889), in a Christmas pageant in Nizhni Novgorod. Two years later, the Nijinsky family moved to Saint Petersburg, and soon afterward her parents separated. Seeking to create a stable environment for her children, Eleonora Nijinsky took Vaslav and Bronislava to audition for the Imperial Theater School, the state academy of dance attached to the Maryinsky Theater. They were accepted as ballet students in 1898 and 1900, respectively.

Nijinska's principal teachers at the Imperial School were Enrico Cecchetti, Nikolai Legat, and Michel Fokine. During the summer holidays she was taught by her brother Vaslav, to whom she remained extremely close during her childhood. As his pupil, she became the first person to know and be influenced by his radically new ideas regarding dance and his desire to substitute a rigorously stylized form of movement for the classical ballet tradition. When Nijinska graduated in 1908, she was given the First Award based on her superior marks in both academics and dancing. Like her brother, she was hired as an artist of the Imperial Theaters and was thereby assured a secure and privileged life in Saint Petersburg.

The following year, in the spring of 1909, the Russian impresario Serge Diaghilev assembled a troupe of dancers organized around the Maryinsky's summer recess. In its first Paris season at the Théâtre du Châtelet, the company—in which Nijinsky was a principal dancer and Nijinska a member of the corps de ballet—introduced Russian ballet to the West and a new concept of performance that integrated dance, music, choreography, and visual design. A second Paris season was presented by Diaghilev in 1910. The following year Nijinska submitted her resignation to the Imperial Theaters and with her brother joined Diaghilev as a member of his newly formed Ballets Russes, a permanent touring company whose base of operation was centered in both Paris and Monte Carlo.

Between 1911 and 1913, Nijinska emerged as a strong and talented dancer. It was also during these years that she assisted her brother as he choreographed his first ballets, *L'Après-midi d'un Faune, Jeux,* and *Le Sacre du Printemps.* In 1914 Nijinska helped Vaslav organize a company of his own in London. In spite of their efforts, the debut season of the Saison Nijinsky was canceled after a two-week run at the Palace Theatre.

Shortly after the outbreak of World War I, Nijinska returned to Petrograd (formerly Saint Petersburg) with her first husband, Aleksandr Kochetovsky, whom she had married in 1912, and their daughter Irina. Husband and wife were engaged as leading dancers by the Petrograd Private Opera Theater in 1915. It was in that year as well that Nijinska presented her first choreography—the solos *La Poupée* and *Autumn Song*—at the Narodny Dom Theater. The following year the couple went to Kiev and worked together staging divertissements and ballets at the State Opera Theater, where Kochetovsky had been appointed ballet master.

Beginning in 1917, Nijinska taught at a variety of institutions, including the State Conservatory of Music, the Central State Ballet Studio, the Yiddish Cultural Center Drama Studio, and the Ukrainian Drama School. Just after the October Revolution, she took a brief trip to Moscow, where she began work on a choreographic treatise titled "On Movement and the School of Movement." It is in this essay that she documents her search for a new means of expression based on the extension of the classical vocabulary of dance steps.

After returning to Kiev, Nijinska resumed teaching, and on 10 February 1919, only three weeks after the birth of her son, Léon, she opened a dance studio that she called the Ecole de Mouvement. Under its aegis, she presented a solo concert that included her first plotless ballet compositions—*Mephisto Valse* (1919) and *Twelfth Rhapsody* (1920)—which may well stand as the first abstract ballets in the history of twentieth-century dance.

In mid-1920, after learning of Nijinsky's tragic mental illness, Nijinska determined that she would leave Russia in order to join him in Vienna. In May 1921 she placed an advanced student in charge of her school and undertook a six-week journey to Austria with her mother and two children. While in Vienna, in September 1921, Nijinska was invited by Diaghilev to rejoin the Ballets Russes in London. In addition to dancing with the company and conducting rehearsals, she arranged several new dance sequences for *The Sleeping Princess* and thus began her tenure as the company's first and only female choreographer.

Between 1922 and 1924, Nijinska served as principal dancer, ballet mistress, and choreographer for the Ballets Russes. During this period she choreographed seven major ballets—*Le Mariage d'Aurore, Le Renard, Les Noces* (The Wedding), *Les Tentations de la Bergère, Les Biches, Les Fâcheux*, and *Le Train Bleu*. Among her collaborators were the composers Igor Stravinsky, Francis Poulenc, Georges Auric, and Darius Milhaud, and the visual artists Mikhail Larionov, Natalia Goncharova, Marie Laurencin, Juan Gris, Georges Braque, Henri Laurens, and Pablo Picasso. In addition to demonstrating her versatility as a choreographer, Nijinska performed leading roles in many Ballets Russes productions.

Nijinska and Kochetovsky separated in 1919 and divorced in 1924. That same year she married Nicholas Singaevsky, a former pupil and dancer with Diaghilev's Ballets Russes; they had no children. The next year, owing to disagreements with Diaghilev over her ideas for abstract ballets, Nijinska resigned from the Ballets Russes and formed her own company, the Théâtre Choréographique Nijinska. For this troupe of eleven dancers she created six short ballets—*Holy Etudes, The Sports and Touring Ballet Revue, Savage Jazz, On the Road, Le Guignol Humoresque*, and *A Night on a Bald Mountain*—which were presented during a summer tour of English resorts, with a selection performed afterward in Paris. Nijinska invited the Russian avant-garde painter Alexandra Exter to design the costumes for these ballets.

From her home in Paris, Nijinska continued to work on a variety of projects. She returned briefly to the Ballets Russes in 1926 to choreograph a modern version of *Romeo and Juliet*, with sets and costumes by the surrealist painters Max Ernst and Joan Miró. That same year she was engaged by the Teatro Colón in Buenos Aires as choreographic director and principal dancer, an association that lasted until 1946.

In Paris, in the summer of 1928, Nijinska was invited to organize and direct the Ida Rubinstein Ballet. She created seven new ballets for the company, including *Le Baiser de la Fée*, to music by Stravinsky, and *Boléro* and *La Valse*, both to the music of Maurice Ravel. The Russian stage designer Alexandre Benois created the sets and costumes for all these productions. The Rubinstein Ballet dissolved a year after its founding but was reactivated in 1931 and 1934, with Nijinska's works remaining in its repertory.

During this period, Nijinska also staged dances for the Opéra Russe in Paris as well as for Max Reinhardt in Berlin. In January 1932 she again founded her own company, which she called the Théâtre de la Danse Nijinska, and which proved to be, in size and repertory, her most ambitious undertaking. This thirty-two-member touring company was in existence from 1932 to 1934 and performed choreography by Nijinska in France, Spain, Italy, and Monte Carlo. Her husband served as the company's business manager.

Although an injured Achilles tendon suffered in 1933 precipitated the end of Nijinska's performance career, she continued to gain recognition as a choreographer and teacher. In 1934 she was awarded the medal of the Archives Internationales de la Danse in Paris for twenty-five years of artistic activity. The following year, working as a guest choreographer, Nijinska created *Les Cent Baisers* for Colonel W. de Basil's Ballets Russes de Monte Carlo, and she was invited to the United States to stage the dance sequences in Reinhardt's feature film *A Midsummer Night's Dream*. Sadly, it was also during this year that she and her family were involved in an automobile accident in which her son Léon was killed and her daughter Irina critically injured.

During the second half of the 1930s, Nijinska was associated with two companies, the Markova-Dolin Ballet, for which she worked as ballet mistress and choreographer, and the Polish Ballet, for which she served as artistic director and choreographer from 1937 to 1938. For the Polish Ballet she created five new works, including *Chopin Concerto*, an abstract ballet conceived in a neoclassical style. On the basis of her work for the company, Nijinska received the Grand Prix for choreography at the 1937 Exposition Internationale in Paris, and her company received the Grand Prix for performance.

With the outbreak of World War II, Nijinska (under contract to de Basil) left Europe and traveled with her family to the United States. Although she was to have continued on to Australia, the contract allowed her to accept an invitation from Lucia Chase in New York to stage her own version of *La Fille Mal Gardée* for the inaugural season of Ballet Theatre (later renamed American Ballet Theatre). The following year Nijinska settled in Hollywood, where she opened the Bronislava Nijinska–Hollywood Ballet School in 1941.

Throughout the ensuing decade, Nijinska continued to choreograph works for companies in Europe—Sergei Denham's Ballet Russe de Monte Carlo, the Markova-Dolin Ballet, and the Grand Ballet de Monte Carlo. In America she choreographed new productions for Ballet Theatre, Ballet Repertory, Chicago, and Ballet International. Nijinska opened a new studio in Beverly Hills in 1951 where, as before, she frequently left her daughter Irina Nijinska in charge while she fulfilled her choreographic engagements. The studio was closed in 1955 after Nijinska moved to Pacific Palisades, but she continued to teach in nearby Brentwood and Pasadena.

During the last decade of her life, Nijinska began to compose her long-planned memoirs. Her work was interrupted in the 1960s when Sir Frederick Ashton, artistic director of Britain's Royal Ballet, asked her to restage *Les Biches* and *Les Noces*. The revival of these two acknowledged masterpieces assured their survival and the continuance of Nijinska's legacy.

After the death of Nijinska's husband in 1968, her daughter became her mother's full-time associate, accompanying her on all her artistic engagements. Between 1968 and 1972, Nijinska restaged *Les Biches, Les Noces, Brahms Variations, Le Mariage d'Aurore*, and *Chopin Concerto* for ballet companies in the United States and Europe. While working on her memoirs, with contracts to restage her ballets pending, Nijinska died in Pacific Palisades, California.

Bronislava Nijinska's remarkable achievements in the world of dance have yet to be fully acknowledged. As one of twentieth-century ballet's great innovators, she transformed the art form and helped move ballet from the nineteenth-century realm of Romantic ballerinas, costumed as swans and sylphs, into contemporary sensibility. By subtly altering classical ballet steps, she extended the line of the dancer's body and introduced a new kind of athleticism and verve to ballet. In the more than eighty works she created, she revealed an authentic individuality of style, and her repertoire introduced a new classicism that made dance a medium of modern art expression. As the twentieth century drew to a close, the contemporary relevance of Nijinska's work was confirmed by the numerous companies—the Dance Theater of Harlem, the Joffrey Ballet, the Oakland Ballet, and the Paris Opera Ballet, among others—that preserved and performed her choreography.

N.V.B.

Albert Jay Nock

[13 OCTOBER 1870–19 AUGUST 1945]

Albert Jay Nock is insufficiently honored for the stylist he indisputably was. His devotion to the English language was total but also discriminating. There was also his copious memory of just about everything there is to be learned about Rabelais or touched on by the classics. He belongs in Oxford, in all the libraries, at deck level B.

WILLIAM F. BUCKLEY, JR.

Albert Jay Nock, critic and writer, was born in Scranton, Pennsylvania, the son of the Reverend Joseph Albert Nock, an Episcopal minister, and Emma Sheldon Jay. When Nock was ten, he moved with his family to Alpena, a lumbering town in Michigan, where his parents provided books and respect for learning. After the family moved again, to Brooklyn, New York, Nock was educated at home until age fourteen. He then attended a boarding school in Illinois before entering St. Stephen's College (later Bard College) in 1887. Having received his B.A. in 1892, he spent several years studying in graduate school, including Berkeley Divinity School, then located in Middletown, Connecticut. He may have played semiprofessional baseball during these years as well. He did not earn a graduate degree but entered the Episcopal ministry in 1897, a profession he pursued until 1909, working in several parishes in Pennsylvania, Virginia, and Michigan. In 1900 Nock married Agnes Grumbine, a native of Titusville, Pennsylvania, with whom he had two children.

This early, quiet career as a minister ended abruptly in 1909, when Nock left the ministry, his wife, and his children to take up journalism. From 1910 to 1914 he wrote for the muckraker journal *American Magazine*, where he worked with Lincoln

Steffens and John Reed, among others. Nock was also associated with progressive politician Brand Whitlock, mayor of Toledo, whom he persuaded to write an autobiography. During this period Nock, a pacifist, supported Woodrow Wilson's campaign for president. He may have worked in the State Department of this Democratic administration for a time, but when Wilson took the United States into World War I, Nock became disillusioned with politics. This disillusionment was an important milestone in his philosophical development, for never again did he trust politics and politicians. Indeed, Nock became a philosophical anarchist, and his criticism of the politics of his day paved the way for future critiques of collectivism and the state. In 1919 he wrote for a short time for Oswald Garrison Villard's magazine, the *Nation*. He then entered a publishing venture with British single-taxer Francis Neilson, whose wife's inherited fortune paid for the launching of the *Freeman* in 1920.

Nock's lofty, formal writing style, acerbic wit, and cosmopolitan interests soon won him a name as a social critic. The critic's function was to do "Isaiah's Job," preaching publicly, assessing culture with "no account of optimism or pessimism." Those who cared to would stop and listen, while the rest of society would pass the critic by. Nock's views combined libertarian notions of politics and social relations with elitist longings for "civilization" and ranged from commentary on elections to literary criticism to attacks on the materialistic bent of American economics. He agreed with Matthew Arnold, from whom he adopted his ideas about a "remnant" of "civilized" individuals who would somehow keep culture and excellence alive. The remnant would consist of people who were able to transcend the materialism and politics of modern society.

Nock was also an admirer of Thomas Jefferson, whose agrarianism and political philosophy were important parts of his own thought. He was also influenced by Herbert Spencer, and for a time he was a supporter of Henry George's single-tax reforms. His attack on the state was further bolstered by the work of anthropologist Franz Oppenheimer, from which he drew his notions of government as the organized plunder and exploitation of society by the ruling class. Nock's critique of the state was derived, then, from nineteenth-century liberalism, and his individualist-anarchism bridged the years when the philosophy of freedom was at its lowest ebb, making him the link between liberalism and the libertarian/conservative movement of the post–World War II era. He was a noninterventionist in foreign policy, but his cosmopolitanism separated him from the popular image of isolationists as provincial populists. He supported women's rights, wrote reports on the education system, and attacked the idea of progress as an impossible myth. Nock's wide-ranging interests included biography, and he wrote biographies of Jefferson and of François Rabelais, as well as numerous biographical essays. This inclination also led to his own autobiography, *Memoirs of a Superfluous Man*, which was published in 1943 and remains his most influential work.

Throughout his later years Nock became increasingly disillusioned with the world around him but refused to give up his hope that the remnant would find him and heed his jeremiads in time to save civilization from decadence and destruction. Nock died at the home of a friend in Wakefield, Rhode Island. His influence has been recognized by the postwar conservative movement, but his contributions to literary criticism, education, and the genre of the essay have been largely ignored. His broad interests and often quirky intellectual musings make Nock an elusive figure whose true place is among the iconoclasts of American literature, a man with whom it is difficult to agree all of the time but impossible to read without being stimulated to thought.

A.J.F.

Fairfield Porter

[10 JUNE 1907–18 SEPTEMBER 1975]

*F*airfield Porter's was one of the most unusual careers in the American art of his time, for it was a career haunted by a sense of belatedness. The advantages he enjoyed in his early life—an elite education in the best schools, European travel, a family that supported his vocation, and a wide acquaintanceship with men of talent and accomplishment in many fields—had the paradoxical effect of postponing the development of his own artistic gifts. When he first emerged as a painter whose work commanded attention and criticism in the 1950s, he was a generation older than most of the painters he exhibited with at the Tibor de Nagy Gallery in New York and the poets who then formed the principle circle of his admirers. Beyond that circle, he still found himself an odd man out on the art scene as a painter who was too traditional for the modernists and too modern for the traditionalists. It would be another twenty years before he began to receive the critical and public acclaim that were his due. Even as late as the 1970s, a curator at the Whitney Museum of American Art characterized his work as "too tame" to be of interest to the museum. It wasn't until 1984, nearly a decade after his death, that he began to attain the status of an American classic with a retrospective exhibition at the Museum of Fine Arts in Boston, "Fairfield Porter (1907-1975): Realist Painter in an Age of Abstraction." By that time, I had been writing about and praising Porter's paintings for nearly a quarter of a century, mainly in the New York Times. Yet on the occasion of that retrospective, I felt obliged to write as follows: "For a critic it is a very odd experience to praise an artist's work over a long period of time and then discover, as I did in Boston, that I had actually underrated it."

HILTON KRAMER

Fairfield Porter painting outdoors on Great Spruce Head Island in the late 1960s. *(James Schuyler Papers, Mandeville Special Collections Library, UCSD)*

airfield Porter, painter and art critic, was born in Winnetka, Illinois, the son of James Porter and Ruth Furness. His father was an architect who built the family's Greek revival home in suburban Chicago and their summer house on Great Spruce Head Island in Penobscot Bay off the coast of Maine. Porter attended and graduated from the Winnetka public schools. When he was fourteen he went to Europe with his father. At the National Gallery in London he was strongly impressed by the works of Italian Renaissance artists and the paintings of J. M. W. Turner. After a year at Milton Academy he entered Harvard University, where he studied art history and philosophy. During the summer before his senior year, Porter traveled and sketched in France and Germany and concluded his trip with a short visit to the Soviet Union. There he heard Leon Trotsky speak, visited the Shchukin Gallery of Modern Art in Moscow, and took careful visual and verbal note of Russian daily life. The trip was fundamental in shaping Porter's leftist views, which matured during the Great Depression.

Porter graduated with a B.S. in fine art from Harvard in 1928 and immediately moved to New York City. There he began taking courses in figure drawing at the Art Students League under the tutelage of Boardman Robinson and Thomas Hart Benton. On his own he became acquainted with the painter John Marin and the critic Paul Rosenfeld, both members of Alfred Stieglitz's circle. Marin's modernist tendency toward abstraction, while retaining some realistic aspects of the subject, initially influenced Porter. Although he continued to admire Marin's work, Porter began to work in a more representational style. During his next trip to Europe (1931–1932), Porter met the art historian Bernard Berenson at his villa outside of Florence, and the two shared their enthusiasm for the Renaissance masters. Porter also spent time learning from these artists by copying their works at the Uffizi Gallery and the Pitti Palace. On his return to the United States in September 1932, Porter married Anne Channing, a poet he had met while he was an undergraduate. They made their first home in New York City and began a family, which eventually consisted of three sons and a daughter.

Porter came into contact with the Socialist Party when he became friends with Alex Haberstroh, a mural painter whom he knew from the Art Students League. Though never a member of the Socialist or Communist parties, Porter painted antifascist placards for a New York City May Day parade and a mural commissioned by the Queens Borough branch of the Socialist Party entitled *Turn Imperialist War into Civil War* (completed in 1935, present whereabouts unknown). In addition, he taught at the Rebel Arts Center in 1933 and 1934 and wrote art criticism for *Arise*, the center's magazine. His first published essay, "Murals for Workers" (1935), described New York City's public art. From 1936 to 1939 Porter worked in Winnetka and became involved in the political theory and activities of a group that promoted Council Communism, a radical, classless form of socialism. But Porter's inability to follow blindly a party line made him unpopular with the group's more zealous adherents.

Porter returned east in 1939, making his home in Peekskill, New York, and renewed a friendship with the then unknown painter Willem de Kooning, whom he had met in New York City in the early thirties. Over the years the two argued about abstraction versus representation in art. Porter had recently seen an exhibit of works by Edouard Vuillard and Pierre Bonnard at the Art Institute of Chicago, and he remained strongly committed to painting figuratively. He especially admired Vuillard's "firmness and wholeness." Despite their aesthetic differences, Porter wrote an article on de Kooning at the request of Clement Greenberg of the *Partisan Review*, but it was rejected by the journal's other editors.

In 1942 Porter moved back to New York City. During World War II he worked for an industrial designer who did jobs for the U.S. Navy. Much of this work was top secret, but Porter's contribution included designs for naval artillery. At night he studied at the Parsons School of Design with Jacques Maroger (the Louvre's painting restorer before the war) to learn about the oils used by Renaissance painters. What Porter learned encouraged him to switch permanently from tempera to oil paint: "It stays wet and it stays put."

Porter came to maturity as an artist in the late 1940s and early 1950s, when representational painting was not in vogue. He specialized in gentle and carefully arranged landscapes, frequently evocative and lyrical, and at times bordering on the sentimental. He preferred a palette of pastel colors. Most of his outdoor scenes—many of the Maine island he had known since his childhood—reveal a soft interplay of light and shadow. Kenworth Moffett has suggested that for Porter "this light was explored for its own sake and for what it did to color."

Despite his figural orientation, Porter pays tribute to abstract expressionism in his use of a flattened pictorial space and the one color–one shape aspect of the canvas's visual components. As in postimpressionist works by Vuillard, Bonnard, or other early moderns, Porter's images lose their integrity as specific objects on too-close scrutiny. John Ashbery believes that "the more one looks at them, the less the paintings seem celebrations of atmosphere and moments but, rather, strong, contentious, and thorny. He painted his surroundings as they looked, and they happened to look cozy. But the coziness is deceiving. . . . The local color is transparent and porous, letting the dark light of space show through." Porter's realism is painterly—he never suggests that one is looking at anything other than a composition whose raison d'être lies in the formal interplay of shape and color. This structural concern is equally evident in his interior views, still lifes, and, to some extent, his portraits, notably those of his family, Frank O'Hara, Larry Rivers, and Elaine de Kooning.

Porter decided to move to Southampton on Long Island in 1949 in order to be close to New York City and to the ocean. Within a year or so he began to show his paintings on a regular basis at the Tibor de Nagy Gallery in Manhattan. Between 1951 and 1970 Porter had fifteen exhibitions in New York and participated in one-man and group shows. In general Porter's work was warmly received by art critics and fellow artists. He frequented the Cedar Tavern in Greenwich Village, where a group of poets including Kenneth Koch, Frank O'Hara, and John Ashbery read their latest work. Porter also wrote verse and critical pieces about the group as well as about the painters (notably Vuillard) associated with the French poet Stéphane Mallarmé for *Semi-colon*, the group's magazine.

In 1951 Porter began to review gallery shows on a regular basis for *ARTnews*, and in 1959 he became the art critic for the *Nation*. In his weekly column he covered a wide variety of artists, styles, and aesthetic issues in an informed and fair manner. As Rackstraw Downes maintains, "it is hard to find instances of him lapsing into adulation, contrariety, indignation, or contempt. Porter kept a calm head in the face of all the novel trends that were so much the preoccupation of criticism in the fifties and sixties; he kept his eye open for fresh individual talents." Porter was elected to the International Association of Art Critics and was the recipient of a Longview Foundation award for his criticism in 1959.

By the early 1960s Porter had firmly established himself as both an artist and a critic. Of note was a retrospective show at the Cleveland Museum of Art in 1966. His paintings sold well, although his friends claimed that he did not ask enough for them. Porter quipped that higher prices would lead to his having to raise his standard of living. He also began to appear as a guest lecturer at colleges, but he had mixed feelings about teaching, which he expressed in his essay "Art and Knowledge." In 1969–1970 Porter was artist-in-residence at Amherst College, and in 1974–1975 he was associated with the School of Visual Arts in New York City. He received honorary degrees from Colby College (1969) and the Maryland Institute College (1970), as well as an award from the National Academy of Design (1970). Later significant exhibits were held at the Hirschl and Adler Galleries (1974), the Heckscher Museum (1974), and the University of Connecticut (1975). He gave a series of lectures in early 1975 that were reworked as his final critical essay, "Technology and Artistic Perception." Porter died later that year at his home in Southampton.

A.R.

Dawn Powell

[28 NOVEMBER 1896–15 NOVEMBER 1965]

It has not gone unnoticed that the work of Dawn Powell excites far greater interest today than it did during her lifetime. This has often, if not invariably, been attributed to the current vogue for what is often, if not invariably, called irony. I, however, would argue that satire as meticulous, as adroit, as downright prosecutorial as that of Powell's stands little chance of popularity in any era, regardless of its tastes, so long as its author, and more importantly, its victims draw breath.

Although she did indeed have her admirers, their number was limited to something closer to that of a coterie than a public. This, combined with the social nature that is the wit's by definition, and the personal bravery that was apparent in both her life and work, enables Powell's literary achievement to come to us, her present-day readers, nearly intact — ruined neither by success nor by failure.

FRAN LEBOWITZ

D awn Powell, writer, was born in Mount Gilead, Ohio, to Roy K. Powell and Hattie Sherman Powell. (Later in life Dawn Powell insisted that the year of her birth was 1897, and this is the date that appears in most reference works, but her official biographer, Tim Page, has confirmed that 1896 is correct.) Her father, charming but feckless, held a series of jobs in area mills before settling into the life of an itinerant salesman, peddling everything from cookies to coffins, after Dawn and her two sisters were born. Following the death of their mother in 1903, the children were cared for by various relatives in villages and farms in the region. When Roy Powell eventually remarried six years later, the children joined him at his new wife's farm near Cleveland. But the life they found there was no better: the second Mrs. Powell proved to be a stereotypically mean step-mother, punishing them severely and subjecting them to endless humiliation. She was especially scornful of Dawn's attempts to write poems and short stories, burning every piece of writing that the child produced.

After more than a year of enduring the situation, Dawn Powell ran away to an aunt's house in Shelby, Ohio, where she was able to attend high school. Her aunt, who worked as a buyer for a major

Publicity photo of Dawn Powell in the 1940s. (*Library of Congress*)

department store in Cleveland and had sophisticated tastes, recognized that Dawn was a thoughtful, gifted child and encouraged her interest in books and writing. With the help of her aunt, Dawn Powell entered Lake Erie College upon graduation from high school in 1914. There she was active in dramatics, edited the college magazine, and earned a bachelor's degree in literature in 1918. She immediately joined the naval reserve as a yeomanette, but after only a few months of service she decided to move to New York City to pursue a writing career, again with the encouragement of her aunt.

In New York Powell found work as a publicist for several organizations, including the Inter-Church World Movement. There she met an advertising executive named Joseph R. Gousha, and the couple were married in 1920. They settled in Greenwich Village, where Dawn Powell would live for the rest of her life, and had one son, born in 1921. The son, who may have suffered brain damage at birth, was exhibiting severe emotional problems by the age of three. Powell and her husband cared for him themselves, educating him at home, until it became impossible for Powell to handle the situation; he was ultimately institutionalized as an adult.

Powell's marriage had enabled her to quit her job as a publicist and devote herself to her own writing, and despite the upheaval caused first by her son's condition and then by her husband's alcoholism, she began to produce fiction, using the Children's Reading Room of the New York Public Library on Fifth Avenue as the place to write. What became the classic elements of Dawn Powell's work were in evidence from the outset. Her first novel, *Whither*, published in 1925, has the characteristic satiric tone, mordant wit, and unforgiving eye for the foibles of middle-class Americans, whether they lived in the Middle West, the setting for her early work, or were newly arrived midwestern émigrés to the big city of New York desperately seeking sophistication.

Fifteen more novels followed over the next thirty-seven years; her last, published in 1962, was *The Golden Spur*. Considered literary rather than popular novels and published by well-established and eminently respectable houses—Farrar and Rinehart, Scribner's, Houghton Mifflin, Viking—many of them received respectful critical notices. Her last novel even earned a favorable review in the *New Yorker* by the eminent Edmund Wilson, who pronounced her on a par with the British writers Evelyn Waugh, Anthony Powell, and Muriel Spark. None of her books, however, were widely read, and by the time of her death all were out of print. Thus to call her a forgotten writer misses the point: during her lifetime she had never been widely recognized. Though Powell's tart gifts earned her praise from the New York literati, they could never command a readership among most of her contemporaries: she was simply not a writer with whom even the most sophisticated readers could feel entirely comfortable. Her comic but ultimately lethal acerbity was simply too off-putting in the early and middle decades of the twentieth century. As the century drew to a close, with irony the watchword of its final decade, it was perhaps not surprising that Dawn Powell began to be discovered and applauded on a larger stage.

Powell seemed to be unhindered by her failure and by her family difficulties. She saw herself as a latter-day Petronius, the scathingly witty Roman writer, and the body of her work as a modern equivalent of his *Satyricon*. Though she suffered through periods of suicidal despair, she possessed a seemingly heroic ability to enjoy life despite its vicissitudes. She had a wide circle of friends and admirers, as well as a longtime lover, and when none of them were around she found diverse interests to keep her occupied, including jazz and modern music, and retained an appealing ability to see the quirky humor in almost every human undertaking. She was also a fan of radio crime dramas. In addition to her novels, she wrote ten plays, only one of which was published, and as many as a hundred short stories, a small collection of which was published as *Sunday, Monday and Always* in 1952.

Powell's health had begun to fail by the late 1950s, and not long after her husband's death in 1962 she was diagnosed with cancer. She was in and out of hospitals in Manhattan before finally succumbing to the illness. Her body was willed to the Cornell Medical Center, but a series of mixups prevented its return to her family in Ohio for final burial. Five years after her death, she was finally interred—in the New York City Cemetery on Hart Island, the final resting place of the city's unwanted and unclaimed dead. It was an ironic end that Powell herself would undoubtedly have appreciated.

The slow "resurrection" of Dawn Powell began in the fall of 1987, with the publication of a long, appreciative essay by Gore Vidal in the *New York Review of Books* and the subsequent reprinting over the next few years of four of her major novels: *The Golden Spur; Angels on Toast*, originally published in 1940; *The Locusts Have No King*, which first appeared in 1948; and *The Wicked Pavilion*, first published in 1954. All are quintessential Powell, peopled with comic New Yorker wannabes looking for both a fast buck and social cachet and animated by ultimately heartbreaking delusions. During the 1990s nearly all of her novels came back into print in paperback form, and their widespread distribution, together with their inclusion on many college reading lists, and the publication of her diaries and letters and a major biography seemed to guarantee an enduring recognition and readership denied to Powell during her lifetime.

A.T.K.

Gisela Richter

[14 AUGUST 1882–24 DECEMBER 1972]

Gisela Richter has inspired me since I first encountered her work on Greek sculpture in college. Like Jane Harrison, the pioneering British classical anthropologist, Richter belonged to a fertile period when enterprising women of great distinction accepted and honored the highest scholarly standards of male tradition.

I admire Richter for her clarity and rigor of mind; her fineness of sensibility and connoisseurship; her attention to detail and her power of observation and deduction; her mastery of form and design.

She revered art and viewed herself as its custodian and transmitter to a wider public. She did not strike sanctimonious political poses about art or interpose gimmicky jargon between viewer and object. If academe is ever to revive, we need to recover Richter's noble ideal of profound erudition, whose lineage extended from nineteenth-century German philology to ancient Alexandria.

CAMILLE PAGLIA

Gisela Marie Augusta Richter, classical archaeologist and art historian, was born in London, England, the daughter of Jean Paul Richter, a historian of Italian Renaissance art, and Louise Schwab, a novelist, translator, and historian of Italian Renaissance art. Gisela's sister Irma, an artist and also a historian of Italian Renaissance art, worked closely with her, teaching her to see like an artist and to understand the value of the "practical side" of art, as Richter called it. Richter later studied pottery with Maude Robinson and learned the techniques of marble carving and bronze casting. This knowledge was invaluable to her in purchasing antiquities and writing her published works. Although their background was German, the members of the family were cosmopolitan and multilingual. They traveled frequently in continental Europe, with lengthy stays in Italy.

Richter's father became associated with the Italian art historian Giovanni Morelli in 1876 and introduced the young American art historian Bernard Berenson to him in 1890. Morelli's approach to connoisseurship, especially his concentration on artists' depiction of anatomical details, had a profound impact on Jean Paul Richter and through him on Gisela Richter's approach to Greek and Roman art history. Examination of the object was primary to Richter. She grouped objects stylistically and then dated the groups chronologically, using both external and internal criteria, including comparisons of sculpture to vase painting and anatomical accuracy.

The Richter family lived in both Rome and Florence, but also traveled a great deal, before they moved back to London in 1892. Richter's education was at Maida Vale School, one of the finest for women at the time. She later recalled, however, that it was her attendance at Emmanuel Loewy's lectures at the University of Rome around 1896 that convinced her to become a classical archaeologist. In 1901 Richter entered Girton College, Cambridge University. Her don there was Katherine Jex-Blake, a prominent classicist and a cotranslator of Pliny the Elder's chapters on the history of art. In 1904 Richter left Cambridge, where as a woman she was ineligible for a degree, to study at the British School in Athens. Although Richter was not allowed to live at the school, she was befriended by its director, Charles Bosanquet, who encouraged her to publish her first article, which appeared in the *Annual of the British School at Athens* (1904–1905). During 1905 Richter traveled in the Peloponnese, Attica, Euboea, and the Greek islands, as well as to Constantinople, Pergamon, Priene, and Mytilene in the Ottoman Empire. However, Richter's most important visit was to the island of Crete. There she met Harriet Boyd, the first woman to direct an archaeological excavation, Gournia. Illness prevented Richter from seeing much of Crete; she saw much of Boyd, though, and the two became lifelong friends. After a vacation with the Richter family, Boyd persuaded Richter to come to the United States, and the two women landed in Boston in 1905. Richter's first attempts to find employment were unsuccessful, but she did meet Edward Robinson, director of the Museum of Fine Arts, Boston. When he moved to become vice director of the Metropolitan Museum of Art in New York, Robinson invited Richter to catalog a newly purchased collection of Greek vases. In 1906 Richter agreed to become a permanent member of the Metropolitan's staff, negotiating three months off each summer to travel to Europe, not only to see family but also to immerse herself in the great collections and make valuable contacts with colleagues.

The years 1906–1928 were heady ones for the Metropolitan, as Robinson and his agent, John Marshall, vastly increased the museum's holdings in Greek and Roman art. Richter was promoted to assistant curator in 1910, and in 1911 her rich flood of publications, inspired by the Metropolitan's classical collection, began. In 1917 Richter became an American citizen, and in 1921 she founded the American Archaeological Club with several friends. Richter's willingness to share her knowledge with others throughout her career was an important reason for her success in keeping abreast of the latest developments in scholarship. Although Richter held only one teaching position, the Annual Professorship at the American School of Classical Studies in Athens (1961), her help to student colleagues was invaluable. She also contributed generously to the financial support of archaeological expeditions.

Richter's rise at the Metropolitan was steady. In 1922 she was promoted to associate curator and then in 1925 to curator, the first woman to hold that high a rank. She arranged for the acquisitions of many masterpieces, among which the Kleitias stand and Lydos krater (1931), the Metropolitan kouros and the Landsdowne Amazon (1932), a Roman portrait of Caracalla (1941), and a Hellenistic Sleeping Eros (1943) particularly stand out. Richter's range of publications expanded as well. In addition to Greek ceramics, she wrote on Roman glass and portraits; Greek, Roman, and Etruscan engraved gems; furniture; bronzes; and above all, Greek sculpture. She dominated the field of Greek sculpture from 1929, when the first edition of *Sculpture and Sculptors of the Greeks* appeared, until her death.

Richter retired from the Metropolitan in 1948 but remained as honorary curator until 1952, when she fully retired and became curator emerita. In 1952 Richter moved to Rome with her sister Irma. Richter's retirement was remarkably fruitful, allowing her to update existing books and write new ones. Her greatest works come from this period: the second edition of *Attic Red-Figured Vases: A Survey* (1958); *Portraits of the Greeks* (3 vols., 1965–1972); the second edition of *Furniture of the Greeks, Etruscans and Romans* (1966); *Korai* (1968); *The Engraved Gems of the Greeks, Etruscans and Romans* (2 vols., 1968–1971); the third edition of *Kouroi* (1970); *Perspective in Greek and Roman Art* (1970); the fourth edition of *Sculpture and Sculptors of the Greeks* (1970); and the posthumous seventh edition of *A Handbook of Greek Art* (1974). Richter received numerous honors over the course of her career, including the AAUW Achievement Award (1944), the American Academy Medal (1955), the Isabella d'Este Award (1965), and the Archaeological Institute of America's gold medal for distinguished archaeological achievement (1968). She died in Rome, never having married.

Richter's descriptions of works are detailed yet concise. She seldom hypothesized. Her categories are so convincing that readers forget that some subsequently discovered works may not fit into her groupings. Her works of synthesis, such as *Sculpture and Sculptors of the Greeks*, depend on the compilation of references from classical texts and reject unprovable attributions based on Roman copies. Richter did not try to relate Greek art to external factors such as history, literature, or philosophy. She saw Roman art through Greek eyes. However, Richter's contributions to the study of Greek art, especially sculpture, are basic for all subsequent scholarship in that field. Her writings and their collections of photographs are fundamental tools in art history.

J.S.C.

Bayard Rustin

[17 MARCH 1912–24 AUGUST 1987]

I met Bayard Rustin and his life-partner when Rustin agreed to speak at a rally protesting the U.S. Supreme Court's 5–4 ruling that gay people could be arrested in their own bedrooms for consensual sex. A gay African American, Rustin was the organizer of America's pivotal civil rights gathering, the historic March on Washington forever associated with Dr. King's "I have a dream" speech. Yet, ironically, the tactician who shaped the public presentation of the civil rights movement in many of its most dramatic moments had spent most of his years agreeing to hide his own sexual identity, rather than handing gay-baiting opponents a weapon against the movement. By 1986, the year before he died, Rustin would no longer capitulate to the closet, choosing instead to place himself on the frontlines of yet another civil rights struggle.

Rustin, too, dreamed of an America that kept its promise of inclusion, equality, and enlarged possibilities for all. He brought to that dream brilliant practical skills and a lifelong commitment to talking and working with people who were different from himself. His selfless and tireless work for equality, despite his experience of dual discrimination, shaped the thinking of many of his colleagues. As an openly gay man, Rustin came to acknowledge his personal stake in the civil right to be both equal and different; so civil rights heroes such as Congressman John Lewis and Coretta Scott King have become outspoken champions of gay people's freedom to marry. Their awareness of the connectedness of all civil rights movements and commitment to full equality for lesbians and gay men fulfill the belief Bayard Rustin shared with Dr. King that "injustice anywhere is a threat to justice anywhere."

EVAN WOLFSON

Bayard Rustin speaking at a civil rights rally in 1965. *(Library of Congress)*

Bayard Rustin, civil rights leader and political activist, was born in West Chester, Pennsylvania, the illegitimate son of an immigrant from the British West Indies. Raised by his maternal grandparents (his grandfather was a caterer), Rustin was educated in the local public schools. He first experienced racial discrimination as a member of his high school football team when he was denied service at a restaurant in Media, Pennsylvania. After high school, he worked at odd jobs, traveled widely, and studied at Wilberforce University in Ohio, Cheney State Teachers College in Pennsylvania, and the City College of New York, never earning a formal degree.

As a young man, Rustin joined the Young Communist League, believing at the time that Communists "seemed the only people who had civil rights at heart." As a Quaker and pacifist, however, his beliefs conflicted with party policy. When Communists demanded U.S. participation in World War II in June 1941 after the German invasion of Russia, Rustin broke with the party. Thereafter he devoted himself to the antiwar and civil rights movements. In 1941 he became field secretary for the Congress of Racial Equality (CORE) and race relations director for the Fellowship of Reconciliation, a nondenominational group founded by the radical pacifist Abraham J. Muste to promote the nonviolent resolution of world problems.

Rustin was soon allied with A. Philip Randolph, president of the Brotherhood of Sleeping Car Porters and an advocate of civil rights for African Americans. Rustin organized young people to participate in Randolph's 1941 March on Washington Movement, an effort to pressure President Franklin D. Roosevelt to ban racial discrimination in employment. When Randolph postponed the scheduled mass protest march because the president established a Fair Employment Practices Committee, Rustin accused the civil rights leader of compromising his principles.

Rustin paid dearly for maintaining his own principles, serving twenty-eight months in a federal prison for refusing to register for the draft. After the war, he continued to promote pacifism and civil rights. In 1947 he participated in the first "freedom ride" (the Journey of Reconciliation) sponsored by CORE, an effort to desegregate interstate bus travel. As a result, a court in North Carolina convicted Rustin of violating the state's Jim Crow laws and sentenced him to labor on a prison chain gang. He also served as executive director of the War Resisters League (1953–1955), an indication of his hesitancy to devote himself solely to civil rights. By the early 1950s, however, Rustin drew closer to Randolph and other African-American civil rights advocates.

Although Rustin remained committed to the use of nonviolent civil disobedience, he increasingly stressed the need for African Americans to build alliances with white reformers, especially with progressive elements in the labor movement. As the civil rights movement intensified in the late 1950s, the importance of Rustin's role heightened. Randolph sent him to

Montgomery, Alabama, in 1955 to aid Martin Luther King, Jr., in organizing a boycott against the city's segregated buses. For the next five years, Rustin worked closely with King, tutoring him in how to organize mass nonviolent demonstrations and also in the importance of building alliances with progressive white reformers. Rustin favored an interracial coalition of poor people because he believed that the achievement of civil rights alone would not lift the mass of African Americans from poverty. Yet until segregation collapsed, he concentrated on the struggle for civil rights. In 1960 Rustin organized civil rights protests at both the Republican and Democratic national conventions. Later he organized the most massive and effective civil rights demonstration in history—the August 1963 March on Washington. More than 250,000 people gathered at the nation's capital to endorse civil rights legislation and to listen to Martin Luther King's "I Have a Dream" speech. The march illustrated Rustin's commitment "to build, through means that are democratic and nonviolent, a just society . . . in which men of all races . . . need not fear each other." In 1964 Rustin organized an equally successful one-day boycott of the New York City public schools in order to speed the process of integration.

The Civil Rights Act of 1964 and the Voting Rights Act of 1965 ended one phase of Rustin's career. Success split the civil rights movement. One element, consisting mostly of younger African Americans, gloried in "black power" and suggested that violent action might be necessary. Rustin insisted that civil disobedience had not failed and that the time had arrived to move from protest to politics. He argued in 1965 that since civil rights legislation had failed to end poverty for African Americans, the movement should turn to coalition politics and join with trade unionists and white liberals to erect a more generous welfare state. Rustin's refusal to endorse "black power" and to reject white political allies caused militant African Americans to condemn him as an "oreo," a black cracker with a white filling. In response, Rustin drew closer to his white allies. During the 1968 New York City teachers' strike, he supported the cause of the United Federation of Teachers against the demands of African-American militants who sought community control of the schools. Rustin forged firm links with the American Federation of Labor and Congress of Industrial Organizations and with the Jewish-American community. Because of his support for the state of Israel and his commitment to multiracialism, Rustin was honored by the American Jewish Committee in 1978 for "illustrious leadership in the cause of racial justice, world peace and human understanding."

From 1964 until his death, Rustin served as executive director of the A. Philip Randolph Institute, which sought to amalgamate the civil rights and labor movements. Only by working with labor, liberal, religious, and reformist business groups, Rustin asserted, could African Americans achieve improved economic and social conditions. Rustin wrote a series of books and pamphlets in defense of a multiracial civil rights movement and a social democratic welfare state, including *Black Studies: Myths and Realities* (1969), *Down the Line* (1971), and *Strategies for Freedom: The Changing Patterns of Black Protest* (1976). Only a few months before his death, Rustin admitted publicly in an interview published in the *Village Voice* that he was a homosexual. He had previously hidden his sexual orientation because public knowledge of it as well as his youthful communism might have ended his influence as a reformer. Rustin died in New York City.

Rustin was a leading exemplar of the African American–Jewish American, civil rights movement–labor movement coalition that did so much to demolish segregation and to build the American welfare state. Moreover, he used nonviolent civil disobedience to mount extremely effective multiracial mass protests.

M.D.

Sequoyah
[1770?–AUGUST 1843?]

Sequoyah, although lacking a formal education, endowed his nation, the Cherokees, with an eighty-six-character alphabet that allowed an entire people to become literate and record their history and culture in a way more lasting than the oral tradition. The only individual, working alone, ever to invent and perfect an entire syllabary, one successfully adopted by a whole society, Sequoyah is so invisible today few people know that the largest tree in North America bears his name (in a variant spelling).

WILLIAM LEAST HEAT-MOON

Sequoyah, inventor of the Cherokee syllabary, was born in the Cherokee town of Tuskegee in present-day eastern Tennessee, of uncertain parentage. He married Sally (maiden name unknown) in 1815, and they had four children. According to Emmet Starr's *History of the Cherokee Indians* (1921), Sequoyah also married U-ti-yu at an unknown date; they had three children. Sometimes referred to as George Guess, or Gist, he was a silversmith by trade, but he had been a warrior. During the Creek War (1813–1814), he enlisted in Colonel Gideon Morgan's Cherokee regiment and served three months.

Accounts of the inspiration for committing Cherokee to writing vary, but Sequoyah revealed to Samuel Lorenzo Knapp in 1827 that his interest stemmed from the capture of a white soldier in a late-eighteenth-century campaign. His war party discovered a letter in the soldier's possession, and the warriors debated "whether this mysterious power *of the talking leaf* was the gift of the Great Spirit to the white man, or the discovery of the white man himself." According to Knapp's account of the conversation, published in his *Lectures on American Literature*

SE - QUO - YAH

A lithograph of Sequoyah holding a copy of the Cherokee alphabet, 1836. *(Library of Congress)*

(1827), "Most of his companions were of the former opinion, while [he] as strenuously maintained the latter." He then decided to develop a system for writing the Cherokee language. After many years of work, Sequoyah finally created a symbol for each syllable, and in 1821 he unveiled a syllabary of eighty-six characters (later reduced to eighty-five), which reportedly could be mastered by a Cherokee speaker in several days.

At the time Sequoyah introduced his syllabary, he was living in Arkansas rather than in his native Southeast. Cherokees had acquired land in Arkansas in the early nineteenth century, and following land cessions in 1808–1810 and 1817–1819, several thousand Cherokees had moved west. A signatory to an unpopular land cession in 1816, Sequoyah had moved west in 1818. He returned east, however, soon after his invention and introduced his syllabary to Cherokees still living there. The Sequoyah syllabary became an immediate success, particularly among Cherokees who had no knowledge of English and little exposure to Anglo-American "civilization." The highly acculturated leaders of the Cherokee nation, the political entity in the Southeast of which three-fourths of the Cherokees were citizens, seem to have known little about the grassroots movement toward literacy. As Cherokee Elias Boudinot recalled in an article in *American Annals of Education* (1 Apr. 1832), by the time they learned of the invention, "the Cherokees had *actually* become a reading people." By 1835 approximately half of the households in the Cherokee nation had members literate in Cherokee.

Rejecting a rival system for writing Cherokee developed by a white philologist, John Pickering, the Cherokee nation embraced the Sequoyah syllabary and incorporated it into the Cherokee renascence of the 1820s. In 1824 the national council voted to honor Sequoyah with a silver medal. The nation also decided to purchase a printing press and types in Latin letters and the Sequoyah syllabary, and in 1828 the *Cherokee Phoenix*, a weekly bilingual newspaper with a circulation of about 200 copies, began publication. Missionaries and Christian Cherokees began to translate hymns and the New Testament into Cherokee. In the West, the Arkansas Cherokee signed a treaty in 1828 that provided for their removal to what is today northeastern Oklahoma. The treaty promised Sequoyah $500 as a reward for his achievement and the western Cherokees $1,000 for a press. The federal government fulfilled neither promise to the western Cherokees, and soon it even cut short the Cherokee renascence in the Southeast.

At the insistence of southern states, particularly Georgia, the United States began to pressure the Cherokee nation to move west. Ultimately, an unauthorized minority of Cherokees agreed to a removal treaty, which the U.S. Senate ratified in 1836. By 1839 the dispossessed Cherokees from the East had arrived west of the Mississippi, where they outnumbered their well-established kinsmen, who included Sequoyah. A struggle for power that verged on civil war erupted. Sequoyah broke with his fellow western Cherokees (or "Old Settlers"), who wanted to impose their government on the far more numerous newcomers, and appealed to the Cherokees for a new government that encompassed all. In a letter reprinted in Grant Foreman's *Sequoyah*, he encouraged the Cherokees to "talk matters over like friends and brothers." His influence helped make possible a compromise that most Cherokees accepted.

In his new role as national conciliator, Sequoyah decided in 1842 to find a group of Cherokees who, according to unsubstantiated reports, were living in Mexico. He died without having located any Cherokee expatriates. The exact place of his death is unknown.

Sequoyah's syllabary remains a source of pride for Cherokees and a medium of cultural preservation. Albert L. Wahrhaftig's survey of four Oklahoma Cherokee communities in 1964–1965 revealed that 36 to 65 percent of adults were literate in Cherokee. Some Cherokees used the syllabary for personal correspondence and gained information through publications in the syllabary, but writing proved most useful in a religious context. While the desire to read the Bible in their own language inspired many Cherokees to learn the Sequoyah syllabary, a writing system also enabled Cherokee medicine men to record their formulas and preserve an ancient religious tradition. These medicine men probably employed writing in such a sacred task because they perceived Sequoyah's accomplishment as mystical rather than mechanical. Whatever the reason, this particular use of the syllabary as well as its continuing viability elevates Sequoyah's invention above mere antiquarian interest to major historical significance.

T.P.

Joseph Smith

[23 DECEMBER 1805–27 JUNE 1844]

If one is not a Mormon believer, then Joseph Smith's success has to be attributed to his extraordinary human qualities. An autodidact and inspired personality, Smith emanated a human force and spiritual intensity that converted and kept loyal to him such extraordinary persons as Brigham Young and Parley Pratt. The mystery of his charisma was and is an enduring fact. Even his own people, he insisted, did not know him, and it is still difficult to apprehend how so much energy of being inhabited a single personality.

Joseph Smith was at once a characteristic American God-seeker of his age and a throwback to the Gnostic and Hermetic visionaries. No other religious imagination of the nineteenth century was as comprehensive and daring as Smith's. Out of Nauvoo came such audacious doctrines as Celestial (plural) Marriage, a new kind of polytheism, and an evolutionary Godhead. Smith contained multitudes: he was as cannily pragmatic as he was visionary, and was both kind and ruthless. A lover of thought and women, Smith's most unique endowment (among American religious founders) was his exuberant good humor and highly developed comic sense.

HAROLD BLOOM

Joseph Smith, founder of the Church of Jesus Christ of Latter-day Saints, known as the Mormon Church, was born in Sharon, Windsor County, Vermont, the son of Joseph Smith, Sr., and Lucy Mack, farmers. Joseph Smith was notable among religious figures for claiming to receive revelations and to translate ancient religious texts. Mormons consider these writings, published as the Doctrine and Covenants and the Book of Mormon, as scripture on a par with the Bible and think of Smith as a prophet in the biblical tradition.

An engraving of Joseph Smith (right) with his brother Hyrum. *(Utah State Historical Society)*

Smith did not consider himself to be either a reformer or the founder of a new religion. In his own eyes, he was restoring the Christian gospel as taught by Jesus and the first apostles. Nothing in Joseph Smith's background prepared him to write scriptures or to head a religious movement. His parents were poor New England farmers who began life with a farm in Tunbridge, Vermont, but lost it in 1803 after a commercial venture failed. When Joseph Smith, Jr., was born two years later, the Smith family lived on a farm rented from a relative. In 1816 they migrated to Palmyra, New York, and in 1818 purchased 100 acres in Farmington (later Manchester) a few miles south of Palmyra village. For the first time in fourteen years they owned land of their own.

Lucy and Joseph Smith, Sr., had drifted to the margins of New England Congregationalism by the time they married in 1796. She was deeply religious but went unbaptized until adulthood, rarely attending meetings. Joseph, Sr., was suspicious of the clergy and of professing Christians. When Lucy joined the Presbyterian Church around 1819, Joseph, Sr., refused to attend. His dreams, recorded in detail by his wife, revealed a yearning for redemption and a frustration at not finding it. Along with his neighbors he searched for buried treasure, a common practice among poor New Englanders at that time. These ventures often blended quests for religious enlightenment with the exercise of magical power. He was seeking something that he could not find. Joseph Smith, Jr., was heir to the yearnings and uncertainties of his parents. He was troubled by the inability of his family to agree on a church when evangelical preaching seemed to demand a decision. At age fourteen, according to his account, he prayed to know which church was right. Two beings of indescribable "brightness and glory" appeared to him, introducing themselves as the Father and the Son. Smith said they forgave his sins and told him to join none of the churches because none of them was right. Latter-day Saints now speak of this event as the First Vision, but at the time it made little impression on the people around Smith, who easily dismissed the visions of a young boy. Ministers, believing that revelation ended with the Bible, disparaged his story and left him to his own devices, more alienated than ever from established Christianity.

From that time to the end of his life, Smith recorded visions and revelations that seemed fabulous to most of his contemporaries but attracted a growing number of believers. In September 1823 he prayed again for direction and received another revelation. According to Smith, an angel who called himself Moroni appeared at his bedside and told him about a record of prophecy from ancient America. Smith was instructed to obtain the record and translate it in preparation for the restoration of Israel and the return of Christ. Moroni, the last of the prophets purported to have written in this record, allegedly said it was engraved on gold plates buried in a hill not far from the Smiths' house. Going there the next day, Smith reportedly found the plates in a stone box and saw Moroni again. The angel told him not to take the plates but to return the next year. For four years Smith went back to the hill on the same day and, according to his account, finally on 22 September 1827 took home the gold plates.

In the interim his ideas about the gold plates underwent a change. He had assisted his father in some treasure-seeking expeditions, among them a search for supposed Spanish treasure near Harmony in northern Pennsylvania. He later reported that on his first trip to see the plates thoughts of their worth crossed his mind, but the angel rebuked him and warned him against the money diggers and thoughts of profit. By the time he obtained the plates in 1827, he had come to focus on their contents and to put aside considerations of their value as gold. While digging for treasure in Harmony, Smith met Emma Hale at the house where he was staying, and an attraction developed between them. She was tall, slender, and dark-haired. He stood over six feet with broad chest and shoulders, light brown hair, and blue eyes. Emma's father was not happy with the match. He had little use for a young man who dug for treasure and claimed to have revelations. Joseph continued to see Emma and married her in 1827 in spite of her father's objections.

For the next two years Smith dictated what he said was a translation of the plates, his words taken down by Emma Hale Smith and then Martin Harris, a prosperous Palmyra farmer, and Oliver Cowdery, a schoolteacher. The Smiths lived in a small house on the Hales' farm in Harmony and later moved to a house in Fayette, New York, belonging to the Whitmer family, who had heard about Smith from Oliver Cowdery. The translation went slowly because of work on the farm and other interruptions until the spring of 1829, when, between April and June, the bulk of the work was accomplished. During the translation Smith permitted no one to see the plates, but in June 1829, according to Harris, Cowdery, and one of the Whitmers, the angel Moroni appeared and showed them the plates, and Smith showed them to eight of his family and close friends. In March 1830 the translation was published as the Book of Mormon.

The undertaking was remarkable in many respects and enough to strain the credulity even of Smith's closest friends. He said the angel provided him with interpreters (Urim and Thummim), "two seer stones set in silver bows" fastened to a "breast plate," to assist him in translation, a claim that scarcely made Smith's account more credible. The entire story could have been dismissed as the fabrication of an overwrought imagination if not for the 5oo pages of printed text that Smith produced. The townspeople considered the book a fraud and refused to buy it. The printer undertook to publish it only because Martin Harris provided financial backing. The book purports to be a scriptural history of the people of ancient America. It was named for the prophet Mormon, who is thought by the Saints to have written the story of his people in the fourth century after Christ. Followers believe that Mormon drew on the records of prophets who had written the history of their own times, beginning with Nephi who migrated to the Western Hemisphere from Jerusalem about 6oo B.C. These prophets taught the Christian gospel and prophesied the coming of Christ to America as well as to Palestine. Mormon wrote that the purpose of the book was to convince its readers that Jesus was Christ and God. The message was especially directed to the remaining descendants of the people in the Book of Mormon, who the Mormons assumed included the American Indians.

Smith collected enough believers by the time the Book of Mormon was published to form a church. On 6 April 183o, at the Whitmers' house in Fayette, he organized the Church of Christ, with himself and Oliver Cowdery as first and second elders. Smith was also given the titles of seer, translator, and prophet. The church set his life on a new course. Until then he had been a young man claiming a divine gift and a mission to translate a book. After 183o he became the prophetic leader of a people.

Smith claimed to lead the church, as he had translated the Book of Mormon, by direct revelation. He received scores of revelations dealing with trivial details of administration and cosmic visions of the life hereafter. Among the first was a command to take the Book of Mormon to the Indian tribes being settled along the frontier in western Missouri. In September and October of 183o four missionaries set out, reaching their destination in midwinter. They preached to the Indians and enjoyed some small success before government agents stopped them, fearing that the presence of Christian preachers would jeopardize the fragile peace with the tribes.

Byproducts of this journey turned out to be even more significant than the mission to the Indians. En route the missionaries stopped in Kirtland, Ohio, and made more converts in a few weeks than Smith had assembled in a year. Smith's claims to restore the authority and spiritual gifts of early Christianity appealed to people confused by competing religious denominations. Some of these new members visited him in New York, and by the end of 1830 Smith received a revelation directing the entire church to move to Ohio. Kirtland was regarded as a temporary location because of another outcome of the Missouri mission. The Book of Mormon had spoken of the construction of a New Jerusalem where all converts were to gather and form a new society called Zion in preparation for the Second Coming of Christ. Revelations had indicated that Zion was to be somewhere in the West, and in the summer of 1831 Smith and other leading figures in the church traveled to Missouri, where he received a revelation designating the exact site for the New Jerusalem near Independence in Jackson County. For the next five or six years church efforts focused on the organization of Zion. While Smith continued to live in Ohio, his ultimate aim was to direct new converts to Missouri where the New Jerusalem was to rise. But the plans for Zion quickly ran into trouble. The people of Jackson County were unhappy at the prospect of Mormons inundating their society and in the fall of 1833 drove them out of the county. The next spring Smith organized a private army called Zion's Camp, which proved to be unsuccessful in its attempt to reinstate his followers on their property. For a few years the Mormons remained in Clay County across the Missouri River from Independence, until the Missouri government agreed to open a new area for them, organized as Caldwell County in north central Missouri. For the time being, church members were required to suspend their hopes for the establishment of Zion at the site of the New Jerusalem.

In Kirtland Smith continued to plan for Zion. He rounded out the organization of the leadership structure, appointing twelve apostles as second in command to himself, sent missionaries throughout the United States and to England, and saw to the construction of a temple in Kirtland, which was dedicated in 1836. Revelations continued to come to him, among them "the Word of Wisdom" cautioning the Mormons (by then known as Latter-day Saints) to avoid tobacco and liquor. He claimed to be visited by ancient prophets, who restored their authority to him, and by Christ himself. Smith also made plans for the Kirtland economy. In Zion property was to be redistributed to people according to their needs, and their surplus each year was to be returned to a common treasury. Although this system had to be abandoned because of the expulsion from Jackson County, Smith had become accustomed to reordering many aspects of ordinary life along religious lines. In Kirtland he organized a bank as part of a broad economic program. Undercapitalization doomed it from the start, and the panic of 1837 sealed its fate. The bank's collapse hurt many of the investors and depositors, and they blamed Smith. The opposition rose to such a pitch that he felt his life was in danger. He and other church leaders fled Kirtland for Missouri in early 1838.

Smith had plans for another temple in Caldwell County at the Mormon settlement of Far West, Missouri, but these ambitions were never realized. Enmity toward the Saints was building once again and broke out in violence at an election in August. The concentration of Mormons in the area had allowed them to dominate voting results, arousing the wrath of other citizens. A bizarre sect could be tolerated in small numbers, but not when it threatened to control all local political offices. In the summer and fall of 1838, pitched battles broke out between the Missourians and the Mormons, claiming lives on both sides. Governor Lilburn Boggs issued an order for the Mormons to leave the state or face extermination. On 31 October 1838 Smith and other leaders were arrested and imprisoned awaiting trial while the Saints fled eastward to Illinois in search of refuge. Languishing in jail for the next five months, Smith had time to contemplate the course of his life to that point. He had always anguished over the state of his own soul; his first prayer for guidance had included a plea to know his standing with God. When traveling he would seek seclusion in the woods to "give vent to all the feelings of my heart in meditation and prayer." In 1839 he was less worried about his sins than about the suffering of himself and his people. Why had God permitted the wicked to separate the Prophet from his people and to drive the Saints from the state? In letters from prison he told his people that their sufferings gave them experience and to remember that Christ had suffered more than any human. The Saints were not to use authority unjustly themselves, but to lead only "by long-suffering, by gentleness and meekness, and by love unfeigned." The Missouri officials allowed Smith to escape his captors in April 1839, and he joined his followers clustered along the banks of the Mississippi near Quincy, Illinois. They were poor, suffering from fever, and uncertain about the future. Ill himself, Smith made efforts to obtain land and eventually arranged for plots at Commerce, Illinois, and across the river in Iowa. From this low point the Mormons began to rebuild their society.

Late in 1839 Smith went to Washington to seek redress from the federal government for the loss of property in Missouri. Denied such redress by President Martin Van Buren, Smith asked the Illinois legislature to charter a new city, to be called Nauvoo, where the Mormons would have control of all the agencies of government. Within the legal walls provided by the charter, he hoped once more to erect a Zion. From Nauvoo Smith launched a renewed missionary effort, and converts soon came flooding in from all over the United States and parts of Europe, especially Great Britain. He organized a female Relief Society and laid plans for another temple. In 1841 he began to teach the doctrine of eternal marriage, including the idea of plural marriage, which he himself practiced. In the temple, faithful Saints would be endowed with a deeper knowledge of the gospel and be sealed as husband and wife for eternity. Living Saints could also be baptized for persons who had died without hearing the gospel of Christ. In March 1844 he organized a Council of Fifty composed of leading Mormons and a few sympathetic non-Mormons to manage the political affairs of the kingdom. All this was more than some of the Saints could accept. Doctrines such as plural marriage went so far beyond conventional Christian teaching, not to mention the bounds of Victorian propriety, that an influential small group came to believe that Smith had betrayed his divine calling. They joined forces with anti-Mormons in surrounding towns who were jealous of the Mormon's growing political influence. The fears of his enemies were only confirmed when Smith announced his candidacy for the presidency in the spring of 1844 and sent missionaries throughout the country to campaign on his behalf. His candidacy meant that Mormons were no longer wooed by Whigs and Democrats, which had made them enemies to whichever party they did not support, and Smith may have believed that, with divine assistance, he could be elected as a preliminary step toward a millennial kingdom.

In April 1844 dissenters in Nauvoo organized a reform church and published a newspaper, the *Nauvoo Expositor*, to expose Smith's errors. The Nauvoo City Council, with Smith presiding as mayor, determined that the *Expositor* was a threat to the peace of the community and a public nuisance. As mayor, Smith was authorized to close the paper and did, which ignited the opposition. On 12 June Smith was charged with inciting a riot for destruction of the press. He ultimately submitted to arrest and was taken to Carthage, the nearby county seat, under the governor's protection. As he left for Carthage, Smith had premonitions of his own death, which proved to be accurate. On 27 June 1844, while he awaited a hearing, a mob with blackened faces stormed the jail, killing him and his brother Hyrum. The mob fled, fearing reprisal from the Mormons, who did not retaliate. The bodies were returned the next day to Nauvoo, where 10,000 Latter-day Saints gathered to mourn the loss of their prophet. Four of his eleven children (two adopted) were living, and a fifth was to be born to Emma Smith four months later.

Joseph Smith was, in the technical sense, a charismatic leader; he exercised authority by virtue of a perceived divine gift. But the movement he began did not rest solely on the strength of his personality. Soon after his death, Brigham Young, as president of the Twelve Apostles and a stalwart friend and defender of Smith, assumed leadership of the church and in 1846 led the Saints west in search of a new place to build Zion. Through the Mormon Church Smith's influence continues to be felt. His followers to this day accept the Book of Mormon and the collection of his revelations in the Doctrine and Covenants as divine writings and honor him as a leader, Christian teacher, and prophet.

R.L.B.

Melvin B. Tolson

[6 FEBRUARY 1900–29 AUGUST 1966]

*H*e *was born in the right place—the United States of America, grand melting pot and Democratic experiment—but at the wrong time: Melvin B. Tolson, black poet and fiery intellectual, had the grave misfortune of publishing his seminal work—* Harlem Gallery, Book I: The Curator—*in 1965, at the height of the Black Power movement. A book-length poem centered around the struggles of three artists and their snooty clientele,* Harlem Gallery *eschews the easy sentiment of unilateral ethnic identity and pride but instead seeks to examine the contradictions and glorious ambivalences that being human embodies per se. Divided into twenty-four sections corresponding to the letters in the Greek alphabet,* Harlem Gallery *contains allusions ranging from Vedic gods to Tintoretto and pre-Columbian pottery, as well as snippets in Latin and French. Spliced into this highly stylized ode are vignettes and dramatic monologues; the extravagant verbiage pays homage to a variety of dictions, with irony and pathos, slapstick and pontification maneuvering side-by-side. Such a complex poetic meditation was unlikely to be a hit in the American social climate of the mid-sixties, with fires raging in Watts, students taking over university buildings, and long-haired youths sticking flowers in the rifle barrels of the National Guard while the war in Vietnam escalated and claimed more and more American lives. The country had no time for subtlety and was in no mood for irony; allegiance and moral rectitude were all too often a matter of black and white.*

"I will visit a land unvisited by Mr. Eliot," Tolson boasted, and lived up to his word. Whereas The Wasteland *became a banner for the post–World War I generation and the psychic landscape it depicts was endemic to the disaffected times that followed such horrific devastation,* Harlem Gallery *takes up the post-postmodern stance, its dazzling array of allusions deliberately complicating our*

259

*preconceived notions of cultural—and, by further comparison, exis-
tential—order. In such a universe, amalgamation is not a dissolution of identity but rather a virtuoso exhibition of one's creativity
and hence, identity . . . a rap on Difference and its edges. The characters that populate Tolson's Brave New World know that survival
involves mother wit and adaptability with self-awareness—in other
words, how to play the American Dream game without disappearing into the melting pot; his Gallery is a global village of the mind.*

*In an interview, Melvin Tolson once stated: "I, as a black poet,
have absorbed the Great Ideas of the Great White World, and inter-
preted them in the melting-pot idiom of my people. My roots are in
Africa, Europe, and America." He was also a prophet of many of
today's pop-cultural phenomena: global interconnections, adven-
turous racial ambiguity, and ethnic squabbling; the high-wire energy of hip-hop and high-speed communication skills required for
survival in our electronic world; even cinematic jump-cuts and the
syncopated signifying known as rap. His linguistic urbanity holds a
mirror up to our multilayered, multitasking times; his meditation on
"the dialectic of / to be or not to be / a Negro" could be applied to
any immigrant group's search for identity in America. To contain
multitudes yet not shy away from the paradoxes of such a convoca-
tion of sensibilities—that is the challenge of our world today. A man
of his times who saw through and beyond his times: Melvin B. Tolson.*

RITA DOVE

Melvin Beaunorus Tolson, poet, teacher, and essayist,
was born in Moberly, Missouri, the son of Alonzo Tolson, an itinerant Methodist minister, and Lera Ann
Hurt, a seamstress. Some sources list his year of birth as 1898.
Although his father's occupation required frequent moves to
various towns in Missouri, Iowa, and Kansas, young Tolson's
childhood was a happy one, relatively unscathed by the various forms of racial prejudice that many African Americans
faced during the early twentieth century. After a brief stint at

Fisk University following his graduation from high school in 1918, Tolson enrolled in 1919 at Lincoln University in Pennsylvania, where he earned a bachelor of arts degree in journalism and theology in 1923. In 1922 he married Ruth Southall, and together they raised four children. Tolson in 1931 entered a graduate program in comparative literature at Columbia University, though he was not overly concerned with the formal aspects of applying for the degree; it was not until 1940 that he was finally awarded the master of arts degree.

Portrait of Melvin B. Tolson. "Tolson's poetic lines and images sing, affirm, reject, predict, and judge experience in America. . . . All history, from Genesis to Munich, is his domain." –Richard Wright. *(Schomburg Center for Research in Black Culture)*

In 1923, fresh from college and only twenty-three years old, Tolson accepted a position as instructor of English and speech at a small African-American college in Marshall, Texas, thus beginning a brilliant teaching career that he would maintain with dedication and energy for more than forty years. Tolson distinguished himself at Wiley College by coaching the debate team to a ten-year winning streak that included victories over champion teams from Oxford University and the University of Southern California. According to Robert M. Farnsworth, his experiences with the debate teams, which included circumventing the color line in racially divided towns throughout the South and the Midwest, often found their way into his creative and journalistic writings, particularly his columns written for the Washington *Tribune* during the 1930s and 1940s.

Tolson remained at Wiley until 1947, when he accepted a position as professor of English and drama at Langston University in the small African-American town of Langston, Oklahoma. Although his years with the celebrated debate teams from Texas had passed, he soon established a solid reputation with the Langston community as a respected teacher and, in 1954, as the town's mayor, an office to which he was reelected three times. The capstone of Tolson's teaching career came in 1965, the year he had planned to retire from Langston University. At sixty-five years of age he accepted the Avalon Chair in Humanities at Tuskegee Institute, an appointment arranged by a former student of Tolson's who now chaired the English Department at Tuskegee.

While his long teaching career provided stability and a consistent income for Tolson's family, it was as a poet that Tolson made a significant contribution to American literature and history. Tolson had tinkered with poetry and painting as a child and had experimented with several literary genres in his early years at Wiley College, but his professional career as a poet began in earnest in the early 1930s with his work on a lengthy manuscript, "A Gallery of Harlem Portraits." Tolson was strongly influenced by Harlem Renaissance poets, including Langston Hughes, Countée Cullen, and Claude McKay, whose writings he had studied extensively while writing his master's thesis at Columbia. "A Gallery of Harlem Portraits" represents an early example of Tolson's conviction that the distinct cultural expressions of the African-American community, particularly the blues, jazz, and gospel forms, provide a wealth of material from which the black poet can draw for inspiration.

Although his first book-length manuscript was praised in a 1938 *Current History* column by fellow writer V. F. Calverton, who lauded Tolson for "trying to do for the Negro what Edgar Lee Masters did for the middlewest white folk over two decades ago," "A Gallery of Harlem Portraits" was rejected by publishers. Determined to continue writing, however, Tolson gained national recognition with "Dark Symphony," a poem that blends a profound historical consciousness of the African-American struggle against adversity with a defiant message aimed at oppressors throughout the world. "Dark Symphony" won first place in a national poetry contest in 1940 and was published in the *Atlantic Monthly* in 1941. Shortly after these initial successes, *Rendezvous with America*, another book-length collection of poems, was accepted by Dodd, Mead and Company. Published in 1944, *Rendezvous* reflected the complexity of the American experience in the context of World War II. While many of the poems allude to the ironies inherent in a racially divided nation that was fighting a war to rid the world of racial supremacy, the book as a whole is also a celebration of America's diversity: "America? / An international river with a legion of tributaries! / A magnificent cosmorama with myriad patterns and colors!" (*Rendezvous*, p. 5). Tolson's book elicited enthusiastic reviews and nearly unqualified praise from prominent African-American writers such as Richard Wright, who opined that "Tolson's poetic lines and images sing, affirm, reject, predict, and judge experience in America. . . . All history, from Genesis to Munich, is his domain."

Following the success of *Rendezvous*, in 1947 Tolson was named "poet laureate of Liberia" at a ceremony in Washington, D.C., and shortly thereafter began work on a poem to celebrate the Liberian centennial. The result was *Libretto for the Republic of Liberia* (1953), a book-length ode that revealed Tolson's broad knowledge of modernist poetry and world history. Although *Libretto* garnered some strong reviews and elicited comparisons with the works of modernists such as Ezra Pound and T. S. Eliot, it was *Harlem Gallery, Book I: The Curator*, released by Twayne Publishers in 1965, that marked the pinnacle of Tolson's poetic career. Tolson envisioned *Harlem Gallery* as a multivolume epic exploring the full experience of African Americans throughout history, but his goal was never realized; he died a year later at a hospital in Dallas, Texas. Nevertheless, the first volume of *Harlem Gallery*, with its innovative use of language and its synthesis of modernist poetics and African-American musical forms, ensured Tolson a place among the highest ranks of American literary masters. In the words of one reviewer, "The book is 'Gibraltarian' in content and apogean in scope. . . . He has taken the language of America and the idiom of the world to fashion a heroic declaration of, about and for Negroes in America."

C.C.D.

Felix Francisco Varela y Morales

[20 NOVEMBER 1788–18 FEBRUARY 1853]

*W*hen *Americans received letters in the year 2000 adorned with a Felix Varela commemorative stamp, most wondered who this foreigner was and why the Postal Service had enshrined his image. But every school child in Cuba for more than a century has known and claimed Varela. Such is the paradox of Latinos in American history: a giant of a man who spent the greatest part of his life in the United States does not figure into American collective memory. Never mind that he produced a magnificent corpus of philosophical, theological and literary texts, nor that he was a pioneer of American Catholicism. Is it because much of his writing was done in the Spanish language? Or that he was a Catholic priest in a then very Protestant, anti-papist country? Or that he did not readily identify with European culture, having been an exponent of the political and cultural independence of the New World? If these reasons were not enough to write him out of our early history, it did not help that he was an early abolitionist and ecumenist.*

The author of the very first historical novel in the Spanish language, Jicoténcal, *and the publisher of one of the first Spanish-language periodicals in the early Republic,* El Habanero, *Varela also published and edited various English-language Catholic magazines. While he was a cerebral and spiritual man, like many Latinos he knew well the plight of the immigrant and the poor, and worked untiringly for their betterment. His progressive ideas on lay governance of the Church and on the abolition of slavery were as unwelcome in some sectors of the United States as his ideas about Spanish American independence were anathema to the Spanish Crown. In fact, it was a criminal offense to utter Varela's name in Cuba, where his writings are thought to have been the first underground bestsellers. Ironically, in the country he knew best and that received the direct benefit of his labors, the United States that is, neither his name, nor his grave marker in St. Augustine, nor his writings stir reaction nor memory.*

For me, Varela embodies most of the ideals that are the pride of American culture. At the same time, he embodies the transculturalism and transnationalism of Latinos and other American ethnic minorities. The life of Varela, and of most Latinos today, transcends the simplistic and exclusionary identity foisted on generations of children growing up within our borders.

NICOLÁS KANELLOS

Felix Francisco Varela y Morales, educator, writer, and pastor, was born in Havana, Cuba, the son of Francisco Varela y Pérez, a military officer, and María Josefa Morales. An orphan by age six, Varela was sent to live with his paternal grandfather, Don Bartolomé, military commander of a Cuban regiment stationed at St. Augustine in the Spanish colony of East Florida. Varela's announcement at age fourteen that he wanted to be a priest was a disappointment to his military-oriented family, but he was sent to Havana, where he attended classes at San Carlos Seminary and the University of Havana. Varela earned his baccalaureate in 1806 and was ordained a Roman Catholic priest in 1811. He was assigned to teach philosophy at San Carlos.

Between 1812 and 1822 Varela earned the reputation as Cuba's foremost philosopher and most illustrious teacher. Taking an eclectic approach to philosophy, he reexamined the philosophers of the past and adapted their thinking to the contemporary situation, thereby combining the works of Aristotle with those of the Enlightenment period to produce a hybrid philosophy. He used this system in his first major published work, *Institutiones philosophical eclecticae ad usum juventutis* (1812), a two-volume logic and metaphysics text. Other philosophical works of the period were *Apuntes Filosóficos* (1818), *Lecciónes de Filosofía* (3 vol., 1818–1819), and *Miscelanea Filosófica* (1819).

Initially uninterested in politics and the upheavals taking place in Latin America over independence, Varela later began, through public speeches, to examine the subject. In *Observaciones sobre la constitución política de la monarquía español seguidas de otros trabajos políticos* (1821) he claimed that justice and individual rights are absolutes originating from God and implanted in the nature of man. His views thrust him into the public forum and led to his election to the Royal Patriotic Society of Cuba (1817) and the Royal Friends of Cuba (1818).

Varela's new interest in politics also resulted in his election, in 1821, as spokesman for Cuba at the Spanish Cortes meeting in Cádiz. Originally convened in 1810 in an effort to stabilize the Spanish state in the wake of Napoleon, the Cortes was a liberal movement that sought change from the traditional order of Spanish monarchical government. At the meeting Varela proposed three separate ideas to the Cortes: a plan for the administration of provincial governments that would lead to virtual autonomy for Cuba; the abolition of slavery; and support for the cause of freedom in Spain's American colonies. Although these plans were never instituted, Varela's advocacy is notable. Ferdinand VII's return to the Spanish throne led to the dissolution of the Cortes, and because of his advocacy of Cuban autonomy, Varela could not return home; he sailed instead for the United States, arriving in New York City on 17 December 1823. Varela arrived as a refugee and without ecclesiastical sanction. Fearful of his progressive views, Bishop John Connolly of New York did not initially grant him clerical faculties. He therefore moved to Philadelphia and, addressing himself to Cuban affairs, began to publish *El habanero, papel político científico y literario*, a political magazine promoting freedom for Cuba.

In 1825 Varela received faculties to minister as a priest in the diocese of New York. He was assigned to St. Peter's Church, where he began to work with Irish immigrants. In 1827 Bishop John Dubois appointed him pastor of Christ Church. Structural failures forced its closure in 1833, after which the bishop purchased a former Reformed Scottish Presbyterian church, rededicated it on 31 March 1836 as the Church of the Transfiguration of Our Lord, and installed Varela as pastor.

Varela was both a zealous priest and progressive in his understanding of the role of the Church. He was known to visit the hospitals each day and in 1832 exhaustively ministered to the victims of a citywide cholera epidemic. He fully supported a board of lay trustees selected to administrate Transfiguration parish, advocated lay participation in parish affairs, and was a pioneer in ecumenism. Varela organized a group dedicated to total abstinence from alcohol a decade before Father Theobald Mathew began to administer "the pledge" to American church congregations in 1849. In support of religious education for youth he supervised the publication of *Children's Catholic Magazine* (1838) and its successor, the *Young Catholic's Magazine* (1840). In April 1841 a third journal, the *Catholic Expositor and Literary Magazine: A Monthly Magazine*, premiered featuring articles in literature and philosophy.

Varela served as co-vicar of the diocese of New York under Dubois and his successor, John Hughes. In this position he fought against anti-Catholic rhetoric, which then circulated widely. In 1840 he initiated, in Hughes's absence, a church campaign to obtain state funds for Catholic schools, arguing that because Catholics pay taxes they have a right to receive a portion of their contribution in the support of church schools. In 1844 Varela was granted administrative control of Transfiguration parish by the lay trustees. For the next six years he worked diligently to liquidate a large debt incurred during the parish's first eight years of operation. His hectic pace of work began to take its toll, however, and his health faltered. In 1850 Transfiguration parish was transferred to the control of Archbishop Hughes, and Varela was allowed to retire to his boyhood town of St. Augustine. He died there three years later.

Varela gave himself totally to his work, whatever it was. The reputation he gained as a teacher drew students to his classes. His philosophical works were widely used in Cuba and until the mid-twentieth century were often reprinted. In his role as pastor he championed the cause of those to whom he ministered and initiated programs, especially English-language magazines, to provide for the religious education of youth. Although he never became a U.S. citizen, Varela embraced a progressive program that was consistent with contemporary American Catholicism, which sought to ground the faith in the American virtues of freedom and democracy.

R.G.

DeWitt Wallace

[12 NOVEMBER 1889–30 MARCH 1981]

De Witt Wallace started a publication from nowhere *that now circles the world and through the years has enlightened and informed readers like no other. I read* Reader's Digest *from cover to cover every month and subscribed to the* Digest *for every editor at* Cosmo *all the years I was there. I pointed out that the* Digest *edited better than any place in the world in terms of pulling in materials (or assigning) and then condensing and even improving, so that the* Digest *version was almost better than the original. Wallace did not buy something and do a rehash — he* created *and had enormous influence on the publishing world that continues to this day.*

HELEN GURLEY BROWN

William Roy (or Roy William) DeWitt Wallace, editor and publisher, was born in St. Paul, Minnesota, the son of James T. Wallace, an educator, and Janet Davis. DeWitt's high marks enabled him to skip two grades in elementary school, but his academic achievements after that were spotty. In high school, he was better known for pranks and athletic skills. Wallace enrolled at Macalester College, a Presbyterian institution where his father was president. After his sophomore year he took a job at a bank in Colorado. In his spare time, he read widely in current publications and formed a habit of making notes on articles he found most appealing and on his own ideas. He then returned to school at the University of California, Berkeley. During a visit to Tacoma, Washington, a friend introduced him to Canadian-born Lila Bell Acheson, who later became his wife and business partner.

Wallace next worked for a small book-publisher in St. Paul, but a critique of the publisher's material got him fired. He was

DeWitt Wallace holding court in his office. In 1922, Wallace's first issue of *Reader's Digest*, sold exclusively by mail and priced at 25¢, including 31 carefully selected articles, including "The Future of Poison Gas," "Wanted: Motives for Motherhood," and "Advice from a President's Physician." *(DeWitt Wallace Library, Macalester College)*

able, however, to extract a $700 credit line from the company to fund a publication of his own, a pocket-sized book *Getting the Most out of Farming*; it was a list of free resource publications on agriculture. A statement that the material had been "prepared by DeWitt Wallace" is believed to have been the only time in his career that he used a byline.

Wallace's marketing strategy was to induce suppliers to affix their names to the booklet and hand it out to customers as a good-will gesture. It worked. In a tour of several states, Wallace and a cousin sold all 100,000 copies printed. There was no tangible profit, but the exercise generated the idea of printing a digest of data that would interest everyone.

During World War I Wallace volunteered for military service and was wounded on the front lines in France. While recuperating in a hospital, he found plenty of time and ample supplies of magazines with which to develop his digest concept. On returning home he immediately headed for the Minneapolis library to put together a prototype, which appeared in January 1920. Several hundred copies were printed with a $600 advance from Wallace's father. The issue's sixty-four pages featured thirty-one articles "of lasting interest," one for each day of the month. They were condensed from articles that had appeared in an assortment of well-known magazines, including the *National Geographic*, *Ladies' Home Journal*, and *Saturday Evening Post*. Wallace titled his creation *Reader's Digest*.

Wallace then tried to find a publishing company to take over the project and pay him to be its editor. He approached many firms without success. The conventional wisdom was that a popular magazine needed advertising, color, illustrations, and fiction—all missing from *Reader's Digest*.

In the meantime Wallace found employment, first as a salesman for a wholesale grocer and later as a promotional writer for Westinghouse in Pittsburgh. He had also reestablished contact with Lila Bell Acheson, a social worker. She was full of enthusiasm for the new publication. The couple married in 1921; they had no children.

A co-worker at Westinghouse who had some experience with direct-mail campaigns was impressed by Wallace's sample and encouraged him to seek subscribers on his own. When a recession forced Westinghouse to cut back, Wallace lost his job. Although dejected over the loss of income, he saw an opportunity to concentrate on his subscription drive. He produced a series of solicitations, using carefully selected mailing lists that targeted business and professional women. Initial returns were not encouraging, but DeWitt and Lila Wallace managed to raise some capital and persevered. *Reader's Digest*, which was to become the world's most widely circulated periodical, began regular monthly publication in February 1922, with a circulation of 5,000.

The Wallaces first had editorial offices in New York City, but they soon moved most of their operations to a Westchester

County village, Pleasantville. Wallace assumed ownership of 52 percent of the new corporation's stock, and his wife assumed the remainder.

The Wallaces adopted a thematic mix for the magazine that remained stable throughout their lives. Articles explored topics from science, nature, art, health, manners, and mores. Descriptions of unusual occurrences, heroic individuals, and lurking dangers were inserted regularly, as were broadly inspirational essays and self-improvement instructions. Humor, often mildly risqué, was another basic ingredient. In general, the content reflected a conservative outlook that emphasized traditional American ideals. The formula attracted a readership of 20,000 in its first four years; that jumped to 216,000 in the next three years.

Eventually the *Digest* began commissioning articles of its own, although it arranged to have them appear first in other magazines. "—And Sudden Death," a major story on the growing dangers of highway travel, alerted the nation in 1935 to the need for auto safety. It was so widely reprinted that the *Digest* later called it "without doubt the most widely read article ever published."

By 1936 circulation reached 1.8 million. A new headquarters building was erected on an eighty-acre site just north of Pleasantville. The *Digest* began publishing overseas with a United Kingdom edition in 1938. In spite of paper shortages during World War II, the *Digest* prospered: from about four million in 1941, its circulation rose to about eight million in 1946.

In 1950 the Wallaces started the highly successful Condensed Book Club. It was followed by a number of other ancillary publishing projects. Through targeting and testing, direct-mail marketing teams were able to predict the sales potential of new products. In 1955 the magazine began accepting advertising. The previous year the *Digest* started to carry articles on the perils of smoking, which have helped millions of Americans to break the tobacco habit.

The Wallaces had a reputation for being generous to their employees and giving large contributions to nonprofit organizations. Macalester College received more than $50 million during DeWitt Wallace's lifetime, and Lila Wallace gave a similar amount to the Metropolitan Museum of Art in New York. DeWitt Wallace died at home in Mt. Kisco, New York.

D.E.K.

Ida B. Wells-Barnett

[16 JULY 1862–25 MARCH 1931]

*Ida Wells strikes so many chords for me, as a woman, a journalist,
and an editor, who was well enough known in her time to be
invited to England to lecture, that I am surprised by how little she is
known today. Every schoolchild in America and Britain knows that
Rosa Parks refused to give up her bus seat to a white man in 1955
and that Martin Luther King organized the famous boycott. Ida
Wells did both these things seven decades before—and that was
only the overture of her lifelong struggle for gender and racial justice.*

*I like the way she tells what happened to her at the beginning of
her adult life. Her parents, both of whom had been slaves, and at
least one sibling in Mississippi were dead of yellow fever. She
boarded a train in Memphis with a first-class rail ticket. This was
during that curious period after the Civil War, before the Jim Crow
laws came in, when it was illegal to discriminate. Still, she was
ordered into the crowded smoking car so a white man could have
her seat: "The conductor tried to drag me out of my seat, but the
moment he caught hold of my arm I fastened my teeth in the back of
his hand. I had braced my feet against the seat in front and was
holding to the back . . ." She was thrown off the train, to white
applause, but she didn't yield to superior power and eventually won
$500 in damages. I like the* Memphis Daily Appeal *headline that
encapsulated the saga: "A Darky Damsel Obtains a Verdict for
Damages Against the Chesapeake Ohio Railroad: What It Cost to
Put a Colored Teacher in a Smoking Carriage for $500."*

*I much admire the way Ida spent her life with her teeth bared,
her feet braced, and her mind in gear. Long before Martin Luther
King, she knew how to affect white opinion through the pocket-
book. When three black storekeepers were lynched in 1892 (because
they were too competitive for a white store), she was the editor of a*

275

Baptist paper. She used her pen to rouse the blacks to boycott the city's streetcar company. Her offices were firebombed, but the Memphis city fathers finally acted against the vigilantes. Consequently there were no more lynchings in Memphis for twenty years. Bravo, Ida!

TINA BROWN

Ida Bell Wells-Barnett, editor and anti-lynching activist, was born in Holly Springs, Mississippi, the daughter of James Wells and Elizabeth Warrenton, slaves. Son of his master, James Wells was a carpenter's apprentice and opened his own shop after emancipation. The eldest of eight children, Ida attended Rust College in Holly Springs until 1878, when a yellow fever epidemic killed her parents and one of her six siblings (another had died some years before). Determined to keep her family together, Wells began teaching in surrounding areas. In 1881 she moved her youngest siblings to Memphis to live with an aunt and took a job as a schoolteacher in nearby Woodstock.

In September 1883, while commuting by train, Wells was asked to leave the "ladies' car" and move to the smoking car, where all African Americans were expected to sit. She refused to leave, bit the conductor who tried to remove her, and then filed a successful suit against the railroad. Although the verdict was reversed by the state supreme court, her accounts of the case in a local black newspaper launched her journalism career. Teaching in the Memphis public schools from 1883 until 1891, Wells wrote articles for black newspapers around the nation under the pen name "Iola." In 1889 she became part owner and editor of the *Memphis Free Speech and Headlight*. Two years later the school board did not renew her contract after she wrote editorials critical of its actions.

Elected secretary of the black-run National Press Association in 1887, Wells became known as the "Princess of the Press" by her mostly male editorial colleagues. Many felt ambivalent toward this attractive young woman, whose writings were militant and uncompromising. In I. Garland Penn's *The Afro-American Press and Its Editors* (1891), fellow editor T. Thomas Fortune noted, "She has become famous as one of the few of our women who handle a goose-quill, with a diamond point, as easily as any man in the newspaper work. . . . She has plenty of nerve, and is as sharp as a steel trap." Never hesitant to criticize anyone, no matter how prominent, Wells collected enemies and suitors in almost equal numbers.

"Where are our 'leaders' when the race is being burnt, shot, and hanged?" Ida B. Wells–Barnett asked of silent government officials during the 1880s in her newspaper *Memphis Free Speech and Headlight*. *(Schomburg Center for Research in Black Culture)*

In 1892 Wells found a focus for her militancy following a triple lynching in Memphis. After three young black men opened the People's Grocery, a white competitor's resentment triggered a chain of events that led to their murders. Earlier lynchings had angered her, but the deaths of three friends brought the evil close to her. She had believed lynchings happened to innocent people but not to respectable ones. Turning the full force of her powerful pen against lynching, Wells attacked the premise that lynching was a necessary deterrent to black rapists. In May she wrote a *Free Speech* editorial in which she suggested that many rape charges arose from the discovery of voluntary sexual liaisons of white women with black men. While Wells was away, angry whites closed the newspaper office and ran her partner out of Memphis.

Afraid to return home, Wells settled in New York and began writing for T. Thomas Fortune's *New York Age*. In June the paper published a lengthy attack on lynching by the thirty-year-old exile. Reprinted as *Southern Horrors: Lynch Law in All Its Phases*, it became the first of several pamphlets on the subject. In it Wells argued that lynching was often used to counteract black achievement and had grown worse as African Americans became more educated and successful. Although raised in less than a third of all lynchings, charges of rape, she noted, "closed the heart, stifled the conscience, warped the judgment and hushed the voice of pulpit and press." Proclaiming that "a Winfield rifle should have a place of honor in every black home," Wells asserted, "The more the Afro-American yields and cringes and begs, the more he has to do so, the more he is insulted, outraged and lynched."

After African-American women in New York gave Wells a testimonial dinner that raised about $400 for her crusade, she received dozens of lecture requests. On one visit to Philadelphia she met Catherine Impey, an Englishwoman who published the journal *Anti-Caste*. Early in 1893 Impey joined with Scottish author Isabelle Mayo to invite Wells to tour Scotland and England in the cause of antilynching. Following her first lecture the women organized the Society for the Recognition of the Brotherhood of Mankind, which invited Wells back the next year for a second tour.

The attention of the English press catapulted Wells to the leadership of the antilynching movement. She used all available platforms for her message. At the World Columbian Exposition in Chicago during 1893, she joined with the famous abolitionist Frederick Douglass and Chicago lawyer Ferdinand L. Barnett to circulate a coauthored protest pamphlet. Even after Wells married Barnett in 1895, she continued her activism. Assuming the editorship of her husband's newspaper, the *Chicago Conservator*, Wells-Barnett remained a militant voice, giving speeches, investigating lynchings, criticizing Booker T. Washington, starting organizations, and joining movements—while bearing four children.

Participating in the founding of such organizations as the National Association of Colored Women (1896), the Afro-American Council (1898), and the National Association for the Advancement of Colored People (1910), Wells-Barnett remained active in few. Her uncompromising attitude alienated many people and prevented effective membership in groups she did not lead. She personally founded the Ida B. Wells Women's Club in 1893; the Negro Fellowship League, a kind of settlement house for black men, in 1910; and the Alpha Suffrage Club in 1913. That year she desegregated a suffrage march in Washington, D.C., by slipping into the Illinois delegation at the last moment. In addition, from 1913 to 1916 Wells-Barnett served as an adult probation officer in Chicago. Always busy, she was active in the Republican Party and, in the three years before her death, began her autobiography and ran for the state senate. For more than four decades Wells-Barnett's militant voice brought worldwide attention to the evil of lynching and influenced the course of American reform. She died in Chicago, Illinois.

L.O.M.

Frank W. Woolworth

[13 APRIL 1852–8 AUGUST 1919]

*F*rank *Winfield Woolworth, revolutionary retailer, entrepreneur, visionary—by the end of his life the concept of the five-and-ten-cent store was synonymous with his name.*

Woolworth's: this was place you went for everything, the most necessary and the absolutely unnecessary. This is where I learned to shop, where my mother, remembering the Woolworth's of her youth, let me loose on Saturday mornings, to wander, to explore. A phantasmagoria, an education, a treasure chest of temptation, a wide expanse with counters that went on forever, wooden floors, oiled to keep dirt from sticking, the whole store filled with the scent of fresh popped popcorn, of roasting peanuts, the sweet tweak of dark chocolates. Every row was an adventure, from buttons and bobbins, to pencil cases, lunch boxes, poster-board, glue and glitter, Halloween costumes, valentines, parakeets and goldfish that seemed to live forever. There was something for everyone and then some, things you could find nowhere else, things you never knew existed, things you never knew you needed until you saw them there.

With more than a thousand stores across the country, Woolworth's was a multi-generational American icon visible in the civil rights struggle when four black students were refused service at a Greensboro, North Carolina, lunch counter. Its red logo lodged deep in our imaginations. The five-and-dime was a general store on steroids, bridging the gap between the nineteenth and twentieth centuries, laying the groundwork for our consumer culture. When the last of the Woolworth's stores closed in the late 1990s, it was as though some piece of the American spirit of had died. The only remaining stores are in Germany and Mexico.

And now, in the early part of the twenty-first century, the Woolworth Building, the tallest building in the world when it was constructed in 1913, stands firm and proud next to the ruins of the

World Trade Center. At night, it glows green, a beacon, a testament to the indomitable nature and passion of Frank W. Woolworth.

A. M. HOMES

Frank Winfield Woolworth, retailer, was born in Rodman, Jefferson County, New York, the son of John Hubbell Woolworth and Fanny McBrier, farmers. At the end of 1858, his paternal grandfather sold the landholdings in Rodman where Woolworth's family lived and farmed, and Woolworth's father had to find a new home. By spring 1859 Woolworth's father had relocated his family to a farm near Great Bend, also in Jefferson County. Woolworth attended common schools in Great Bend, New York. When he was sixteen years old, his mother paid for him to spend a few months studying commerce at a commercial college in Watertown, New York.

While he worked on the family farm until he reached age twenty-one, Woolworth also worked for two winters as an unpaid assistant at a general store in Great Bend owned by Daniel McNeill. In March 1873 Woolworth was offered a job on the farm of his uncle, Albon S. McBrier. However, Woolworth detested farmwork and did not accept the offer. Instead, he tried hard to find a job in the retail trade. Later in 1873 he succeeded in obtaining a six-month trial with the merchants Augsbury & Moore in Watertown, New York. His position was unpaid for the first three months, and during the second three months he received $3.50 a week—this was just sufficient to pay his board. When the six months were completed, Woolworth's remuneration was increased by fifty cents a week. At the beginning of his third year, Augsbury's interest in the store was acquired by Perry R. Smith, and the business became Moore & Smith.

In the fall of 1875 Woolworth was appointed senior clerk at A. Bushnell and Company, a dry goods and carpet store in Watertown. In 1876 Woolworth returned to his position with his previous employer. Poor health, however, forced him to take a prolonged period of unpaid sick leave and to return to his father's farm. While recuperating on the farm, Woolworth married Jennie Creighton, a 23-year-old seamstress from Picton, Ontario, in 1876. They had three daughters.

In 1877 he returned to Watertown as senior clerk with Moore & Smith. In the spring of 1878 he helped introduce a five-cent counter in the store: this was to prove a revolutionary new concept in retailing. (It had been developed by a former salesman at A. Bushnell and Company.) Woolworth saw its commercial potential and adapted it by displaying goods on counters so customers could select items themselves. This meant that there was no longer any requirement for skilled clerks in the stores that he was to open. Relatively well-paid clerks were to be replaced with low-paid young women, who, in the long run, were to be an important cost advantage in a business with very low profit margins.

On 22 February 1879 Woolworth opened his first "Great 5-Cent Store" in Utica, New York, with $350 worth of goods purchased with a note underwritten by his former employer, W. H. Moore. This store was unsuccessful because it was poorly located; it was closed after three months. In June 1879, however, Woolworth opened a second store in Lancaster, Pennsylvania, which was a success. By 1882 three out of Woolworth's first five stores had failed, due to an insufficient number of customers and a lack of buying experience; of the remaining two, one was a great success and the other only partially successful.

During the 1880s Woolworth expanded his business partly through the use of partners. In 1885 Moore—now sole proprietor of his business—was on the verge of bankruptcy. Woolworth helped Moore save his business by assisting him in the establishment of a five-and-ten-cent store. By 1886 Woolworth controlled seven stores with various partners. His business strategy had some similarities with the modern-day franchising concept because the use of partnerships helped minimize his personal outlay of capital. In 1886 his expanding business led to the establishment of an administrative and purchasing office in New York City.

In 1888 stress and overwork made Woolworth ill, which persuaded him to incorporate his business in order to ensure its survival. (It was not until 1905, however, that he finally formed F. W. Woolworth & Co.) In 1890 Woolworth moved to Brooklyn, New York. During the 1890s the five-and-ten-cent stores started to adopt a diamond with a "W" in the center as a trademark. The same decade also saw a considerable improvement in the terms and conditions of employment for the Woolworth staff. In 1896 Woolworth, in response to upward pressure on wages in the retail sector, introduced a Christmas bonus, one week's paid vacation per annum for those with service of six months or longer, and a minimum wage of $2.50 a week for the female clerks. In 1898 Woolworth expanded into New England with the purchase of a group of nine stores from E. P. Charlton.

During the 1890s Woolworth began a series of annual visits to Europe. On his first trip, in 1890, he discovered that Germany had a comparative advantage over the United States in the manufacture of toys and Christmas decorations. As a result, he started to import large quantities of toys and decorations from Germany. During this visit to Europe Woolworth also discovered that the Austrian Kingdom of Bohemia would be a good source of cheap vases and glass goods. By 1911 Woolworth was purchasing three-quarters of all the Christmas tree decorations made in Germany for his stores. In his quest to keep costs as low as possible he began to purchase "German toys" made in Japan. By this time he was employing seven buyers in foreign countries to purchase such items as china, toys, laces, and agate ware.

Woolworth's European visit in 1890 revealed to him the potential for five-and-ten stores in Great Britain. His first foreign store, however, was actually opened in Canada in 1897. It was not until 1909 that he founded a British chain, F. W. Woolworth & Company Ltd. His first British store was opened in November 1909 in Liverpool; many more were established thereafter.

In 1900 Woolworth began to adopt a uniform appearance for his stores, which now numbered fifty-nine. After some experimentation, he adopted a fast and brilliant carmine red for his store fronts and show windows. In 1901 he purchased a new thirty-room mansion on New York City's Fifth Avenue. The following year, he increased the minimum wage in his stores to $3 a week. In 1904 Woolworth acquired over forty stores in the Midwest, Pennsylvania, and Massachusetts, bringing the total number of stores in the Woolworth syndicate to 120. In 1912 Woolworth merged his stores with rival five-and-dime stores owned by Moore, C. S. Woolworth, F. M. Kirby, S. H. Knox, and E. P. Charlton, to form the F. W. Woolworth Co. The new company had 596 stores. During the early part of the same year Woolworth suffered a nervous breakdown. In May he left New York City to spend six weeks taking the cure in the West Bohemian spa towns of Carlsbad and Marienbad. After a motor tour of Switzerland and France, he returned to New York City. But in October he was taken ill again and was sent on another vacation to Europe by his doctor. By the spring of 1913 Woolworth had recovered sufficiently to attend the opening of the new Woolworth Building by President Woodrow Wilson on 24 April. Commissioned by Woolworth in the spring of 1910 and designed by the architect Cass Gilbert, the skyscraper was 787 feet tall, making it the tallest structure in the world at the time. Woolworth himself financed the construction, which cost more than $13 million.

World War I caused considerable disruption to Woolworth's business because he was cut off from his European suppliers. It proved difficult to find suitable American substitutes for much of his imported merchandise. Nonetheless, the number of Woolworth stores continued to grow, and by 1919 the company controlled 1,081 five-and-ten stores in the United States and Canada.

During the summer of 1919 Woolworth was taken ill with a number of maladies, including bad teeth. He refused to have his teeth treated and developed septic poisoning, which contributed to his death at his country home in Glen Cove, Long Island, New York. He left a net estate of $27 million. In addition to his share of the eponymous company, at the time of his death he was also one of the largest stockholders in the Broadway-Park Place Company—which owned the Woolworth Building and other New York City real estate—and in the Irving National Bank and Irving Trust Company.

In helping to develop mass retailing, Woolworth was less an innovator than an entrepreneur whose genius lay in successfully adapting new ideas. He personally identified ways of reducing costs through the use of counter displays of merchandise and through the importation of cheap goods, which afforded him profit margins his competitors could not match.

R.A.H.

AUTHORS OF ARTICLES
from the
AMERICAN NATIONAL BIOGRAPHY

H.B. Hugh Barbour (Lindley Murray)

N.V.B. Nancy Van Norman Baer (Bronislava Nijinska)

R.L.B. Richard L. Bushman (Joseph Smith)

C.C. Clayborne Carson (Malcolm X)

C.W.C. Charles W. Carey, Jr. (Paul Laurence Dunbar)

J.S.C. John Stephens Crawford (Gisela Richter)

M.C.C. Mark C. Carnes (Leon F. Czolgosz)

P.W.C. Patrick W. Carey (John England)

C.C.D. Christopher C. De Santis (Melvin B. Tolson)

M.D. Melvyn Dubofsky (Bayard Rustin)

N.D. Norman Dorsen (Roger Nash Baldwin)

A.J.F. A. James Fuller (Albert Jay Nock)

R.G. Richard Gribble (Felix Francisco Varela y Morales)

R.L.G. Robert L. Gale (John Jay Chapman)

C.E.H.-S. Charles E. Hambrick-Stowe (Charles Grandison Finney)

L. H. Lilian Handlin (George Bancroft)

R.A.H. Richard A. Hawkins (Frank W. Woolworth)

A.T.K. Ann T. Keene (Murray Kempton, Dawn Powell)

D.E.K. David E. Kucharsky (DeWitt Wallace)

E.K. Ellen Knight (Béla Bartók)

S.A.K. Sheryl A. Kujawa (Jessie Daniel Ames)

A.L. Alan Levy (Charles Tomlinson Griffes)

M.E.L. Mamie E. Locke (Fannie Lou Hamer)

K.G.M. Katherine G. Morrissey (Adolphus Washington Greely)

L.O.M. Linda O. McMurry (Ida B. Wells-Barnett)

P.C.M. Pauline C. Metcalf (Dorothy Draper)

S.V.M. Sherrill V. Martin (James Gibbons Huneker)

P.D.N. Paul David Nelson (Nathanael Greene)

H.P. Hans Pols (Adolf Meyer)

T.P. Theda Purdue (Sequoyah)

A.R. Arthur Rubenfeld (Fairfield Porter)

B.R. Barry Rivadue (Dorothy Fields)

C.R. Charles Rosenblum (Henry Hornbostel)

J.W.R.	James W. Reed (Robert L. Dickinson)	R.S.	Ronald Steel (Walter Lippmann)
S.A.R.	Steven A. Riess (Rocky Marciano)	R.S.	Robert Stepto (Sterling Brown)
T.M.R.	Terrie M. Romano (William Halsted)	W.S.	William Stott (James Agee)
C.G.S.	Carolyn G. Shapiro (John Hoskins Griscom)	S.C.T.	Steven C. Tracy (Blind Lemon Jefferson)
D.L.S.	David L. Stebenne (Arthur J. Goldberg)	A.R.W.	Alice Ruth Wexler (Emma Goldman)
J.S.	John Sugden (Handsome Lake)	C.K.W.	Charles K. Wolfe (A. P. Carter and Sara Carter)
J.M.S.	James S. Salem (Johnny Ace)	D.W.	Dennis Wepman (DuBose Heyward)
K.B.S.	Keir B. Sterling (Herman Haupt)	N.L.Y.	Neil L. York (Oliver Evans)

SOURCES AND FURTHER READINGS

Johnny Ace

The most complete accounts of Johnny Ace's career and contributions to American popular music may be found in James M. Salem, "Death and the Rhythm-and-Bluesman: The Life and Recordings of Johnny Ace," *American Music* (Fall 1993): 316–67, and "Johnny Ace: A Case Study in the Diffusion and Transformation of Minority Culture," *Prospects: An Annual of American Cultural Studies* 17 (1992): 211–41. In addition, Galen Gart and Roy C. Ames, *Duke/Peacock Records: An Illustrated History with Discography* (1990), provides valuable information about Ace and his relationship with record owner Don D. Robey. For an account of the beginning of his career by Duke Records founder David James Mattis, see George A. Moonoogian and Roger Meeden, "Duke Records — The Early Years: An Interview with David J. Mattis," *Whiskey, Women, and . . .* , June 1984, pp. 18–25. For overviews of Ace's life and death, see Nick Tosches, *Unsung Heroes of Rock 'n' Roll (1984)*; Peter Grendysa, "Johnny Ace, the 'Ace' of Duke," *Goldmine*, 25 Sept. 1987, pp. 28 and 91; and Colin Escott, "Johnny Ace: The First Rock 'n' Roll Casualty," *Goldmine*, 21 Nov. 1986, pp. 16–17. Excellent photographs of Ace and his associates can be found in "Strange Case of Johnny Ace," *Ebony*, July 1955, pp. 63–68. The most complete and accurate discography of Ace's twenty-one recorded sides may be found in *American Music* (Fall 1993): 353–57. Useful obituaries are in the *Tri-State Defender*, 8 Jan. 1955; the *Pittsburgh Courier*, 1, 5, and 15 Jan. 1955; the *Chicago Defender*, 8 Jan. 1955; and the *Houston Informer*, 1 and 8 Jan. 1955. Newspaper coverage about his death and career is in the *Cleveland Call and Post*, 15 Jan. 1955; the *Pittsburgh Courier*, 5 Feb. 1955; and the *Tri-State Defender*, 5 Mar. 1955.

James Agee

Most of Agee's manuscripts and letters are in the Humanities Research Center of the University of Texas at Austin. Other libraries and individuals with Agee manuscripts and letters are listed in Laurence Bergreen, *James Agee: A Life* (1984). Bergreen's biography, the most complete yet published, is unsympathetic to Agee and raised a storm of criticism when it appeared. Ross Spears, whose documentary film *Agee* (1979) contains interviews with Agee's wives and friends, points out many errors in Bergreen's book in "Fiction as Life," *Yale Review* 74 (Winter 1985): 296–306. See also Alan Spiegel, *James Agee and the Legend of Himself: A Critical Study* (1998). Five of Agee's film scripts are collected in *Agee on Film*, vol. 2 (1960). *Remembering James Agee,* ed. David Madden (1974), collects essays by Agee's last wife and his important friends and co-workers. Agee's second wife, Alma Neuman, describes Agee's life while he was writing *Let Us Now Praise Famous Men* in "Thoughts of Jim: A Memoir of Frenchtown and James Agee," *Shenandoah* 33, no. 1 (1981–1982): 25–36. Richard Pells, *Radical Visions and American Dreams* (1973), and William Stott, *Documentary Expression and Thirties America* (1973), analyze *Let Us Now Praise Famous Men* and the intellectual and cultural contexts in which it was made. The 18 May 1955 issue of the *New York Times* has an obituary.

Jessie Daniel Ames

The Jessie Daniel Ames Papers are in the Southern Historical Collection at the University of North Carolina, Chapel Hill, and contain materials related to her personal and public life. The CIC papers, 1919–1944, and the ASWPL papers, 1930–1942, are in the Robert W. Woodruff Library at the Atlanta University Center; they are also available through University Microfilms, Ann Arbor, Michigan. The Texas State Library, Austin, holds Ames's papers related to the League of Women Voters and the Texas Equal Suffrage Association. Papers concerning her suffrage work are at the Dallas Historical Society. An interview with Ames, c. 1965/1966, is in the Southern Regional Council Papers, Southern Oral History Program, University of North Carolina, Chapel Hill. Ames's publications include *Cast Down Your Bucket Where You Are* (1932) and *The Changing Character of Lynching* (1942), both published by the CIC, and *Southern Women Look at Lynching* (1937), published by the ASWPL. For additional information, see Jacqueline Dowd Hall, *Revolt against Chivalry: Jessie Daniel Ames and the Women's Campaign against Lynching* (1979; rev. ed., 1993), and Hall, "Second Thoughts on Jessie Daniel Ames," in *The Challenge of Feminist Biography: Writing the Lives of Modern American Women*, ed. Sarah Alpen (1992).

Roger Nash Baldwin

Baldwin's papers are in the Roger Nash Baldwin Papers and the ACLU Collection, Seeley Mudd Library, Princeton University. His oral history, recorded in the mid-1950s, is in the Oral History Collection, Columbia University. Peggy Lamson's *Roger Baldwin: Founder of the American Civil Liberties Union* (1976) is an extended interview with commentary. See also the interviews of Baldwin by Alan Westin, "Recollections of a Life in Civil Liberties," pt. 1, *Civil Liberties Review* 2 (Spring 1975): 39–72; pt. 2 (Fall 1975): 10–40. The annual reports of the American Civil Liberties Union, 1920–1969, published in seven volumes (1970), contain valuable material on Baldwin's work as well as his introduction, "The Meaning of Civil Liberties." Articles by and about Baldwin are in *The American*

Civil Liberties Union: An Annotated Bibliography, ed. Samuel Walker (1992). See also Walker, *In Defense of American Liberties: A History of the ACLU* (1990), and *The Pulse of Freedom: American Liberties 1920–1970s*, ed. Alan Reitman (1975). For biographical information, see Robert C. Cottrell, *Roger Nash Baldwin and the American Civil Liberties Union* (2000). Dwight Macdonald wrote a long and insightful two-part article on Baldwin in the *New Yorker*, 11 July and 18 July 1953. An obituary is in the *New York Times*, 27 Aug. 1981.

George Bancroft

The bulk of material related to Bancroft's life is divided among the Massachusetts Historical Society, the New York Public Library, Cornell University Library, and the American Antiquarian Society in Worcester, Massachusetts. The Bancroft-Bliss papers and the papers of Andrew Johnson in the Library of Congress provide additional documentation. A great deal of material is scattered among the collections of major American political and intellectual nineteenth-century figures. Lists of Bancroft's published writings can be found in Robert H. Canary, *George Bancroft* (1974), pp. 133–35. The standard biographies include Mark Anthony deWolfe Howe, *The Life and Letters of George Bancroft* (2 vols., 1908); Russel B. Nye, *George Bancroft, Brahmin Rebel* (1944); and Lilian Handlin, *George Bancroft, the Intellectual as Democrat* (1984).

Béla Bartók

The principal collection of Bartók papers is located at the New York Bartók Archives in Cedarhurst, New York. The collection has been cataloged by Victor Bator in *The Béla Bartók Archives: History and Catalogue* (1963). Published studies by Bartók include his classic *Hungarian Folk Music*, trans. M. D. Calvocoressi (1931); his work on Romanian music in Benjamin Suchoff, ed., *Rumanian Folk Music*, vol. 5 (1967–1975); and, with A. B. Lord, *Serbo-Croatian Folk Songs* (1951). See also Suchoff, ed., *Béla Bartók Essays* (1976); and János Deményi, ed., *Béla Bartók Letters* (1971). An autobiography was published in German and Hungarian journals (1918–1927). A complete catalog of Bartók's compositions and published writings and an extensive bibliography appear in *The New Grove Dictionary of Music and Musicians*, 2d ed. (2001). A partial list of books about Bartók and his music, in English, includes: Emil Haraszti, *Béla Bartók: His Life and Works* (1938); Serge Moreux, *Béla Bartók* (1949; trans. 1953); Halsey Stevens, *The Life and Music of Béla Bartók* (1953; rev. ed., 1993); Agatha Fassett, *The Naked Face of Genius: Béla Bartók's American Years* (1958); Lajos Lesznai, *Béla Bartók* (1961; trans. 1973); Ferenc Bónis, ed., *Béla Bartók: His Life in Pictures and Documents* (1964; trans. 1972); Jósef Ujfalussy, *Béla Bartók* (1965; trans. 1971); E. Lendvai, *Béla Bartók: An Analysis of His Music* (1971); J. McCabe,

Bartók Orchestral Music (1974); Gyorgy Kroó, *A Guide to Bartók* (1974); Todd Crow, ed., *Bartók Studies* (1976); Vilmos Juhasz, *Bartók's Years in America* (1981); T. Tallian, *Béla Bartók: The Man and His Work* (1981); Hamish Milne, *Bartók: His Life and Times* (1982); Elliott Antokoletz, *Béla Bartók: A Guide to Research (1988); David Yeomans, Bartók for Piano: A Survey of His Solo Literature* (1988); Malcolm Gillies, *Bartók in Britain: A Guided Tour* (1989) and *Bartók Remembered* (1991); and Paul Wilson, *The Music of Béla Bartók* (1992).

Sterling A. Brown

Brown's papers are housed at Howard University, chiefly in the Moorland-Spingard Collection. Robert G. O'Meally's "Annotated Bibliography of the Works of Sterling Brown" appears in Brown's *Collected Poems* (1980) and in *Callaloo* 14/15 (1982): 90–105, an issue with a special section devoted to Brown. Joanne Gabbin, *Sterling A. Brown: Building the Black Aesthetic Tradition* (1985), and Mark A. Sanders, *Afro-Modernist Aesthetics and the Poetry of Sterling A. Brown*, are book-length studies of his work. Robert Stepto assesses Brown in "'When de Saints go Ma'chin' Home': Sterling Brown's Blueprint for a New Negro Poetry," *Kunapipi* 4, no. 1 (1982): 94–105, and in "Sterling Brown: Outsider in the Renaissance," in *Harlem Renaissance Revaluations*, ed. Amritjit Singh et al. (1989). See also Henry Louis Gates, Jr., *Figures in Black: Words, Signs, and the "Racial" Self* (1987). A later discussion is in Gayl Jones, *Liberating Voices: Oral Tradition in African American Literature* (1991). An obituary is in the *New York Times*, 17 Jan. 1989.

A. P. Carter and Sara Carter

The Carter Family's songs were collected in Alvin Pleasant Carter's *The Carter Family Album of Smokey Mountain Ballads* (1934–1937) and *The Carter Family Album of Smokey Mountain Ballads, No. 3* (1944). For additional information on A. P. and Sara's career, see John Atkins, "The Carter Family," in *Stars of Country Music*, ed. Judith McCulloch and Bill C. Malone (1975); Atkins, ed., *The Carter Family* (1973); and Charles K. Wolfe's liner notes for *The Carter Family: The Complete Victor Recordings* (Rounder Records; 9 vols., 1995–1996).

John Jay Chapman

Most of Chapman's voluminous papers are at the Huntington Library in San Marino, California, and in libraries at Columbia University, Johns Hopkins University, the University of Pennsylvania, and Yale University. *The Selected Writings of John Jay Chapman*, ed. Jacques Barzun (1957), reprints representative works by Chapman with an analytical introduction. Owen Wister, *Two Appreciations of John Jay Chapman* (1934), is a tribute by a lifelong friend.

M. A. DeWolfe Howe, another close friend, in *John Jay Chapman and His Letters* (1937), quotes extensively from "Retrospections," Chapman's unpublished autobiography. Richard B. Hovey, *John Jay Chapman: An American Mind* (1959), is the standard biography and contains a select bibliography. Edmund Wilson, *The Triple Thinkers: Ten Essays on Literature* (1938; rev. ed., 1948), contains the best short essay on Chapman. Daniel Aaron, "'Strongly-Flavored Imitation Cynicism': Henry Adams's *Education* Reviewed by John Jay Chapman," *New England Quarterly* 93 (June 1990): 288–93, prints for the first time and comments on Chapman's adverse opinion of *The Education of Henry Adams*. An obituary is in the *New York Times*, 5 Nov. 1933.

Leon F. Czolgosz

Newspaper accounts and other materials on the assassination can be found at the Buffalo and Erie County Public Library, the Buffalo and Erie County Historical Association, and also the Courthouse Archives of Erie County, N.Y. (*People v. Leon F. Czolgosz* [1901], repr. in *American State Trials*, ed. John D. Lawson [1923]). The major biography is A. Wesley Johns, *The Man Who Shot McKinley* (1970). For the official report positing Czolgosz's sanity, see Joseph Fowler et al., "Official Report of the Experts for the People in the Case of the *People v. Leon F. Czolgosz*" (1901), reprinted in *American State Trials*. On the posthumous claim that he was insane, see Walter Channing, "The Mental State of Czolgosz, the Assassin of President McKinley," *American Journal of Insanity* 59 (Oct. 1902); and L. Vernon Briggs, *The Manner of Man That Kills* (1921). See also Robert J. Donovan, *The Assassins* (1952), and Sidney Fine, "Anarchism and the Assassination of McKinley," *American Historical Review* 60, no. 4 (July 1955).

Robert Latou Dickinson

Dickinson's papers are in the Countway Library of Medicine, Boston, Massachusetts. For his biography, see "Robert L. Dickinson and the Committee on Maternal Health," part 3 of James Reed's *From Private Vice to Public Virtue: The Birth Control Movement and American Society since 1830* (1978). On Dickinson's work with the Committee for the Study of Sex Variants, see Jennifer Terry, "Lesbians under the Medical Gaze: Scientists Search for Remarkable Differences," *Journal of Sex Research* 27, no. 3 (Aug. 1990): 317–39. Obituaries are in the *New York Herald Tribune* and *New York Times*, both 30 Nov. 1950.

Dorothy Draper

The firm of Dorothy Draper and Company, Inc., also known as Carlton Varney, New York City, has the records of the firm, scrapbooks containing articles about Dorothy Draper, and some renderings of her commissions. Two of her drawings for the Convair airplane interior are at the Cooper-Hewitt Museum in New York City. A biography is Carleton Varney, *The Draper Touch: The High Life and High Style of Dorothy Draper* (1988). See also Mark Hampton, *Legendary Decorators of the Twentieth Century* (1992), and Robert A. M. Stern et al., *New York 1960* (1995). Draper was interviewed by Edward R. Murrow on CBS's "Person to Person" on 17 May 1957. An obituary is in the *New York Times*, 12 Mar. 1969.

Paul Laurence Dunbar

Dunbar's papers are in the archives of the Ohio Historical Society. His poems are gathered in *The Collected Poetry of Paul Laurence Dunbar*, ed. Joanne M. Braxton (1993). Many of his letters appear in Jay Martin and Gossie H. Hudson, eds., *The Paul Laurence Dunbar Reader* (1975), which also contains a good biographical sketch of Dunbar and a complete bibliography of his work. Another good biographical source is Tony Gentry, *Paul Laurence Dunbar* (1989). Kenny J. Williams, *They Also Spoke: An Essay on Negro Literature in America, 1787–1930* (1970), places Dunbar's work in the tradition of black writing as well as American literature in general. His obituary is in the *New York Times*, 10 Feb. 1906.

John England

England's letters and unpublished correspondence are located primarily in the Archives of the Archdiocese of Baltimore, the Diocese of Charleston, Propaganda Fide (Rome), and the University of Notre Dame. His published collected works are available in Ignatius Aloysius Reynolds, ed., *The Works of the Right Rev. John England, First Bishop of Charleston* (5 vols., 1849), and Sebastian Messmer, *The Works of the Right Reverend John England* (7 vols., 1908). The most extensively documented biography is Peter Guilday, *The Life and Times of John England, First Bishop of Charleston (1786-1842)* (2 vols., 1927; repr. 1969). Other studies of his life and thought include Patrick Carey, *An Immigrant Bishop: John England's Adaptation of Irish Catholicism to American Republicanism* (1982), and Peter Clarke, *A Free Church in a Free Society* (1982).

Oliver Evans

Evans's papers are scattered in various libraries around the country. Evans's descriptions of his milling and steam engine inventions can be found in, respectively, *The Young Mill-Wright and Miller's Guide*, first published in 1795 with subsequent editions through the fifteenth in 1860, and *The Abortion of the Young Steam Engineer's Guide* (1805). Henry Howe, *Memoirs of the Most Emi-*

nent American Mechanics (1840), and Coleman Sellers, Jr., "Oliver Evans and His Inventions," *Journal of the Franklin Institute* 122 (July 1886): 1–16, celebrate Evans as a heroic inventor. In *March of the Iron Men* (1938) and, more especially, in *Machines That Built America* (1953), Roger Burlingame continued that tradition. Siegfried Giedion's classic *Mechanization Takes Command* (1948) more successfully put Evans into the larger technological context. Giedion, however, concentrated on Evans as a pioneer of the automated assembly line and passed over Evans's equally important work with steam engines; not so Carroll W. Pursell, Jr., *Early Stationary Steam Engines in America* (1969). Giedion, like Burlingame, took much of his information from Greville Bathe and Dorothy Bathe, *Oliver Evans: A Chronicle of Early American Engineering* (1935; repr. 1972). For Greville Bathe, himself an engineer, this was a labor of love. He tried to trace every surviving snippet of Evans's life and included long excerpts from dozens of documents in his text. The Bathes note all the repositories of Evans papers. Although their study remains the best source, Eugene S. Ferguson's brief *Oliver Evans: Inventive Genius of the American Industrial Revolution* (1980) is a fine introduction to Evans's work. A scale model of an Evans flour mill is on display at the Henry Clay Mill of the Hagley Museum, outside Wilmington, Delaware.

Dorothy Fields
Several of Fields's libretti are available for study in the Billy Rose Theatre Collection at the New York Public Library for the Performing Arts, Lincoln Center. Max Wilks's *They're Playing Our Song* (1973) and Virginia L. Grattan's *American Women Songwriters* (1993) provide significant portraits of Fields's contribution to songwriting. An insightful understanding of the evolution of the lyricist's craft can be found in Lehman Engel, *Words with Music* (1972). Armond Fields and L. Marc Fields's *From the Bowery to Broadway: Lew Fields and the Roots of American Popular Theater* (1993) is the primary source on the theatrical legacy of Fields's family and an essential source on her own life and career. See also Deborah Grace Winer, *On the Sunny Side of the Street: The Life and Lyrics of Dorothy Fields* (1997). An obituary is in the *New York Times*, 29 Mar. 1974.

Charles Grandison Finney
The Charles Grandison Finney Papers, including correspondence and sermon and lecture notes, are in the Oberlin College Archives. In addition to his published books, the *Oberlin Evangelist* contains hundreds of sermons, letters, and lectures by him. Several books of sermons were published after his death, including *Sermons on Gospel Themes* (1876), *Sermons on the Way of*

Salvation (1891), and a paperback series that includes *Reflections on Revival* (1979) and *The Promise of the Spirit* (1980). *The Memoirs of Charles G. Finney*, ed. Garth M. Rosell and A. G. Dupuis (1989), is the most important source on his life. Biographies include George F. Wright, *Charles Grandison Finney* (1891); Keith J. Hardman, *Charles Grandison Finney, 1792–1875: Revivalist and Reformer* (1987); and Charles E. Hambrick-Stowe, *Charles G. Finney and the Spirit of American Evangelicalism* (1996). On Finney's upstate New York revivals, see Whitney R. Cross, *The Burned-Over District: The Social and Intellectual History of Enthusiastic Religion in Western New York, 1800–1850* (1950), and Paul E. Johnson, *A Shopkeeper's Millennium: Society and Revivals in Rochester, New York, 1815–1837* (1978). Leonard I. Sweet, *The Minister's Wife: Her Role in Nineteenth-Century American Evangelicalism* (1983), discusses Finney and his first two wives. See also Nancy A. Hardesty, *Your Daughters Shall Prophesy: Revivalism and Feminism in the Age of Finney* (1991); Glenn A. Hewitt, *Regeneration and Morality: A Study of Charles Finney, Charles Hodge, John W. Nevin, and Horace Bushnell* (1991); and David L. Weddle, *The Law as Gospel: Revival and Reform in the Theology of Charles G. Finney* (1985). For Finney at Oberlin, see Robert Samuel Fletcher, *A History of Oberlin College: From Its Foundation through the Civil War*, 2 vols. (1943).

Arthur J. Goldberg

Goldberg's papers are in the Library of Congress. His two major books are *AFL-CIO: Labor United* (1956) and *Equal Justice under Law: The Warren Era of the Supreme Court* (1971). For his career and life, see Dorothy Goldberg, *A Private View of a Public Life* (1975), and Daniel P. Moynihan, ed., *The Defenses of Freedom: The Public Papers of Arthur J. Goldberg* (1966). For a comprehensive list of Goldberg's writings, see Tim J. Watts, "A Bibliography of Arthur J. Goldberg," *Law Library Journal* 77, no. 2 (1984–1985): 307–38. The most complete scholarly assessment is David L. Stebenne, *Arthur J. Goldberg: New Deal Liberal* (1996). See also Robert Shaplen's two-part profile, "Peacemaker," *New Yorker*, 7 and 14 Apr. 1962; the reminiscences collected in *In Memoriam: Honorable Arthur J. Goldberg*, Proceedings before the Supreme Court of the United States, 15 Oct. 1990; "In Memoriam: Arthur J. Goldberg," *Northwestern Law Review* 84, no. 3–4 (1990): 807–31; and Emily Field Van Tassel, "Justice Arthur J. Goldberg," in *The Jewish Justices of the Supreme Court Revisited: Brandeis to Fortas*, ed. Jennifer M. Lowe (1994). An obituary is in the *New York Times*, 20 Jan. 1990.

Emma Goldman

The Emma Goldman Papers are available on seventy reels of microfilm from Chadwyck-Healy, along with an extensive guide and index. All the Goldman biographies include useful bibliographies. Richard Drinnon's pioneering *Rebel in Paradise* (1961) stresses Goldman's identity as an American radical. Candace Falk's *Love, Anarchy and Emma Goldman* (1984) focuses more on her erotic life. Alice Wexler's two-volume biography, *Emma Goldman in America* (1984) and *Emma Goldman in Exile* (1989), emphasizes her feminism and offers a more critical perspective. José Peirats, *Emma Goldman: Anarquista de ambos mundos* (1978), stresses the Spanish Civil War years. There are two Twayne studies of Goldman, one by Martha Solomon (1987) and another by Marion Goldman (1992). Published collections of Goldman's writings include Alix Kates Shulman, ed., *Red Emma Speaks* (1972; rev. ed. 1983); Richard Drinnon and Anna Maria Drinnon, eds., *Nowhere at Home: Letters from Exile of Emma Goldman and Alexander Berkman* (1975); and David Porter, ed., *Vision on Fire: Emma Goldman and the Spanish Revolution* (1983). Goldman's *My Disillusionment in Russia* (1925) offers an anarchist critique of the civil war years. For a provocative essay on *Living My Life*, see Blanche H. Gelfant, "Speaking Her Own Piece: Emma Goldman and the Discursive Skeins of Autobiography," in *American Autobiography: Retrospect and Prospect*, ed. Paul John Eakin, (1991). Alice Wexler considers the process of writing about Goldman in "Emma Goldman and the Anxiety of Biography," in *The Challenge of Feminist Biography*, ed. Sara Alpern et al. (1992).

Adolphus Washington Greely

The main collection of Greely's papers, which includes personal papers, military papers, and the most complete list of his published articles, is in the Library of Congress; smaller collections are located at Dartmouth College, Hanover, New Hampshire, and the National Geographic Society Library, Washington, D.C. Additional materials from the Lady Franklin Bay expedition are located in the National Archives. Records, journals, and scientific materials left at Fort Conger and retrieved in 1899 by Robert E. Peary are located in the Explorers' Club, New York City. Greely's autobiographical writings include *Three Years of Arctic Service: An Account of the Lady Franklin Bay Expedition of 1881–84, and the Attainment of the Farthest North* (2 vols., 1886) and *Reminiscences of Adventure and Service: A Record of Sixty-five Years* (1927). His extensive published work includes popular books on arctic exploration, such as *Handbook of Arctic Discoveries* (1896) and *True Tales of Arctic Heroism* (1912); general surveys, such as *American Weather* (1888) and *Handbook of Alaska* (1909); and official reports, such as *Isothermal Lines of the United States, 1871–1880* (1881) and U.S. Army, Pacific Division, *Earthquake in California, April 18, 1906* (1906). William Mitchell, who served under Greely in the signal corps, wrote a laudatory biography, *General Greely: The Story of a Great American*

(1936). The prominent published primary accounts of the Lady Bay Franklin expedition include an edited version of David L. Brainard's diary, *The Outpost of the Lost: An Arctic Adventure*, ed. Bessie Rowland James (1929); Charles Lanman, *Farthest North; or, The Life and Explorations of Lieutenant James Booth Lockwood, of the Greely Arctic Expedition* (1885), based on Lockwood's journal; and W. S. Schley and J. R. Soley, *The Rescue of Greely* (1885).

Nathanael Greene

Greene's papers are in the William L. Clements Library at the University of Michigan, the National Archives, the Library of Congress, and the American Philosophical Society Library. His correspondence is being published in *The Papers of General Nathanael Greene*, ed. Richard K. Showman et al. (1976–). The best biography is Theodore Thayer, *Nathanael Greene: Strategist of the American Revolution* (1960). In addition, Thayer has written a fine short sketch, "Nathanael Greene: Revolutionary War Strategist," in *George Washington's Generals*, ed. George A. Billias (1964). See also G. W. Greene, *The Life of Nathanael Greene, Major-General in the Army of the Revolution* (3 vols., 1867–1871); William Johnson, *Sketches of the Life and Correspondence of Nathanael Greene, Major General of the Armies of the United States in the War of the Revolution* (2 vols., 1822); Douglas S. Freeman, *George Washington: A Biography* (7 vols., 1948–1957); M. F. Treacy, *Prelude to Yorktown: The Southern Campaign of Nathanael Greene, 1780–81* (1963); and John S. Pancake, *This Destructive War: The British Campaign in the Carolinas, 1780–1782* (1985).

Charles Tomlinson Griffes

There are several biographies of Griffes. For years the only work on the composer was John T. Howard, *Charles Tomlinson Griffes* (1923). Written shortly after Griffes's death, the work was very much a memorial and more a narrative of Griffes's life than an analytical study of his music. D. Boda, "The Music of Charles Griffes" (Ph.D. diss., Florida State Univ., 1962), capably analyzes many of the composer's works, as does an article by W. T. Upton, "The Songs of Charles T. Griffes," *Musical Quarterly* 9 (1923): 314. Two excellent books that thoroughly cover both Griffes's life and his music, as well as integrate the composer's career into the context of his era, are Donna K. Anderson, *Charles T. Griffes: A Life in Music* (1993), and Edward Maisel, *Charles T. Griffes: The Life of an American Composer* (1984).

John Hoskins Griscom

Few manuscript letters of John Griscom survive; these are located in the New York Public Library, the New-York Historical Society (Gulian Verplanck

Papers), the Henry E. Huntington Library of San Marino, California, and in the Francis A. Countway Library of Medicine, Harvard University, (Edward Jarvis Papers). The *Medical and Surgical Reporter* (Jan.–Apr. 1866) and the *New Jersey Medical and Surgical Reporter* (Feb. 1856–Mar. 1858) contain Griscom's printed letters. In the latter he published under the name of J. Gotham, Jr. His other published works include *First Lessons in Human Physiology* (1846), *Anniversary Discourse before the New York Academy of Medicine* (1855), *The Memoir of John Griscom, L.L.D.* (1859), and *Sanitary Legislation, Past and Future* (1861). Duncan Robert Jamieson, "Towards a Cleaner New York: John H. Griscom and New York's Public Health, 1830–1870" (Ph.D. diss., Mich. State Univ., 1972), provides a detailed chronology of Griscom's life as well as a primary bibliography and an annotated secondary bibliography. See also James H. Cassedy, "The Roots of American Sanitary Reform, 1843–1847: Seven Letters from John H. Griscom to Lemuel Shattuck," *Journal of the History of Medicine* 30 (Apr. 1975): 136–47; Charles E. Rosenberg and Carroll Smith Rosenberg, "Pietism and the Origins of the Public Health Movement: A Note on John H. Griscom and Robert M. Hartley," *Journal of the History of Medicine* 23 (Jan. 1968): 16–35; and Samuel W. Francis, "John H. Griscom," *Medical and Surgical Reporter* 15 (1866): 118–22.

William Halsted

Halsted's surgical papers are collected in *Surgical Papers in Two Volumes* (1924; repr. 1961). Information relevant to Halsted's life can be found in an unpublished book manuscript by William Osler, "The Inner History of the Johns Hopkins Hospital" at the Osler Library, McGill University, Montreal, Quebec, and in the papers of Harvey Cushing at Yale University. Halsted's original biographer, William George MacCallum, published *William Stewart Halsted: Surgeon* (1930) and "William Stewart Halsted," National Academy of Sciences, *Biographical Memoirs* 17 (1936). Another biography is Samuel James Crowe, *Halsted of Johns Hopkins: The Man and His Men* (1957). Short biographical notices include Irving B. Rosen and Mark Korman, "Halsted: His Success and His Secret," *Annals of the Royal College of Physicians and Surgeons of Canada* 29, no. 6 (1996): 348–51; and Wilder Penfield, "Halsted of Johns Hopkins," *Journal of the American Medical Association* 210 (1969): 2214–18. Penfield was the first to publicly reveal Halsted's long-term addiction to drugs. A particularly engaging account of Halsted's life is Sherwin B. Nuland, *Doctors: The Biography of Medicine* (1989), chap. 13. For an overview of his contributions to surgery, see Owen H. Wangensteen and Sarah D. Wangensteen, *The Rise of Surgery: From Empiric Craft to Scientific Discipline* (1978).

Fannie Lou Hamer

Hamer's papers are in the Amistad Research Center at Tulane University, the Mississippi Department of Archives and History, and the Wisconsin State Historical Society. Other papers and speeches are in the Moses Moon Collection at the National Museum of American History of the Smithsonian Institution and the Civil Rights Documentation Project at the Moorland-Spingarn Research Center at Howard University. For full-length biographical accounts, see Kay Mills, *This Little Light of Mine: The Life of Fannie Lou Hamer* (1993), and Chana Kai Lee, *For Freedom's Sake: The Life of Fannie Lou Hamer* (1999). Hamer is the subject of a chapter in George Sewell, *Mississippi Black History Makers* (1977); three articles in Vicki L. Crawford, ed., *Women in the Civil Rights Movement* (1990); and a short sketch in Juan Williams, *Eyes on the Prize: America's Civil Rights Years, 1954–1965* (1987). See also Jerry DeMuth, "Tired of Being Sick and Tired," *Nation*, 1 June 1964, pp. 548–51; J. H. O'Dell, "Life in Mississippi: An Interview with Fannie Lou Hamer," *Freedomways*, Spring 1965, pp. 231–42; Susan Johnson, "Fannie Lou Hamer: Mississippi Grassroots Organizer," *Black Law Journal* 2 (Summer 1972): 155–62; and Art Peters, "Marked for Murder," *Sepia*, Apr. 1965, pp. 29–33. An obituary and a follow-up article are in the *Washington Post*, 17 Mar. 1977 and 19 Mar. 1977.

Handsome Lake

The primary sources for Handsome Lake's initial visions are printed in A. F. C. Wallace, ed., "Halliday Jackson's Journal to the Seneca Indians, 1798–1800," *Pennsylvania History* 19 (1952): 117–47, 325–49. There are interesting differences between the prophet's message as reported in the contemporary materials and the versions reworked and written after 1840. Chief among these last are the reminiscences of Blacksnake in Thomas S. Abler, ed., *Chainbreaker: The Revolutionary War Memoirs of Governor Blacksnake* (1989), and Arthur C. Parker, ed., *The Code of Handsome Lake* (1913). A. F. C. Wallace, *The Death and Rebirth of the Seneca* (1970), is the standard secondary work, but Merle H. Deardorff, "The Religion of Handsome Lake: Its Origin and Development," in *Symposium on Local Diversity in Iroquois Culture*, ed. William N. Fenton (1951), and Elisabeth Tooker, "On the Development of the Handsome Lake Religion," *Proceedings of the American Philosophical Society* 133 (1989): 35–50, are worth consulting. Attempts to fit Handsome Lake in the contemporary Indian and non-Indian revivalism are made by A. F. C. Wallace, "Handsome Lake and the Great Revival in the West," *American Quarterly* 4 (1952): 149–65, and Gregory E. Dowd, *A Spirited Resistance* (1992).

Herman Haupt

The bulk of Haupt's papers are in the archives of the Yale University Library. Smaller collections are in the National Archives and at the Minnesota Historical Society. A complete biography is James A. Ward, *That Man Haupt* (1973). Francis A. Lord, *Lincoln's Railroad Man: Herman Haupt* (1969), focuses on Haupt's Civil War career. See also sketches of Haupt in Ezra J. Warner, *Generals in Blue* (1964), and Roger J. Spiller et al., eds., *Dictionary of American Military Biography* (1984). Haupt's work is also discussed in George E. Turner, *Victory Rode the Rails: The Strategic Place of the Railroads in the Civil War* (1953); Thomas Weber, *The Northern Railroads in the Civil War* (1952); and Bruce Catton, *Mr. Lincoln's Army* (1951). Other sources of information include Richard Snow, "American Characters: Herman Haupt," *American Heritage* (Feb.–Mar. 1985); George H. Burgess and Miles C. Kennedy, *Centennial History of the Pennsylvania Railroad Company, 1846–1946* (1949); and William Henry Haupt, *The Haupt Family in America* (1924). An obituary appears in the *New York Times*, 15 Dec. 1905.

DuBose Heyward

Heyward's correspondence and manuscripts can be found in the DuBose Heyward Papers and the John Bennett Papers at the South Carolina Historical Society in Charleston, in the Yates Snowden Papers at the University of South Carolina in Charleston, and in the Hervey Allen Papers at the University of Pittsburgh Library. Heyward's life is detailed in Frank Durham, *DuBose Heyward: The Man Who Wrote Porgy* (1954), and his work is critically examined at length in William Slavick, *DuBose Heyward* (1981); see also James M. Hutchisson, *DuBose Heyward: A Charleston Gentleman and the World of Porgy and Bess* (2000). Other sources of information include Emily Clark, "DuBose Heyward," *Virginia Quarterly Review* 6 (Oct. 1930): 546–56, and Harlan Henthorne Hatcher, *Creating the Modern American Novel* (1935). Obituaries are in the *New York Times* and the *New York Herald Tribune*, both 17 June 1940.

Henry Hornbostel

Significant repositories of Hornbostel's papers and drawings are in the Avery Architectural and Fine Arts Library at Columbia University and the Architecture Archives at Carnegie Mellon University in Pittsburgh. The latter collection also contains a comprehensive collection of articles on Hornbostel's work from the professional press, the forum that has seen the most thorough coverage of his accomplishments. These include Francis S. Swales, "Master Draftsmen XVII—Henry Hornbostel," *Pencil Points*, Feb. 1926, pp. 73–92, a well-illustrated biographical assessment of the architect at mid-late career. James D.Van Trump, *Life and Architecture in Pittsburgh* (1983), contains three articles on Hornbostel's life and work, including a detailed obituary. Clark V. Poling, *Henry Hornbostel, Michael Graves: An Exhibition of Architectural Drawings, Photographs and Models* (1985), uses buildings at Emory University as a lens through which to view the careers of Hornbostel and postmodern architect Michael Graves. The 14 Dec. 1961 issue of the *New York Times* has an obituary.

James Gibbons Huneker

Huneker's personal papers, including literary manuscripts, notebooks, photographs, correspondence, press clippings, and 175 volumes from his library are in the Huneker collection, Baker Memorial Library, Dartmouth College; 800 books from his library, pamphlets on music and literature, and his scrapbooks are at the New York Public Library at Lincoln Center. A selection of his writings appears in *Americans in the Arts, 1890–1920: Critiques by James Gibbons Huneker*, ed. Arnold T. Schwab (1985). The most complete modern assessment is Schwab, *James Gibbons Huneker: Critic of the Seven Arts* (1963), which includes a complete list of Huneker's books, an extensive bibliography, and a note on sources. See also Benjamin De Casseres, *James Gibbons Huneker* (1925; repr. 1980), and the obituary in the *New York Times*, 10 Feb. 1921.

Blind Lemon Jefferson

All but four of Jefferson's released recordings are collected on *Complete Recorded Works in Chronological Order* (vols. 1–4, Document DOCD 5017–5020). The most complete discussion of his life and career is Bob Groom's *Blind Lemon Jefferson* (1970). See also the section on Jefferson by Alan Govenar in *Bluesland: Portraits of Twelve Major American Blues Masters*, ed. Pete Welding and Toby Byron (1991); Stephen Calt's liner notes to *King of Country Blues* (Yazoo CD 1069); Sheldon Harris, *Blues Who's Who* (1979); and Sam Charters, *The Bluesmen* (1967). David Evans, *Big Road Blues* (1982), discusses the changing nature of Jefferson's lyrics throughout his career. Max E. Vreede, *The Paramount 12000/13000 Series* (1971), explores the Paramount blues series, and R. M. W. Dixon and John Godrich, *Blues and Gospel Records 190–1942* (1982), offers complete discographical details.

Murray Kempton

For biographical information, see "Kempton, Murray" in the 1973 and 1997 editions of *Current Biography Yearbook*; *Contemporary Authors*, vols. 97–100 (1981), and vol. 158 (1998); and *Contemporary Authors: New Revision Series*, vol. 51 (1996). An obituary appears in the *New York Times*, 6 May 1997.

Walter Lippmann

Lippmann's papers, including private correspondence and many original manuscripts, are at Sterling Memorial Library, Yale University. A major portion of his published works is available from the library on microfilm. An important part of his correspondence can be found in *Public Philosopher: Selected Letters of Walter Lippmann*, ed. John Morton Blum (1985). Gilbert Harrison compiled both *Early Writings* (1970), a selection of Lippmann's articles for the *New Republic*, and *Public Persons* (1976), a collection of portraits by Lippmann of figures ranging from William James to John F. Kennedy. The transcripts of Lippmann's seven network television broadcasts from 1960 to 1965 are compiled under the title *Conversations with Walter Lippmann* (1965). The most complete biography, based on Lippmann's private papers and conversations with him, is Ronald Steel, *Walter Lippmann and the American Century* (1980). A number of significant books have been written about different aspects of Lippmann's thought and career, including Stephen Blum, *Walter Lippmann: Cosmopolitanism in the Century of Total War* (1984); Barry Riccio, *Walter Lippmann: Odyssey of a Liberal* (1994); Anwar Seyd, *Walter Lippmann's Philosophy of International Politics* (1963); Hari Dam, *The Intellectual Odyssey of Walter Lippmann* (1973); Charles Wellborn, *Twentieth Century Pilgrimage: Walter Lippmann and the Public Philosophy* (1969); Edward L. Schapsmeier and Frederick H. Schapsmeier, *Walter Lippmann: Philosopher-Journalist* (1969); Benjamin Wright, *Five Public Philosophies of Walter Lippmann* (1973); and Francine Curro Cary, *The Influence of War on Walter Lippmann, 1914–1944* (1967). Clinton Rossiter and James Lare, *The Essential Lippmann* (1963), is a spotty collection of Lippmann's writings, focusing on the books and largely ignoring the articles and columns. The 15 Dec. 1974 issue of the *New York Times* has an obituary.

Malcolm X

In addition to the works mentioned in the text, see Clayborne Carson, *Malcolm X: The FBI File* (1991); Michael Friedly, *Malcolm X: The Assassination* (1992); and Bruce Perry, *Malcolm: The Life of a Man Who Changed Black America* (1991). An obituary is in the *New York Times*, 22 Feb. 1965.

Rocky Marciano

For biographical information on Marciano, see Everett M. Skehan, *Rocky Marciano: Biography of a First Son* (1977), and Bill Libby, *Rocky: The Story of a Champion* (1971). His career was carefully followed by *Ring* magazine, which published the following articles: "Marciano Has Problems," Jan. 1953; Ted Carroll, "Food for Thought," Aug. 1953; Dan Daniel, "Power vs. Cleverness,"

Oct. 1953; and Lester Bromberg, "Crafty Seconds," Nov. 1954. For a controversial examination of Marciano's personal life, see William Nack, "The Rock," *Sports Illustrated*, 23 Aug. 1993, pp. 52–56ff. An obituary is in the *New York Times*, 1 Sept. 1969.

Adolf Meyer

The Johns Hopkins University Medical School holds a collection of Meyer's papers; the G. Stanley Hall Papers at the Clark University Archives include some material related to Meyer. See *The Collected Papers of Adolf Meyer*, ed. Eunice E. Winters (1950–1952), for a published edition of his papers. Published works by Meyer that are worth noting include "The Dynamic Interpretation of Dementia Parecox," *American Journal of Psychology* 21 (1910): 2–3 and 139–57; and *The Commonsense Psychiatry of Dr. Adolf Meyer*, ed. Alfred Lief (1948), for which Lief also wrote a biographical article. See also Ruth Leys, "Types of One: Adolf Meyer's Life Chart and the Representation of Individuality," *Representations* 34 (1991): 1–28; and Eunice E. Winters, "Adolf Meyer's Two and a Half Years at Kankakee: May 1, 1893–Nov. 1, 1895," *Bulletin for the History of Medicine* 40 (1966): 441–58. An obituary is in the *New York Times*, 18 Mar. 1950.

Lindley Murray

Murray outlined his own life in six "Letters" to his secretary Elizabeth Frank, to which she added accounts of his last days for his *Memoirs* (1827). Murray's *Compendium of Religious Faith* (1817) for young Quakers was shaped by the *Principles of Religion* (1805) by Henry Tuke, whose biography Murray wrote in 1816. His other books written specifically for Quakers made little mark. The definitive biography, Stephen Allott, *Lindley Murray, 1745–1826* (1991), is supplemented in Hugh Barbour et al., *Quaker Crosscurrents* (1995). See also Mary R. Glover, *The Retreat, York* (1984); Michael Belok, "The Most Successful Grammar," *Educational Forum* 21, no. 1 (Nov. 1966): 107–11, and "Lindley Murray's English Readers," *Education* 87 (1966–67): 496, 501. Peter Davis's unpublished paper is in the Haverford College Quaker Collection. Twenty-one letters from Lindley Murray to John Murray, Jr., are in the Haviland Records Room of New York Yearly Meeting.

Bronislava Nijinska

The Bronislava Nijinska Archives are in Pacific Palisades, California. *Bronislava Nijinska: Early Memoirs*, translated and coedited by her daughter Irina Nijinska and Jean Rawlinson, was published posthumously (1981; repr. 1993). Biographical treatments include Nancy Van Norman Baer, *Bronislava Nijins-*

ka: A Dancer's Legacy (1986); Jack Anderson, "The Fabulous Career of Bro-
nislava Nijinska," *Dance Magazine*, Aug. 1963, pp. 40–46; Peter Williams,
"Nijinsky/Nijinska," *Dance Gazette*, July 1984, pp. 16–19; and Gunhild
Schuller, "Bronislava Nijinska: Eine Monographie" (Ph.D. diss., Univ. of
Vienna, 1976). Discussions of Nijinska can be found in several works focus-
ing on Diaghilev, among them Richard Buckle, *Diaghilev* (1979); Lynn
Garafola, *Diaghilev's Ballets Russes* (1989); and Serge L. Grigoriev, *The
Diaghilev Ballet, 1909–1929* (1953). On Nijinska's choreography see her own
"On Movement and the School of Movement," *Ballet Review* 13 (Winter 1986):
75–81, and Garafola, "Choreography by Nijinska," *Ballet Review* 20 (Winter
1992): 64–71. Also see A. V. Coton, *A Prejudice for Ballet* (1938), and Arnold L.
Haskell, *Ballet – To Poland* (1940). The 23 Feb. 1972 issue of the *New York Times*
has an obituary.

Albert Jay Nock

The Albert Jay Nock Papers are in the Library of Congress, and Yale University possesses an Albert Jay Nock Collection. Nock's writings, sources for
understanding his life, include *A Journal of These Days: June 1932–December
1933* (1934); *Journal of Forgotten Days: May 1934–October 1935* (1948); *Letters from
Albert Jay Nock, 1924–1945, to Edmund C. Evans, Mrs. Edmund C. Evans, and
Ellen Winsor*, ed. Frank W. Garrison (1949); and *Selected Letters of Albert Jay
Nock*, ed. Francis Jay Nock (1962). For collections of Nock's important works,
see *The State of the Union: Essays in Social Criticism*, ed. Charles H. Hamilton
(1991) and *Our Enemy the State* (1935; repr. 1994). Other editions of his essays
include *The Freeman* (1920), *The Myth of a Guilty Nation* (1922), *On Doing the
Right Thing and Other Essays* (1928), *The Book of Journeyman: Essays from the
New Freeman* (1930), *Free Speech and Plain Language* (1937), *Snoring as a Fine
Art and Twelve Other Essays* (1958), and *Cogitations from Albert Jay Nock* (1970).
For Nock's work as a biographer and historian, see *Jefferson* (1926), *Francis
Rabelais: The Man and His Work* (with Catherine R. Wilson, 1929), *A Journey
into Rabelais's France* (1934), and *Henry George: An Essay* (1939). Other works
edited or coedited by Nock include *Selected Works of Artemus Ward* (1924) and
The Urquhart–Le Motteux Translation of the Works of Francis Rabelais (1931).
The best source on Nock himself remains his autobiography. Other impor-
tant biographical accounts include Van Wyck Brooks, *Days of the Phoenix*
(1957); Frank Chodorov, *Out of Step* (1962); Robert M. Crunden, *The Mind and
Art of Albert Jay Nock* (1964); J. Sandor Cziraky, "The Evolution of the Social
Philosophy of Albert Jay Nock" (Ph.D. diss., Univ. of Pennsylvania, 1959); and
Michael Wreszin, *The Superfluous Anarchist: Albert Jay Nock* (1971). The 20
Aug. 1945 issue of the *New York Times* has an obituary.

Fairfield Porter

Porter's only book is *Thomas Eakins* (1959). The best single-volume work on him is John T. Spike, *Fairfield Porter: An American Classic* (1992); a more recent biographical account is Justin Spring, *Fairfield Porter: A Life in Art* (2000). A good selection of Porter's paintings is also found in *Fairfield Porter: Realist Painter in an Age of Abstraction* (1982), with essays by John Ashbery, Kenworth Moffett, and others. Rackstraw Downes edited and wrote the introduction for *Fairfield Porter: Art in Its Own Terms: Selected Criticism, 1935–1975* (1979). See also Joan Ludman, *Fairfield Porter: A Catalogue Raisonné of His Prints* (1981), and Ludman, *Fairfield Porter: A Catalogue Raisonné of the Paintings, Watercolors, and Pastels* (2001); Hilton Kramer, "The Duality of Fairfield Porter," *Art in America* (June 1963); Patricia Mainardi, "Fairfield Porter's Contribution to Modernism," *ARTnews* (Feb. 1976); and Louis Finkelstein, "The Naturalness of Fairfield Porter," *Arts Magazine* (May 1976). An obituary is in the *New York Times*, 20 Sept. 1975.

Dawn Powell

The Dawn Powell Collection at the Columbia University Library is the repository of her papers. The most accurate source of biographical information on Powell is Tim Page's biography, *Dawn Powell*, published in 1998. Powell's largely autobiographical novel, *My Home Is Far Away*, first published in 1944 and reprinted in 1995, gives an even more focused insight into her early years. See also Tim Page, ed., *The Diaries of Dawn Powell, 1931–1965* (1995), and *Selected Letters of Dawn Powell, 1913–1965* (1999). For appreciations of her work, see especially Gore Vidal, "Dawn Powell: The American Writer," *New York Review of Books*, 5 Nov. 1987, and Edmund Wilson, "Dawn Powell: Greenwich Village in the Fifties," *New Yorker*, 17 Nov. 1962. An obituary appears in the *New York Times*, 16 Nov. 1965.

Gisela Richter

Richter's personal papers are on deposit in the library of the American Academy in Rome. Documents on her work at the Metropolitan Museum are in the files of the Department of Greek and Roman Art. The most complete primary sources are those written by Richter herself: *My Memoirs: Recollections of an Archaeologist's Life* (1972) and "The Department of Greek and Roman Art: Triumphs and Tribulations," *Metropolitan Museum Journal* 3 (1970): 73–95. Short biographies have appeared: Ingrid E. M. Edlund et al., "Gisela Marie Augusta Richter (1882–1972): Scholar of Classical Art and Museum Archaeologist," in *Women as Interpreters of the Visual Arts, 1820–1979*, ed. Claire R. Sherman (1981; with selected bibliography); and Evelyn Harrison, "Gisela Richter," in *Notable American Women*, ed. Barbara Sicherman and Carol H. Green (1980). Mary Allsebrook, *Born to Rebel: The Life of Harriet Boyd Hawes* (1992), written by Harriet Boyd Hawes's daughter, has information on Richter not found elsewhere. Perceptive obituaries are in Frank E. Brown, *Studi Etruschi* 41 (1973): 597–600; Homer Thompson, *American Philosophical Society Yearbook* (1973): 144–50; and Cornelius C. Vermeule III, *The Burlington Magazine* 115 (1973): 329.

Bayard Rustin

There is no single collection of Rustin's papers. Much material on him may be found in the records of the A. Philip Randolph Institute in the Library of Congress and in the Congress of Racial Equality Papers at the State Historical Society of Wisconsin. For a full-length account of his life, see Jervis Anderson, *Bayard Rustin: Troubles I've Seen* (1997). His contributions to the civil rights movement and to political coalition building can also be followed in Paula F. Pfeffer, *A. Philip Randolph, Pioneer of the Civil Rights Movement* (1990), and David J. Garrow, *Bearing the Cross: Martin Luther King, Jr., and the Southern Christian Leadership Conference* (1988). Obituaries are in the *New York Times*, 25 Aug. 1987; *Jet*, 7 Sept. 1987; *New Leader*, 7 Sept. 1987; and the *New Republic*, 28 Sept. 1987.

Sequoyah

Sequoyah left no collection of papers, but the Thomas Gilcrease Institute in Tulsa, Oklahoma, has four manuscripts attributed to him. The best biography of Sequoyah, although it contains no citations for lengthy quotations, remains Grant Foreman, *Sequoyah* (1938). Recent studies are Willard Walker and James Sarbaugh, "The Early History of the Cherokee Syllabary," *Ethnohistory* 40 (1993): 70–94, and Theda Perdue, "The Sequoyah Syllabary and Cultural Revitalization," in *Perspectives on the Southeast: Linguistics, Archaeology, and Ethnohistory* (1994). On the use of the Cherokee syllabary, see Willard Walker, "Notes on Native Writing Systems and the Design of Native Literacy Programs," *Anthropological Linguistics* 11 (1969): 148–66, and Albert L. Wahrhaftig, *Social and Economic Characteristics of the Cherokee Population of Eastern Oklahoma* (1970).

Joseph Smith

The papers of Joseph Smith, located in the Church Archives, Salt Lake City, Utah, are being edited by Dean C. Jessee, who published *The Personal Writings of Joseph Smith* in 1984 and the first volume of the *Papers* in 1989 and the second in 1992. Lucy Mack Smith narrated reminiscences later published as

Biographical Sketches of Joseph Smith the Prophet (1853). The best complete biography is Donna Hill, *Joseph Smith, the First Mormon* (1977). See also Fawn M. Brodie, *No Man Knows My History* (1945), for a critical view by a disaffected Mormon, and Richard L. Bushman, *Joseph Smith and the Beginnings of Mormonism* (1984), for a sympathetic account.

Melvin B. Tolson

Tolson's papers are in the Library of Congress. In addition to the volumes of poetry published during his lifetime, readers should consult *Caviar and Cabbage: Selected Columns by Melvin B. Tolson from the Washington Tribune, 1937–1944* (1982) and *A Gallery of Harlem Portraits* (1979), both edited by Robert M. Farnsworth. The most complete critical biography is Farnsworth, *Melvin B. Tolson, 1898–1966: Plain Talk and Poetic Prophecy* (1984). See also Joy Flasch, *Melvin B. Tolson* (1972), for a general assessment of Tolson's life and writings. For critical analyses of Tolson's writings, see Mariann Russell, *Melvin B. Tolson's Harlem Gallery: A Literary Analysis* (1980); Michael Berube, *Marginal Forces/Cultural Centers: Tolson, Pynchon, and the Politics of the Canon* (1992); and Craig Hansen Werner, *Playing the Changes: From Afro-Modernism to the Jazz Impulse* (1994). An obituary is in the *New York Times*, 30 Aug. 1966.

Felix Francisco Varela y Morales

Records of Transfiguration Church in New York City, the archives of the Archdiocese of Baltimore, and the papers of John Hughes in the archives of the Archdiocese of New York hold documents pertaining to Varela. Literary works by Varela include *Elenco* (1816) and *Lección Preliminar* (1819). The most recent biography is Joseph McCadden and Helen McCadden, *Father Varela: Torchbearer from Cuba* (1969). Other sources that describe aspects of his life are Jay P. Dolan, *The Immigrant Church: New York's Irish and German Catholics, 1815–1865* (1975), which outlines Varela's pastoral work in New York City; Vincent P. Lannie, *Public Money and Parochial Education* (1968), which describes Varela's efforts to obtain public monies for Catholic schools; José Ignacio Rodríguez, *Vida del Presbítero Don Felix Varela* (1878), a biography; William Francis Blakeslee, C.S.P., "Felix Varela — 1788–853," *Records* 38 (1927): 15-46, a biographical summary, Sister Gemma Marie Del Duca, S.C., "A Political Portrait: Felix Varela y Morales, 1788–1853" (Ph.D. diss., Univ. of New Mexico, 1966), an analysis of Varela's political views; and Joseph J. McCadden, "The New York-to-Cuba-Axis of Father Varela," *The Americas* 20 (Apr. 1964): 37–62, a summary of Varela's advocacy for Cubans.

DeWitt Wallace

Most of Wallace's papers are held by *Reader's Digest* at its headquarters in Chappaqua, New York. Though replete with hearsay, John Heidenry, *Theirs Was the Kingdom* (1993), is a thorough, insightful, and well-documented history of the Wallaces and their publishing enterprise. James Playsted Wood, *Of Lasting Interest: The Story of the Reader's Digest* (1967), is a friendlier account. See also John Bainbridge, *Little Wonder; or, The Reader's Digest and How It Grew* (1945), Samuel A. Schreiner, Jr., *The Condensed World of the Reader's Digest* (1977), and Walter H. Weintz, *The Solid Gold Mailbox* (1987). Major articles about the Wallaces and the *Reader's Digest* appeared in *Fortune*, Nov. 1936, and in *Time*, 10 Dec. 1951. An obituary is in the *New York Times*, 1 Apr. 1981.

Ida B. Wells-Barnett

Wells-Barnett's papers are in the Regenstein Library at the University of Chicago. Her published writings are reprinted in *Selected Works of Ida B. Wells-Barnett*, ed. Trudier Harris (1991), and Mildred Thompson, *Ida B. Wells-Barnett: An Exploratory Study of an American Black Woman, 1893–1930* (1990). Some of her private writings are in *The Memphis Diary of Ida B. Wells*, ed. Miriam DeCosta-Willis (1995). Her *Crusade for Justice: The Autobiography of Ida B. Wells* (1970) was edited by her daughter, Alfreda M. Duster. For a full-length biography, see Linda O. McMurry, *To Keep the Waters Troubled: The Life of Ida B. Wells* (1998). See also Gail Bederman, "'Civilization,' the Decline of Middle-Class Manliness, and Ida B. Wells's Antilynching Campaign (1892–94)," *Radical History Review* 52 (1992): 5–30, and McMurry, "Ida Wells-Barnett and the African-American Anti-Lynching Campaign," in *American Reform and Reformers*, ed. Randall M. Miller and Paul A. Cimbla (1996).

Frank W. Woolworth

For a full-length biography, see John K. Winkler, *Five and Ten: The Fabulous Life of F. W. Woolworth* (1941). James Brough, *The Woolworths* (1982), is a narrative history of the Woolworth family. The following are popular accounts of the history of Woolworth's company: John Peter Nichols, *Skyline Queen and the Merchant Prince: The Woolworth Story* (1973); and Nina Brown Baker, *Nickels and Dimes: The Story of F. W. Woolworth* (1954). Information about Woolworth's career can be found in *Fortieth Anniversary Souvenir, F. W. Woolworth Company: 1879–1919* (1919); *1879–1929: Fifty Years of Woolworth* (c. 1929); *Celebrating 60 Years of an American Institution: F. W. Woolworth Co.* (c. 1939); *Woolworth's First 75 Years: The Story of Everybody's Store, 1879–1954*

(1954). A feature article on Woolworth and his business can be found in the *New York Times*, 1 Jan. 1911. A report on the opening of the Woolworth skyscraper is in the *New York Times*, 25 Apr. 1913. An obituary is in the *New York Times*, 9 Apr. 1919.

THE SELECTORS

Joan Acocella, dance critic for the *New Yorker*, is the author of *Mark Morris* and the editor of *The Diary of Vaslav Nijinsky*.

Richard Avedon is an award-winning photographer who began in fashion with *Harper's Bazaar* and *Vogue* before moving on to the stark portraiture seen in the reformatted *New Yorker*, where he was appointed staff photographer, the first to hold the post.

Jacques Barzun, University Professor Emeritus of Columbia University, has written and edited critical and historical studies on a wide variety of subjects culminating in his book *From Dawn to Decadence: 500 Years of Western Cultural Life, 1500 to the Present*, a surprise bestseller.

Sven Birkerts is director of students and core faculty writing instructor in the Master of Fine Arts Program at Bennington College as well as an instructor in Emerson College's Master of Fine Arts Writing Program.

Cultural, literary, and religious critic **Harold Bloom** is the Sterling Professor of the Humanities in the English Department at Yale University.

Alan Brinkley is the Allan Nevins Professor of History at Columbia University and the author of four books on twentieth-century American history.

Helen Gurley Brown, the editor-in-chief of *Cosmopolitan* for thirty-two years, is now Editor-in-Chief of *Cosmopolitan International* with forty-six editions all over the world. She is the author of eight books, and a chair has been endowed in her name at the Medill School of Journalism at Northwestern University.

Katie Brown, author of *Katie Brown Entertains* and former host of *Next Door with Katie Brown*, is currently dispensing her crafty knowledge from Katie Brown Studio in New York.

Magazine publisher and past editor of *Vanity Fair* and the *New Yorker*, **Tina Brown** launched *Talk* magazine in 1999.

Syndicated columnist, television host, and author **William F. Buckley, Jr.**, founded the *National Review* in 1955.

Mark C. Carnes is Ann Whitney Olin Professor of History at Barnard College and General Editor of the *American National Biography*.

Former U.S. Senator **Alfonse D'Amato** is the managing director of Park Strategies LLC, a business development and strategic consulting firm based in New York City.

Author of seven books, including the recent bestseller *Supreme Injustice: How the High Court Hijacked Election 2000*, **Alan Dershowitz** currently teaches at Harvard Law School.

Rita Dove received the 1987 Pulitzer Prize in poetry and served as poet laureate of the United States from 1993 to 1995. A 1996 National Humanities Medalist, she is at present Commonwealth Professor of English at the University of Virginia.

Distinguished Professor of History at the City University of New York and the founder of The Center for Lesbian and Gay Studies (CLAGS), **Martin Duberman** is the author of some twenty books, including *Paul Robeson, Cures, Stonewall, Black Mountain,* and *Left Out*.

Michael Eric Dyson is the Ida B. Wells-Barnett Professor at DePaul University. He is most recently the author of *Holler If You Hear Me: Searching for Tupac Shakur*.

Harold Evans wrote the best-selling book *The American Century*, established new standards of investigative reporting as the editor of the *Sunday Times* of London, was vice-chairman of *U.S. News & World Report*, the *New York Daily News*, the *Atlantic Monthly*, and *Fast Company*, and is now writing a book and television series on innovators.

Bryan A. Garner is the president of LawProse Inc. and Editor-in-Chief of *Black's Law Dictionary*; he is also the author of more than ten books, including *A Dictionary of Modern American Usage*.

The first African American to earn a doctorate in English at Cambridge University, **Henry Louis Gates, Jr.**, is the chair of Afro-American Studies and the director of the W.E.B. Du Bois Institute for Afro-American Research at Harvard University.

Gary Giddins, a writer for the *Village Voice* since 1973 and co-founder of the American Jazz Orchestra, is the award-winning author of several books on music and popular culture, including *Visions of Jazz* and *Bing Crosby: A Pocketful of Dreams*.

Terry Golway is a columnist and city editor at the *New York Observer* and is the author of four books. He is currently working on a biography of his invisible giant, Nathanael Greene.

Internationally known architect and Princeton University professor **Michael Graves** gained additional fame in the last decade as a designer of household products and was awarded the National Medal of the Arts in 1999 and the 2001 Gold Medal from the American Institute of Architects.

A priest, distinguished sociologist, and bestselling author, the Reverend **Andrew M. Greeley** is Professor of Social Sciences at the University of Chicago and the University of Arizona.

The author of three critically acclaimed and bestselling works of American literature, **William Least Heat-Moon** has taught literature, writing, and journalism at several colleges in addition to the University of Missouri at Columbia.

A. M. Homes is the author of the critically acclaimed novels *The End of Alice*, *In a Country of Mothers*, *Jack*, and the short story collections *The Safety of Objects* and the forthcoming volume *Things You Should Know*. She teaches in The Writing Program at Columbia University.

Nicolás Kanellos is Director of Arte Público Press and the Brown Foundation Professor of Hispanic Literature at the University of Houston. He is the general editor of the recently published *Herencia: The Anthology of Hispanic Literature of the United States*.

The Donald J. McLachlan Professor of History at Stanford University, **David M. Kennedy** received the Pulitzer Prize in History for his book *Freedom from Fear: The American People in Depression and War, 1929–1945*.

Former congressman and New York City mayor **Ed Koch** is the author of many books and a lawyer, professional public speaker, columnist, and television and radio personality.

Professor of English at the City University of New York Graduate Center, **Wayne Koestenbaum** is the author of three books of poetry and five books of prose including, most recently, *Andy Warhol*.

Hilton Kramer, the editor and publisher of the *New Criterion*, currently serves as the art critic for the *New York Observer* and for many years has written the "Critic's Notebook" column in *Art & Antiques* magazine.

Fran Lebowitz, the author of *Metropolitan Life* and *Social Studies*, still lives in New York City, as she does not believe that she would be allowed to live anywhere else.

Poet and professor at both Bennington College and the New School for Social Research, **David Lehman** is the series editor of *The Best American Poetry* annual.

Wilma Mankiller, former principal chief of the Cherokee Nation of Oklahoma, the second largest tribe in the United States, was the first female in modern history to be elected to lead a major Native American tribe. She has served on board of the Ms. Foundation for Women and is currently a member of the Ford Foundation and the Freedom Foundation.

Renowned Civil War scholar **James M. McPherson**, author of the Pulitzer Prize–winning *Battle Cry of Freedom*, is the George Henry Davis Professor of American History at Princeton University, where he has taught since 1962.

The author of many books on American colonial history, **Edmund S. Morgan** is the Sterling Professor of History Emeritus at Yale University.

Sherwin B. Nuland is a Clinical Professor of Surgery at the Yale School of Medicine; his essential study of the modern way of death, *How We Die: Reflections on Life's Final Chapter*, won the National Book Award and has been translated into sixteen languages.

Poet **Sharon Olds** won the National Book Critics Circle Award for her collection *The Dead and the Living*, helped found the Writing Program at Goldwater Hospital for the severely physically disabled, and is the current chair of New York University's Creative Writing Program.

Camille Paglia is University Professor of Humanities and Media Studies at the University of the Arts in Philadelphia and the author of four books, including *Sexual Personae: Art and Decadence from Nefertiti to Emily Dickinson* and *Vamps & Tramps: New Essays*.

The author of eleven books and a correspondent, writer, and producer for CBS News, **Andy Rooney** has won three Emmy Awards and six Writer's Guild Awards for his unique television essays, which he has been composing since 1964.

The winner of two Pulitzer prizes and former special assistant to President Kennedy, **Arthur M. Schlesinger, Jr.**, has taught history at Harvard and at the City University of New York Graduate School.

Walter Shapiro is the political columnist for *USA Today*. In prior incarnations, he has worked for *Esquire*, *Time*, *Newsweek*, and the *Washington Post*, as well as serving as a presidential speechwriter for Jimmy Carter.

Film and theater critic **John Simon** frequently writes for *New York Magazine* and the *National Review*.

The author of eleven works of fiction including *Fair and Tender Ladies*, **Lee Smith** has recently retired from her creative writing post at North Carolina State University.

Andrew Solomon's most recent book, *The Noonday Demon: An Atlas of Depression*, won the 2001 National Book Award.

Composer and lyricist **Stephen Sondheim** has made a career of reinventing the musical with successful theater productions such as *West Side Story*, *Gypsy*, *A Funny Thing Happened on the Way to the Forum*, *Company*, *Follies*, *Into the Woods*, and *Assassins*.

Writer and social activist **Gloria Steinem** co-founded *New York* magazine and *Ms.* magazine, where she serves as a contributing editor today. She also was the founder of the National Women's Political Caucus, The Ms. Foundation for Women, and The Coalition of Labor Union Women and is the author of many articles and books.

Composer, playwright, and author **Elizabeth Swados** has received acclaim for her many creative projects. She is the winner of five Tony award nominations, three Obie awards, and an Outer Critics Circle Award for her work in theater.

Mike Wallace is a professor of history at John Jay College, City University of New York, founder of The Gotham Center, and coauthor of the Pulitzer Prize–winning *Gotham: A History of New York City to 1898*.

Simon Winchester's most recent books include *The Professor and the Madman* and *The Map That Changed the World*.

Formerly the marriage project director for Lambda Legal Defense & Education Fund and co-counsel in the historic Hawaii marriage case, **Evan Wolfson**—named one of the 100 most influential lawyers in America by the *National Law Journal*—has been awarded a grant to explore the next step for winning the freedom to marry.